digitalSTRUCTURES
Data and Urban Strategies of the Civic Future

Wendy W Fok
霍渭瑜

"We can only see a short distance ahead, but we can see plenty there that needs to be done."

- *Alan Turing*

ORO Editions
Publishers of Architecture, Art, and Design
Gordon Goff: Publisher

www.oroeditions.com
info@oroeditions.com

Published by ORO Editions

Authors:
Wendy W. Fok (霍渭瑜)

Guest Contributors (Written/Interviews):
Amber Bartosh, Lydia Kallipoliti, Jimenez Lai, Greg Lynn, Mik Naayem, Jesse Reiser, Saskia Sassen, Minerva Tantoco, Andrew Witt

Graphics Layout & Research Design Team:
Rachel Pendleton, Jessica Marquez, Yarzar Hlaing (ရာဇာတင်မောင်လှိုင်),
JJ Jin (金智杰), Isabelle 'Iza' Dabrowski, Sevil Tara Akdora

Digital Content & WebAR R&D Team:
Lucy Liu (刘场瑞), Juan Villatoro

Cover Design:
Hyun Jung Ahn (안현정)

Language & Copy Editor:
Irina T. Oryshkevich

Project Manager:
Jake Anderson

10 9 8 7 6 5 4 3 2 1 First Edition

ISBN: 978-1-954081-81-9

Color Separations and Printing: ORO Group Ltd.
Printed in China.

ORO Editions makes a continuous effort to minimize the overall carbon footprint of its publications. As part of this goal, ORO Editions, in association with Global ReLeaf, arranges to plant trees to replace those used in the manufacturing of the paper produced for its books. Global ReLeaf is an international campaign run by American Forests, one of the world's oldest nonprofit conservation organizations. Global ReLeaf is American Forests' education and action program that helps individuals, organizations, agencies, and corporations improve the local and global environment by planting and caring for trees.

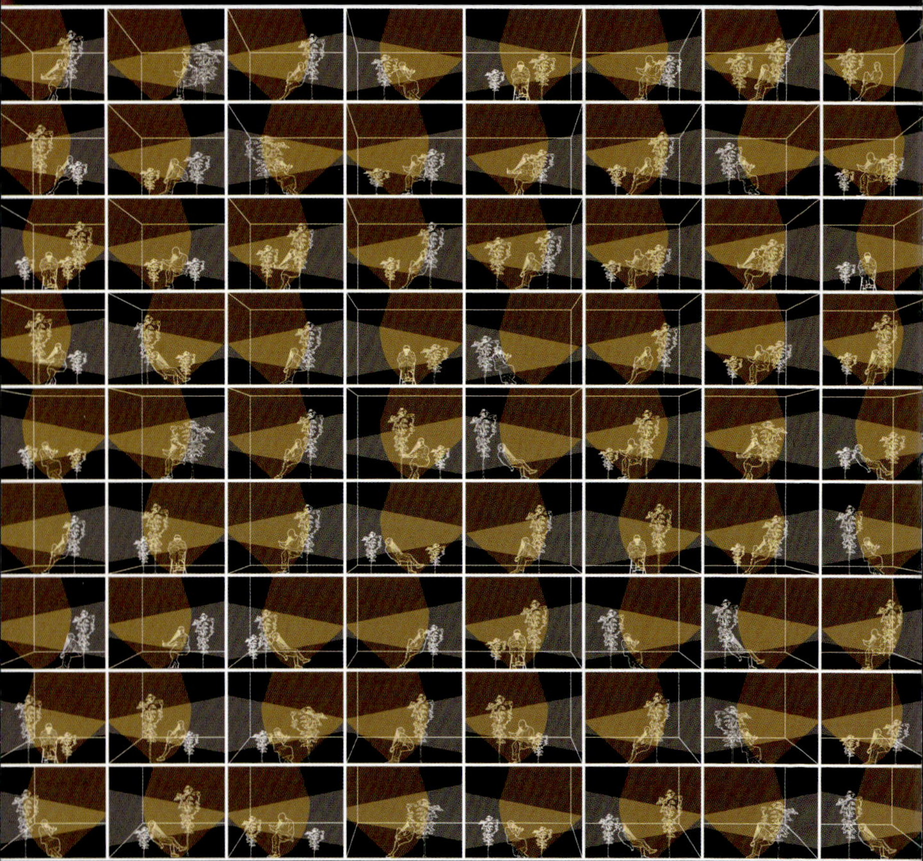

a

Points on Architecture and Technology

Jesse Reiser and Julian Harake

The advent of digital computation in architecture is commonly credited to an architect who, most likely, has never used a computer. Unironically, Frank Gehry has always been more personally invested in physical model making; his intentness on capturing the exact, unrationalizable configurations of his hand-built paper models led him to solicit the help of the most advanced digital scanning and three-dimensional modeling technologies available. Yet as is commonly done, it would be a disservice to dismiss his working method as some strange coincidence of high and low means of making and doing. For his is the most compelling and prolific example in recent memory of an architect pushing technology to get what they wanted, and of technology making possible a previously undoable, let alone previously unimaginable, architecture.

Gehry's is not an isolated case. In our office, we often use scripting to digitally replicate the geometric specificity of our handcrafted wax study models. As metallurgist Cyril Stanley Smith reminds us, from the pyramids of Giza to the Forbidden City and Baalbek, technological advancement is frequently at the behest of aesthetic and spiritual (and political) impulses. Or so goes for the most compelling monuments of all times.

Closer to ours, the Apollo 11 moon landing was one such endeavor. Standing today less likely in Giza—or on the moon, for now—and more likely in a shopping mall Zara or an exuberantly "high-tech" airport, the inverse appears equally valid. Against the placemaking prerogative of great architecture, a placeless nature, driven by rational thinking, typifies much of our built world. Genius has thus given way to the focus group.

For those in other fields, this might constitute a positive change. From experiences with clients, we are privy to the heuristic thinking which, though perhaps useful for other disciplines, betrays architecture's requisite specificity and by which it is frequently marketed. Unlike science or the clarity of advertising, and closer to art, architecture is not the product of general principles and clear explanations. Fittingly, machine-obsessed Le Corbusier sought "ineffability." We therefore might revise some common assumptions regarding architecture's relationship with technology:

1. *Computers are intelligent → Computers are dumb*

In *What Computers Can't Do* (HarperCollins, 1972), philosopher Hubert Dreyfus predicted that so long as artificial intelligence was rooted in rule-based and systematic thinking, it would fail to reach the higher-level capabilities of human cognition. As Dreyfus argues, this is because human intelligence is based less on persistent data acquisition and pattern recognition and more on intuition to deal with novel, entirely singular situations.

By that measure, rule-based computational procedures and optimization are not inherently intelligent design methods. Their results must ultimately be interpreted by an intelligent designer, who might then judge whether they are good or bad. This critical second step of evaluation is often forgotten by architects when faced with the novelty and marvels of algorithmic thinking. As computation has evolved over a span of decades, our gut reactions have evolved over millennia.

2. *There must be a reason for every form → Post rationalization is rational*

When laying out the exterior wall perforations in our O-14 tower, we initially tried using computer algorithms to negotiate structural, shading, and aesthetic concerns. Because our algorithm was rule based and incorporated competing performance criteria, we were able to justify any and all results to the developer while amassing a vast quantity of potential options that might otherwise be unavailable. There was only one issue: the results didn't look good. After running iteration after iteration on our computers, applying more rules to the algorithm, and nearly driving our computer-savvy employee insane, we realized that the only solution was to craft a composition directly based on what we wanted and thought looked good. That same employee accused us of engaging in "random play," but the resulting composition exhibited an incontrovertible intelligence, one that was paradoxically out of the computer's reach.

In this instance, all possible design iterations were rational on some basis of performance. More generally, we find that all forms are good for something. With this attitude, design might then become a process of elaboration and mining a project for potential uses and expressions, possible only through its formal development toward higher degrees of resolution.

3. *Science births technology → Technology precedes science*

As noted by Stanley Smith, the invention of steel predates knowledge of its molecular composition. Japanese swordsmiths, believing that steel was a form of purified iron, were blissfully ignorant of the fundamental importance of their coal fueled furnaces, which expelled carbon and warped the crystalline composition of iron molecules in their swords, hardening them at the cost of ductility. Despite a contemporary understanding of the molecular properties of steel, the technology used to create Japanese swords has effectively remained unchanged. Scientific understanding has had but little impact in the face of centuries of technological refinement.

As exemplified above, a design need not be entirely rational nor comprehended fully to be useful. As with the swordsmiths before them, many structural engineers we have worked with similarly rely first on visual and intuitive understandings of form, structure, and material behavior, using mathematical and computational analyses as but final checks to their gut reactions. They remind us too that the exact behavior of a structure can never be fully predicted by science. Their job is rather to provide an acceptable degree of certainty as to whether or not a building might stand the test of time and its concomitant forces.

4. *Necessity is the mother of invention → Invention mothers its own necessity*

As with the evolution of species, utility only follows the introduction of an arbitrary mutation. To do otherwise is to limit the structural, aesthetic, and thermodynamic possibilities of an architecture at the outset in favor of conventional design solutions.

Similar to that of the opposable thumb, the births of the slinky, guncotton, penicillin, microwave oven, pacemaker, and post-it note resulted from accidental occurrences which were then formalized and iteratively elaborated. Arbitrariness and chance operations are thus means to escape the trappings of rational thought, often toward greater, previously unforeseeable alternatives.

5. *Meaning is fixed in symbolic form → Physics is fixed, meaning is transient*

Working with "imagineers" for Disney's Shanghai campus, we were privileged to gain insight into their working methods and procedures. One which had a particularly strong impact on us concerned the park's numerous rides, which were often themed around characters and movies drawn from the full extents of Disney's vast universe. As we were told, though the rides varied widely in content, they were all nearly identical in terms of their physics and sequence of movements, all obeying approximately the same narrative structure of physical effects. This resulted in an interchangeability of content, allowing the imagineers to continually swap out characters, themes, and storylines while leaving the rides more or less intact.

The transience of meaning with regard to physical form in this context suggests its conditionality in all instances. Like the amassed totems of Jason's Argo and Ahab's Pequod, content is separable from the physical structure onto which it is applied, and is entirely dependent on the specific circumstances of its encounter. The same might be said of program in relation to the hard physical reality of architecture. As explicated by Aldo Rossi, a Roman coliseum might one day house a city on its interior, its exterior walls adapted as ramparts against foreign invaders.

6. *The city is a laboratory* → *The city is not a laboratory*

By definition, a laboratory is an environment where variables are limited and controlled, such that phenomena and behaviors might be studied in isolation. This allows the experimentalist to deduce specific causes of particular effects, and to make generalizations regarding future events irrespective of circumstantial particularities.

Unlike science, architecture operates at a contaminated scale. It is ultimately a thing in the world and entirely conditional on the specific circumstances of its engenderment, betraying the requisite isolation necessary for scientific analysis. A successful architecture is thus always an urban proposition.

These points do not constitute a disavowal of technology, nor of science and technology. Rather, our intent here is simply to resituate architecture in relation to peripheral developments in other fields, and to strongly assert its disciplinary specificity. As evidenced by the need to spell it out in this very text, never before has the unique expertise of architecture been so gravely at risk, and by extension so abundant in opportunity.

Jesse Reiser FAIA FAAR is a registered architect in New York and a principal of RUR Architecture DPC. He received his Bachelor of Architecture degree from the Cooper Union in New York, and completed his Masters of Architecture at the Cranbrook Academy of Art. He was a fellow of the American Academy in Rome in 1985, and he trained in the offices of John Hejduk and Aldo Rossi prior to forming Reiser + Umemoto with Nanako Umemoto. Jesse is a Professor of Architecture at Princeton University and has previously taught at various schools in the US and Asia, including Columbia University, Yale University, Ohio State University, Hong Kong University, and has lectured widely at various educational and cultural institutions throughout the United States, Europe and Asia. He is also an honorary fellow at the University of Tokyo's School of Engineering.

Scan the icon to view dynamic content

Background

It was around 2010 that I first began formulating and doing research on *blockchains*, digital property, and the issues surrounding data infrastructure in the ownership and authorship of both digital and real property in Architecture and Intellectual Property (IP) law. It was then, too, that I dabbled in the cryptocurrency of the time–back when one *bitcoin* was worth $118–without really understanding that the complementary software program in *Unity3D* that I was developing for my doctoral candidacy, with the help of my research assistant, was, in fact, a research application of what would now be considered a multi-user decentralized *blockchain* platform that offers architects and designers an opportunity to engage with building technology and the internet cloud.

At the time, the culture surrounding discussions of *Non-Fungible Tokens* (NFT) in digital art and museums/art galleries/auction houses was less developed. While perhaps myopic, my principal advisor at the Doctor of Design program at Harvard's Graduate School of Design had little to no faith in the possibility that blockchains would ever be used in the field of Architecture, Engineering, and Construction (AEC). By contrast, my primary advisors at the Harvard Law School, Professors William 'Terry' Fisher and Yochai Benkler, and my secondary advisor at the GSD, Professor Martin Bechthold, found the topic promising and encouraged me to look at how other fields were getting ahead of the curve in both the theoretical and practical application of blockchain-like systems. Martin specifically suggested that I look into a case study of *Boeing*. Between 2010 to 2017, digital ledgers were used primarily in logistics and distribution, finance and law, and focused on production issues within the larger infrastructural distribution networks of supply chains.

Now, in 2022, three years into the COVID-19 pandemic, the exponential impact of digital infrastructure and supply-chain conundrums has generated greater awareness of the woes of builders, real estate developers, contractors, and architects and the ways in which micro and macro distribution channels affect architecture and construction driven by an uncertain global economy, policy, and climate laws.

The foreword to this book is written by my long-time mentor, Jesse Reiser (with Julian Harake) from my days at Princeton University's School of Architecture, while the video interviews for the book, originally recorded, collected, and edited by my co-chair Biayna Bogosian and me for the *Things Left Unsaid* talk series are accessible on the open-access digital platform that complements it.

An abridged selection of the interviews with Saskia Sassen, Michael Young & Kutan Ayata (Young & Ayata), Amber Bartosh, and Jimenez Lai, in which they voice their opinion on cities' engagement with data and ownership, is included in the print version, while interviews with Paola Antonelli, Sarah Williams, Kate Crawford, Indy Johar, and others are available on the open-access database, designed to be read alongside the book. Essays and oppositions by Minerva Tantoco, Andrew Witt, Mik Nayeem (edited by Margo Spiritus), and Lydia Kallipoliti are sandwiched at the end of related chapters. A next steps interview with Greg Lynn, both a friend and mentor, takes us to discussions about the beyond.

Is it fair to say that the internet in the world of *Web 3.0* has become practically as necessary as oxygen? *digitalSTRUCTURES* is a curious attempt to break down, probe, and map out the international force of digital property and data infrastructure. It looks into how we can apply strategies to constructing our urban built environment. It is also a stab at questioning the power of the ownership and authorship of digital and physical goods, and the way in which our digital infrastructure (the internet) is evolving in relation to both the physical construction of our built environment and the private corporations and public states that extend and expand our digital network of fiber-optic cables to connect the modern Web 3.0 world of *phygital* (physical and digital) space.

Introduction

The Current Iteration and Contemporary Relevance

digitalSTRUCTURES provokes a larger body of work that engages with digital property and data infrastructures. Digital currencies (cryptocurrencies) and digital property require large amounts of land, resources, data centers, and infrastructures for storage purposes. The larger and more urgent architectural and urban infrastructural question lies in how to mediate these various kinds of digital exchanges in order to limit the damage they do to our everyday resources.

If our everyday objects are digital and no longer physical, what is the challenge to ecological issues?

How does this affect the future of urban living?

The case studies, interviews, and guest contributions presented here continue the discussions initiated at *CityX Venice, Sezione del Padiglione Italia,* at the *17th La Biennale di Venezia*, and in the talk series *Things Left Unsaid*, organized by co-chair Biayna Bogosian and me. Guest contributors were prompted to challenge and provoke topics related to the issue of open innovation models for operating cities, robotics and artificial intelligent systems, supply chains affected by digital storage, data infrastructure and other matters that play an important role in our Web 3.0 urban digital and real landscapes.

Elaborating on and testing the theme *How do We Live Together*, proposed by the biennale's chief curator, Hashim Sarkis, this book and mixed digital media project explores the contemporary issues surrounding the definition of work and urban living in both Western and Eastern countries. The research provokes interrogations of the post-COVID-19 digital era as it pertains to supply chains, data structures, urban strategies, construction, and the civic planning of future cities.

Taking a mixed-media approach, the book couples a novel exploration of XR (mixed-reality) and AR (augmented reality) in diagrammatic mapping and graphic cartography to examine how data interacts with various open-innovation models in digital property and real property.

This research explores broader developmental topics affecting the humanities and social sciences, such as ethical trade routes and policies of materiality, in order to engage with interdisciplinary and cross-cultural concerns that question the policy challenges facing "democracies" in the 21st century.

As the world is becoming a more circular economy in terms of both information (data) and economic, political, and material exchange, this study is meant to promote greater awareness of the interconnected activities that impact the material (hard goods and soft goods) and technical information exchange of trade in our built environment.

Building materials have significant influence on our world of construction. Trade and material exchange are key to understanding the impact of data and information, that works together with climate change and economic growth. My research is ongoing and part of a larger investigation of two different infrastructural structures - that of the present (contemporary) and that of the past (historic) data infrastructural structures were designed as a systemic network of power. One that increases the modern economies of trade, and the second where urban political dispersion of architectural exchange, in hope, will inform larger discussions by future generations.

As we re-mapped and re-drew the ever-evolving connections of the submarine cable network–the basis of the internet and the future of Web 3.0–we began to see the larger economic and climatic effects on architecture and construction, ones that go beyond supply chains, and are hit by greater digital infrastructural needs as we progress towards a more connected society.

Digital and Real:

Property, Ownership, Authorship - An Operating Definition for the Age of Digital Architecture

Chapter 1 explores the principles of ownership and authorship as they relate to architecture, and the concerns that arise from their legal and economic applications. The chapter also discusses the ways in which the public domain, in the physical and digital realm, exists within, and is impacted by the basic parameters of ownership and authorship, and is applicable to the discussion of collective works and the participatory dialogue within digital works. The future, it argues, will be characterized by the bounds of *participatory* authorship, enabled by multi-user contributions to design goods within the public domain, and *automatic authorship* overseen by economic and legal theories that provide circumstantial support for the distribution of rights to the property of digital and physical contributions.

Megastructures and Infrastructures:

The Internet as Megastructure?

Chapter 2 explores the architecture of data centers and infrastructures, their ongoing popularity as individuals use and save more data, and their impact on climate change.

1964 was the Megayear–the year, according to Reyner Banham, in which Fumihiko Maki coined the term "megastructure" in his *Investigations in Collective Form* **1**. The word is generally believed to derive etymologically from the "megaton" of atomic weaponry, as Ralph Wilcoxon guesses in his *Bibliography: mega(structure)*, and from "infrastructure." Curiously, the term has given rise to other similar terms that are variations of it, and Maki (along with Masato Otaka) and various Metabolists use the term "compositional form" together with "monumentality" to mean "megastructure".

Now, in 2022, the major US technology companies invested in the internet and its privatized expansion are mostly corporations and conglomerates: *Google* (Alphabet), *Microsoft*, *Facebook* (Meta), *Twitter*, *Amazon*, *Cloudflare*, and *Yahoo* (2016). In the late 2010s and early 2020s **2** significant Chinese actors and Chinese state-owned companies, such as Huawei Marine, grew rapidly around the investment and build-out of submarine internet cable structures.

These cables, which crawl the depths of the oceans, are what we call digital infrastructure or substructures, used to connect networked societies trans-continentally and trans-oceanically. The construction of these infrastructures has a dramatic and climatic toll

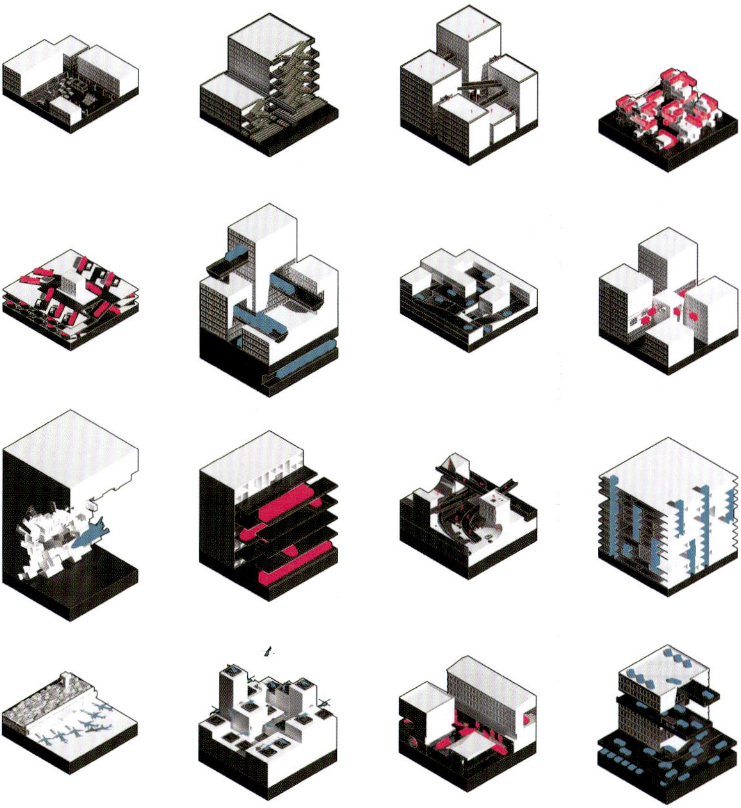

b

on marine life because it requires dredging and thus damaging the ocean floor. Yet, these same megastructures are what allow the trade and supply chains of the architecture and construction industry to perform various formulations.

As we proceed into the world of Web 3.0 and phygital (physical and digital) space, it is difficult not to ask how democracies will continue to hold and freely distribute information, and how logistic channels will distribute our raw materials–especially if digital technologies and data infrastructures are to be soft powered and built by private corporations and select nation-states. Since the internet and data distribution varies from country to country, information aligned with digital governance, and on what is defined as the "western" interpretation of the internet, is still a widely debated topic.

Are Kenzo Tange's Tokyo Bay or Boston Harbor megastructures or architectural infrastructures? The larger complexity of the term in relation to the phygital is further examined in this chapter. Both terms will be continually misinterpreted and playfully interrogated throughout the book to exhaust the nature of *how we are living together* today in a world in which digital property and data infrastructures compound our daily lives. In reference to Hashim Sarkis' brief for the *17th La Biennale di Venezia*.

Robots, Software, Manufacturing:
Can Architecture Be Licensed as a Commodity?

Chapter 3 looks at robotics, software, manufacturing, and construction. As advancements in robotics, automation technologies, and manufacturing capabilities have emerged, so too have questions on what effects these may have on the workforce, especially with regard to the emergence of new means of architectural construction. Meanwhile, the recent shift in architecture towards coding, programming, and both algorithmic and parametric modeling, owe much to computer science. The impact of new technologies on U.S. economic development has been extensively discussed, but the scope and pace of new advances adds additional dimensions to this already familiar conversation.

This chapter considers: 1) whether traditional industrialized workforces will adapt to new automated technologies; 2) whether robotic technologies will displace laborers; 3) the benefits that can be expected from widespread deployment of these technologies; 4) whether architecture can be viewed as a commodity; and 5), if it can, then what insights can architecture glean from computer science and software licensing.

Beginning with a brief history of robotic development, primarily in terms of automation's impact on traditional fields such as industrial manufacturing, the chapter will proceed to examples of how new technologies may affect labor forces that were once considered impervious to them. After examining the relationships between them, the chapter will investigate the macroeconomic effect of robotics and automation as a rapidly advancing and potentially labor-disrupting technology. Finally, the chapter considers the economic interest of licensing and royalties for architecture and questions the commodification of architecture.

Access, Permission, Distribution of Design in Architecture:

How Are We Affected by Cryptocurrency and Digital Exchange?

Chapter 4 highlights and examines the economic and automation trade-offs that the speedy arrival of big data and the next phase of Web 3.0 will generate as both become approachable, asks whether organizations leverage data from the outset to drive value, and examines how machine learning developed from big data and machine-driven design is the best approach for the AEC industry of the future.

The chapter summarizes case studies that demonstrate the importance of architectural CAD software, the *Internet of Things* (IoT), and their role in the ever more fast-paced digital turn of architectural design and the building industry. The case studies discussed in this section reveal how data has grown in scale and across platforms. Specific explorations will include the lineage of architectural software that contributed to digital fabrication and the expedition of manufacturing, 3D printing, the mechanical realities of robotics that are contributing to experimental architecture and construction, the business of distributing and accessing design in the open source and digital world, and finally, the way in which open data affects the governance of our cities.

Within the field of digital media and architecture, there will need to be more discoveries and experimentation made through understanding iteration and versioning. Applications already have the potential to access user-information and distribution of design information through meta-data. Big data has been on the rise as more organizations store, process, and extract value from data of all kind.

From Platform to Phygital:
Realities of Web X.0 in Architecture

Chapter 5 questions the issue of digital/physical property in Web 2's Internet of Things and its transformation into the architecture.

In 2006, *Time* magazine, designated the collective digital "YOU" as the "Person of the Year." By doing so, it referred to the millions of people who, in earlier iterations of the internet, controlled and created the media and financed the new digital democracy.

These same citizens of digital innovation built the new platforms–as can be seen in the early beta developments of Kickstarter, Twitter, Wikipedia, and Facebook–and contributed to the manipulation of international power and information exchange, creating value propositions beyond the traditional product complexity of the ideas and commodity market.

By the early 2000s, peer exchange and crowd organizational strategies were being used to innovate the built environment. The shift has only grown since. Architecture and the construction industry would do well to recognize and benefit from this emerging trend as this kind of open innovation and new media have proven invaluable for consumer goods and corporate vendors.

Whereas the last chapter discussed the relationship of architecture-related software and applications, this one brings together theories about digital collaboration that lead to research that can be applied to the realities of urban and everyday life.

The case studies show a shift from Web 2.0 to Web 3.0, including its (i.e. Web 3.0's) wide-scale adoption in markets The case-studies raise questions about the future direction of the built environment with the advances made by data analytics, which have led to growth in Big Data and phygital (physical and digital) space, with respect to what it means to engage with the meta.

Finally, this chapter elaborates on whether digital collaboration and the IoT will inform or disrupt the evolution of the building industry beyond 3D printing houses and the commodification of architecture In doing so, it will dive into what "digital" really means and does in our digital culture, look at what open data contributes to public infrastructure and civic opportunities, and ask whether architects need to care about the environmental damage caused by data centers if they are not regulated soon.

Conclusion: Whose Digital Property?

From IoT Web 2.0 to Blockchains involving Cryptocurrency in Web 3.0, this inconclusive chapter takes us back to the ways in which our lives are intrinsically connected to data. Data is not fossil fuel; it is not a limited resource, but a great deal of energy is required to store and keep it alive.

Both within the practice of architecture and the world of Web 3.0, it is practically impossible to delineate the future of labor (both visible and invisible) without the coalescence of data infrastructure and digital property. Power is forged from and against the contingencies of invisible labor, the inoperability of platforms and automation, supply-chain disruptions, fractures in infrastructural systems, etc.

The sense of geopolitical urgency in architecture has recently come closer to the brink of rupture thanks to the field's intricate connections to the larger systematic source of data and information. Platforms and clouds of infinite kinds connect in minute daily operations that dictate the function of software and data storage.

Architects and designers are often hired to consult and offer insight on both the physical and virtual real world–a world that we are building with our invisible labor.

Innovations in and the rapid development of the Internet since 1989 have allowed architecture to overcome the traditional limitations of physical space and professional hierarchy. Today the discipline is practiced increasingly in digital space. Online collaboration across industries has led to innumerable advances in both global manufacturing and architecture by facilitating the distribution of electronic files and the exchange of information across borders. However, online collaboration has also increased the vulnerability of creators and innovators, who can do little to protect themselves from the dangers of duplication, illicit file-sharing, and high-speed transfers.

For me, the key takeaway from all this research over the past decade and a half lies in the details of how our information is intrinsically linked to both the physical and digital properties of an evolving data-infused world. Neither law, policy, and/or design can always resolve these issues. This suggests that the practice of architecture and design has become more difficult to define from both generated data and the data generated by its automated systems (be these GAN style software, processing, Grasshopper, G-codes, etc.).

Although we may not always have a chance to take ownership of data, we should still be aware of how data is owned, where it is stored, and potentially, what it is doing to our world (physical and digital) in terms of climate and policy.

References

1 Reyner Banham, "Megayear 1964," in *Megastructure: Urban Futures of the Recent Past*, (Monacelli Press, 2020 [1976]), Chapter 4, Page 76.

2 Doug Brake, "Submarine Cables: Critical Infrastructure for Global Communications," ITIF (Information Technology and Innovation Foundation) Policy Report, April 2019.

Image Credits

a Isolation Rooms - Tara Akdora

b Isolated Infrastructural Cities - JJ Jin & Wendy W Fok

How to Use This Book

There are infographics, charts, maps, and contents that have evolving information, such as the submarine cable map that takes the reader to an online open-access digital platform, accessible to owners of this physical book.

Please scan the QR to activate all the digital contents within the book. This will activate the camera to "see" the digital contents within the book.

Once you have activated the camera, look out for these icons throughout the book. These icons will take you to the enhanced reality digital content areas of the physical book:

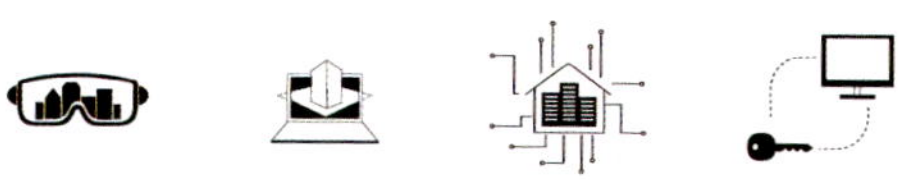

Pro Tip: If you see these icons, scan the entire page to ensure best experience.

1. Scan QR

2. Find Icons

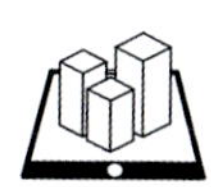

3. Access Enhanced Content

The design of the book can be viewed in chapters or sections. Each chapter comes with a title image. The title image has 'easter eggs' embedded within the image that can be scanned by the reader to reveal a relevant imagery and 3D artifacts that relate to the chapter contents and readings. 2D Diagrams are scannable and complemented by an AR 3D artifact when activated.

Contents will be promised to be updated up to a 3-year period from the publication date.

Scan the icon to view dynamic content

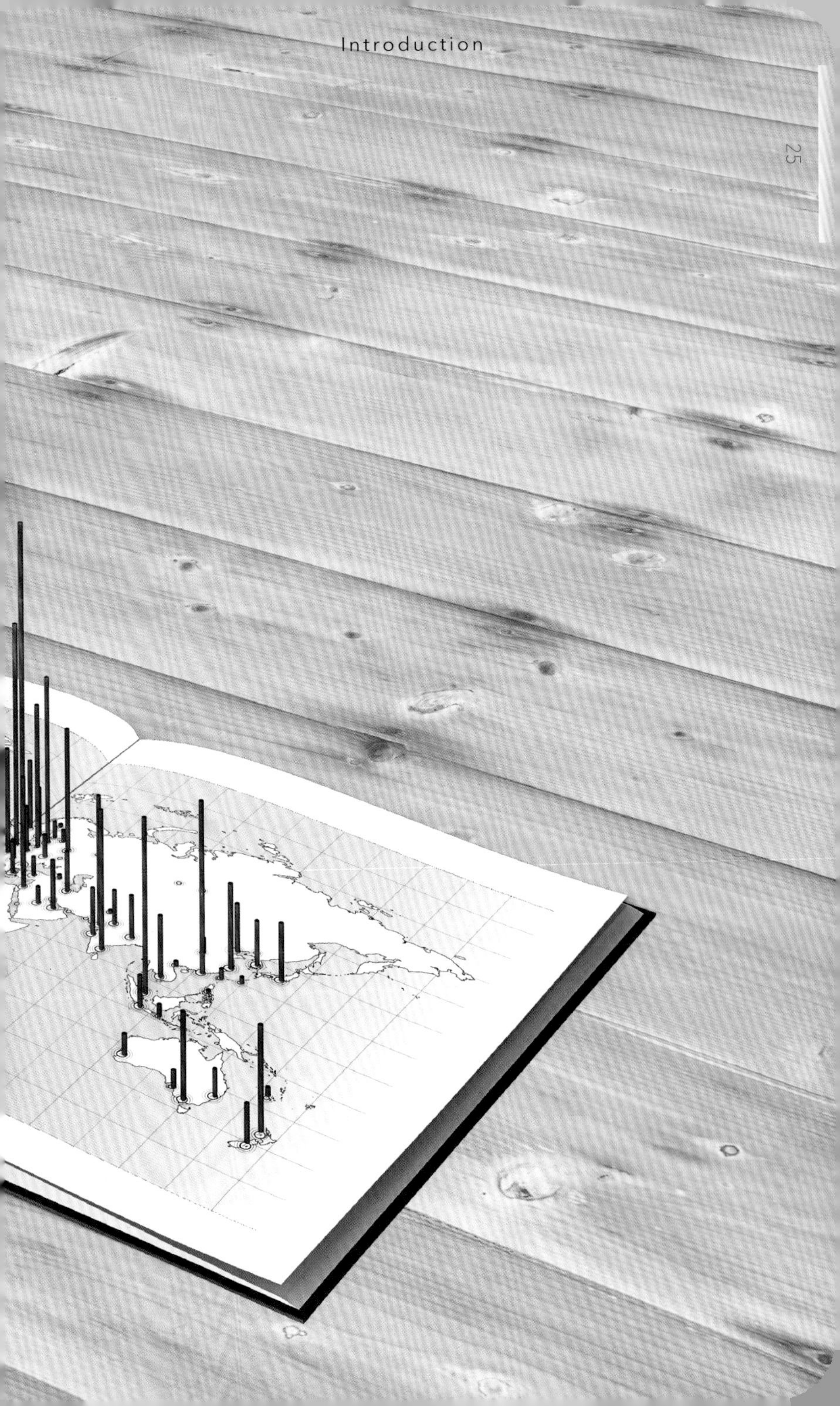

1. Digital and Re
An
6-4138
4649
3-0678
6-2256
7-1410

Property / Ownership / Authorship

rating Definition for the Age of Digital Architecture

1.

"Distance means less and less in the digital world. In fact, an Internet user is utterly oblivious to it. On the Internet, distance often seems to function in reverse ... When a delivery system that looks more like the Internet is used in the general world of entertainment, the planet becomes a single media machine."

– Nicholas Negroponte 1

Ownership / Authorship in the Age of Digital Architecture

This chapter explores the principles of *ownership* and *authorship* as they relate to architecture as well as the consequent concerns that arise from their legal and economic applications. The chapter also discusses how the public domain, in its physical and digital realm, exists within–and is impacted by–the basic parameters of ownership and authorship, while bearing application to the discussion of collective works, and the participatory dialogue within digital works. What is more, the future will be characterized by the bounds of *participatory* authorship, enabled by multi-user contributions to designed goods in the public domain, and *automatic authorship* overseen by economic and legal theories that provide circumstantial support for the distribution of rights to the property of digital and physical contributions.

Authorship in the Collaborative Digital World of Architectural Practice

Authorship and its Characterization in Architecture and Design

The architect, as singular author, has been integral to the traditional concept of architecture as a field. However, this traditional paradigm is quickly growing obsolete and the notion of authorship destabilized. In the current regime of digital design, more architects play multiple roles as programmers, designers, and users of digital and transferable files. Moreover, today, the interpretation of *how* an architect designs and *what* an architect does with architecture has larger implications–as does what happens to a digital file–especially as more collaborators and contributors participate in the development of a digital file or digital architecture before it becomes physical.

Authorship takes a startlingly different shape once multiple media start inter-correlating between forms and platforms. In such a scenario, architects must contemplate the play among themselves as they are now both the consumers and producers of digital files. The line between the two becomes increasingly porous as the notion of authorship becomes diffused due to the multiple roles and media in which architects work. Their task is manifold; they will download a script, edit the code, and apply a transformative nature between code (GAN style, neural networks, etc.) and physical form. Once they are given the tools of the computer and programming language, architects are no longer linear practitioners.

Mario Carpo's *The Alphabet and the Algorithm* addresses the contemporary state of architectural practice and its struggle with authorship. What Carpo calls the "modern paradigm" the architectural authorship that emerged from Leon Battista Alberti's obsession with the author became obsolete with the "digital turn" of the 1990s (Allen, 2011) **2**. Discussions of art and ownership certainly have antecedents in art history and philosophy. One may turn to none other than Walter Benjamin in *Works of Art in the Age of Mechanical Reproduction* to see the degree to which social and technological change has led to various means of interpretating the emerging state of file-sharing and the digital property of authorship.

The important shift from authorship is also the concern of ownership. How one obtains control of the distribution of files and uses digital distribution in an ethic manner lies at the center of the authorial enigma. Identical copies of an architectural design can proliferate on the Internet because technological measures enable the distribution of the file, even as the legal rights of that file and its author are still being determined. Authorship allows for attribution, but ownership is where the equity–or economics–of the discussion is taking a new turn.

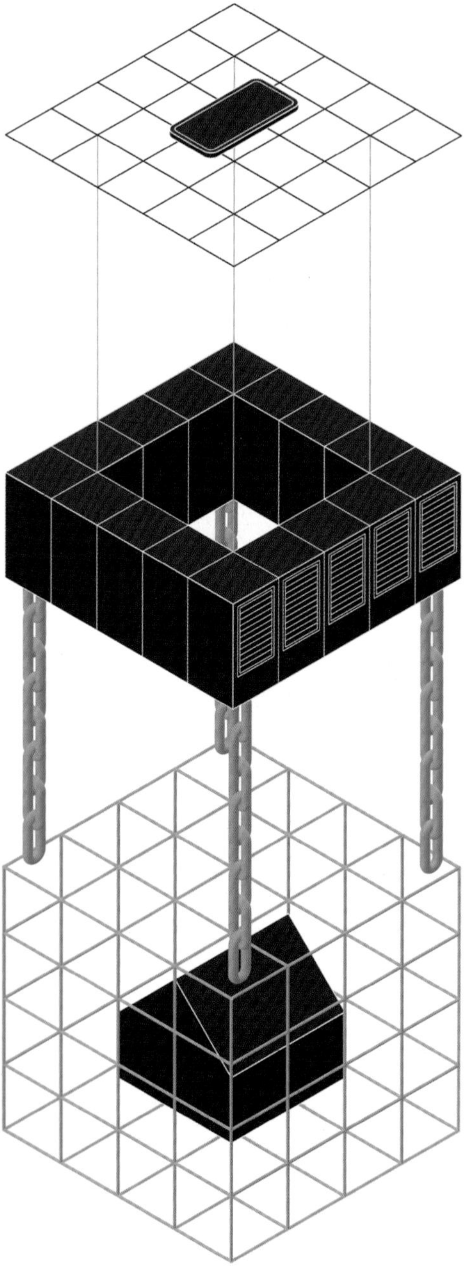

a

In 2004, Google announced plans to scan the contents of several of the largest academic libraries, make those titles not under copyright available online, allow searches within them, but also display excerpts of books still under copyright to the public (Banner, 2011) **3**. By 2009, Google had scanned over ten million books. The result was public outrage, an ongoing lawsuit, and an outcry for legal reform by authors and publishers who claimed that the move had undermined the ownership of the texts.

The larger questions of this case study consider how its impact could undermine the practice of architecture. If one were to 3D scan, then build an entire empire of 3D models of the world's buildings by less and more famous designers and architects, how would this affect the explicit direction of architecture as a field? Who would control those designs? The answers would be full of holes since in the world of law, the practice of architecture is simplistic, and most cases of duplication, as in choreography and fashion, are covered by extralegal norms. *The Architecture Act of 1990* is very new, compared to other copyright laws, and much of the protection of the law is duly covered only to the built, constructed, and physical building.

Property, in the form of both digital and physical goods and exchange, has come under assault in the Digital Age. The networked state of the contemporary world has a framework of physical and tangible entities that are overloaded with intangible and non-physical information that is richly explored and solely available online. In the Wealth of Networks, Yochai Benkler claims that peer production is the wave of the future, and the fact that this "emergence of more effective collective action practices that are decentralized but do not rely on either the price system or a managerial structure for coordinationii" (Benkler, 2006) **4** allows for a third way (Banner, 2011) of getting things done. In *Intellectual Property in the Information Age: The Politics of Expanding Ownership Rights*, Debora Halbert similarly supports this claim. Examining the expansion of intellectual property rights in the Information Age, she criticizes the theoretical foundations of copyright law as well as the current U.S. approach to it, and suggests that we should not extend copyright law without critically assessing the impact of such a move on the free exchange of information.

The question, then, is should *intangible* information be free for distribution, online and through digital formats? The internet and digital platforms of exchange promises an economic imbalance in the form of market exchange, in which the information generated is, to some degree, less equitable and is less likely to be distributed as duplicates are more easily accessible. If intangible information is free then the internet and digital platform of exchange may lead to economic imbalance. In such case, a good will not necessarily be produced to be sold on the market, "not because someone higher up in the chain of authority ordered its production, but rather as a result of the uncoordinated choices of the producers themselves" (Banner, 2011). Central to this discussion are programmers and competition-crazed designers and architects who produce for the sake of production and to formalize their notoriety and status, rather than for economic exchange. In this scenario, the proliferation of property as a means of authorship would greatly diminish its role in a world characterized by this form of transfer.

Participatory Authorship and Automatic Authorship

Creative agency within architecture and the crucial issue of authorship in architecture often tie in with the problem of the architect's role in cultural production. The discussion on authorship also reflects the tension between the architect as the mediator between art and the ethics of social responsibility (a mediator generally mediates between two things/entities).

The authorial rights of physical objects, especially within architecture, thus become a means to an end, especially when the file can be produced from a digital copy. The physicality of buildings provides protection against violations of intellectual property; buildings are, by their material nature, tangible objects that are more easily quantifiable in legal discourse. The discriminating governance of the community's ability to access a file, in such case as open-access of files through digital authorship, then becomes a notion of diminishing means. If the authority of an author permit for the publication or manufacture of a digital good through an embedded directory of data, the public ownership of the good must be borne by all members of the public, and no member can divest themself of that ownership (Alchian, 2007) **5**. The economic thought of property, in the ownership of a public property, therefore, is not voluntary. As in public property, like digital information on the internet, is accessible to all, but is also not owned by all.

Carpo argues that the "primary author" sets up a generic system, while "secondary authors" or "interactors" merely specify the manifestations we call buildings.v To define this, I will consider two kinds of authorship that formalize the current collaborative state of contemporary digital architecture: 1) participatory authorship and 2) automatic authorship.

Rachel Elizabeth Meyers wrote in her 2014 thesis, *"In Search of an Author: From Participatory Culture to Participatory Authorship"* that, similar to video games, *Participatory Authorship* encompasses variable authors who contribute to a combined or an already prescribed creation. The rights management here is similar to the legal theory of collective property arrangement. Participatory authorship requires active participation of audience members in the creation, expansion, and adaptation of another's creative work.

The 2011 Yale School of Architecture conference, *"On Architecture and Authorship: A Conversation"* was devoted to the concept of participatory authorship and its relationship to creative and collective property in architecture and design. Its organizers, Nikolaus Hirsch, Jorge Otero-Pailos, and David Adjaye, discussed in depth how architecture and buildings emerge within each other through acts of creative agency. Rather than focus on the *artist-as-author,* they stressed the importance of *creative agents*, namely, all those who intervene.

> The question is not who is the author? But who creates the creator? As creative agents engaged with an existing work, you might say that we help create the creator the moment we begin to intervene – the moment we begin to determine the scope of the project, to process the brief, and to analyze what is historically significant and worth preserving about the existing building or city, which might very well be the intervention of a previous author. There are also institutional mechanisms of

> creating the creator – museum curators, gallerists, critics, government bureaucrats, funders – all these external actors or clients who determine authorship, who participate in creating the creator. There is a very strong political and social field that emerges when we begin to think of a work of architecture as a co-authored work.
>
> – Jorge Otero-Pailos

As discussed by Hirsh, Adjaye, and Otero-Pailos, the cultural implications of co-authorship reveal the blurred boundaries of "multi-authorship" in traditional architecture. As Otero-Pailos observes, "every work of architecture is a work of co-authorship, even if some co-authors often remain structurally hidden... the sequence is clear: first planning, then construction, and then eventually the architect hands the building over to the client."

The three architects also ask whether architectural practice truly embraces the opportunity to improve form or bring transparency to co-authorship. What they do not address is whether the ownership of information should be transferred and made transparent to multiple "co-authors." They also offer no suggestions or examples of how the future of the AEC industry might become more about co-authorship. In my opinion, co-authorship is inherently structured into the collaborative model of this industry. Nonetheless, AEC will continue to lag behind its potential–especially if compared to start-up models (as discussed in Chapter 5) – until it sees the systemization of new business models and greater awareness within its practice. The industry should also explore the use of *Blockchain* (as discussed in Chapter 5) and means of integrating it, borrowing systematic influences of organization, and that AEC should look towards the technology sector for help with systematic organization. Meanwhile, it should do either that or innovate its modes of digital tooling (as discussed in Chapter 3 and 4).

Automatic Authorship is a term derived from the world of computer science, from the "automatic authorship attribution" code as it is commonly understood on Google+ and other social media sites. These sites use a form of online profiling that allows users and creators to attribute their work "automatically," that is, have their works instantly labelled and attributed to their authorship in the digital sphere. This type of automatic authorship allows users and creators to be identified by their digital codes, which are

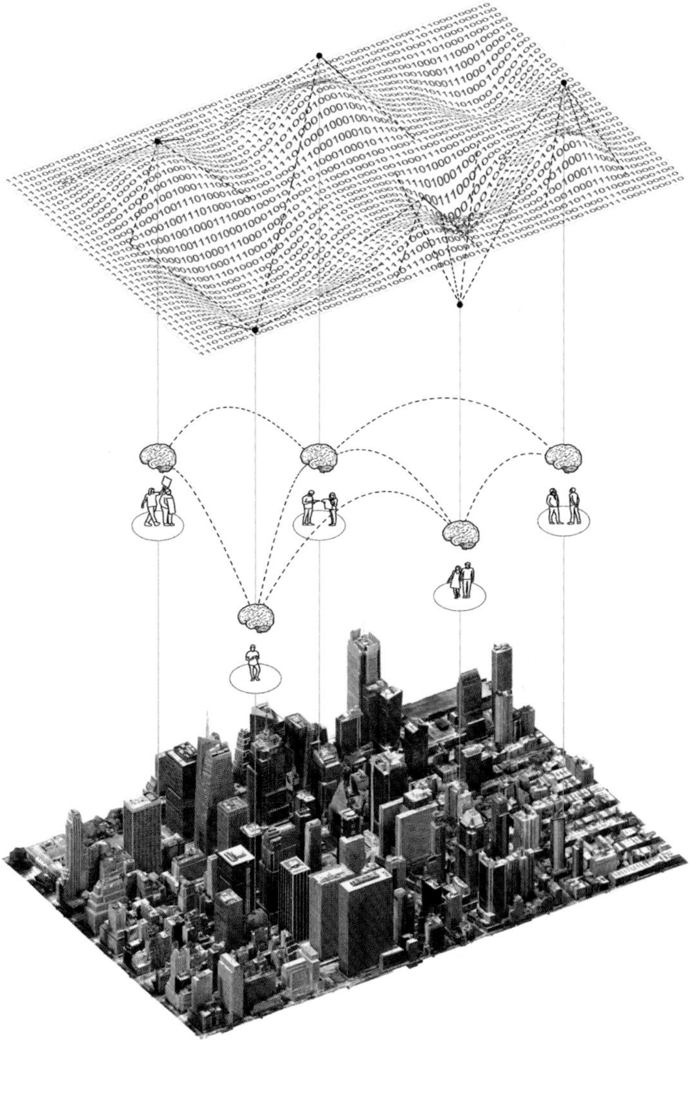

b

connected to their online accounts or IP addresses, as well as to the computers or programs that allow them to create these works. Unlike participatory authorship, automatic authorship does not allow users and creators to remove their rights of authorship. This form of attribution and contribution is also not anonymous.

Due to the perpetual speed and struggles of the technology of current digital culture, authorship may now be a dream of the past. For architects and designers, the endeavor to obtain authority over their work is still an imperative battle in those design fields that could benefit from participatory exchange and collaboration. Issues of control are central to the discussion of property and attribution within the field of architectural file transfer, while ownership can be governed through various purviews. The discerning fact of our digital culture, however, is the struggle with the limitations of the new efficiencies of manufacturing. Although the speed of production allows for more rapid production, as does 3D printing or rapid prototyping tooling (due to the expiration of the laser sintering patent), for example, the realities of producing formal translations of digital files through replication offers a truly seamless transferal of quality to the lived world. Digital files can easily be duplicated in new media. The digital rights of the files embedded within these files, as in the case of Meta data, can be transferred within the intangible world. Still, many of these manufacturing methods limit the transfer of these rights from the digital format to the production of physical objects from digital files.

Authorship Without Ownership

Is authorship without ownership of the works produced possible in the field of architecture and design? This is an idea that is often fantasized, but hardly ever put into practice. According to Otero-Pailo, a sense of authorship emerges in the political and social sphere when the public begins thinking of a piece of architecture as a co-authored work. **6** This leads to the question of *who creates the creator*–a point of entry into a larger architectural discussion on the direct intervention of the author.

In copyright law, the *creator of a work* and the *owner of the legal rights* to the work are specifically defined. The author is not necessarily the owner. Many of the determining factors in modern-day design rules are determined through contracts and the assigned rights of the work. Loosely speaking, the *creator of the work* (an author, a photographer, an artist, a musician, etc.) is referred to as the *creator* or *author,* while the entity with the *ownership of legal rights* to publish, modify, and republish the work is referred to as the owner.

Although the English philosopher John Locke does not discuss the rights of ownership with reference to the division of labor, there are several indications that the problem would not have troubled him. He argues that property is part of a known "common stock" derived from the context of medieval commons. **7** The fact that a laborer worked on a product does not automatically make that product his/her property. Locke continues:

> We see in Commons, which remain so by compact, that this taking any part of what is common, and removing it out of the state of nature leaves it in, which begins the property; without which the common is of no use. And the taking of this or that part, does not depend on the express consent of all the Commoners. Thus the grass my horse has bit; the turfs my servant has cut and the ore I have dug in any place where I have right to them in common with others, becomes my property...
>
> - John Locke, *Second Treatise of Government*

Today, technology has entered the dialogue around property rights. As Diane Zimmermanix points out, digital technology has provided *prosumers*, **8** that is, prospective consumers, with the power to easily transmit creative and informational works, thanks not only to the "radical diminution in the cost of producing," but also to unlimited transferability in the world of digital platforms. The multiplication of works also raises questions about authorship and its relation to the ownership of works.

The very notion of authorship is, in fact, an invented one. Defining authorship with respect to art and architecture, Mario Carpo and Walter Benjamin emphasize "reproduction." Carpo writes about authorship as an early modern pursuit of identical reproduction of data and information. Similar to Alberti's obsession with authorship and the 1990's digital turn's obsession with authorship. *In the Architecture in the Age of Printing* (MIT Press, 2001), Carpo argues in the *Alphabet* (Carpo's book) argues that the desire to reproduce effortless variability in production and authorship caused by technological advancements is the result of the automated systems, generative forms, and algorithms offered by modern computational innovations.

Authorship as a concept has its roots in the Industrial Revolution. Benjamin wrote extensively about copy and reproduction as they related to the invention of the printing press. In his 1936 essay, he grappled with the impact of the Industrial Revolution on early concepts of authorship. The Digital Age has seen another paradigm shift, to digital reproduction. The current possibilities of reproduction are multifold. Options for digital file transfers include Adobe Photoshop, online appropriation, and social media exchange. Reproduction has facilitated a new form of exchange in architecture and design as well—an exchange of innovations

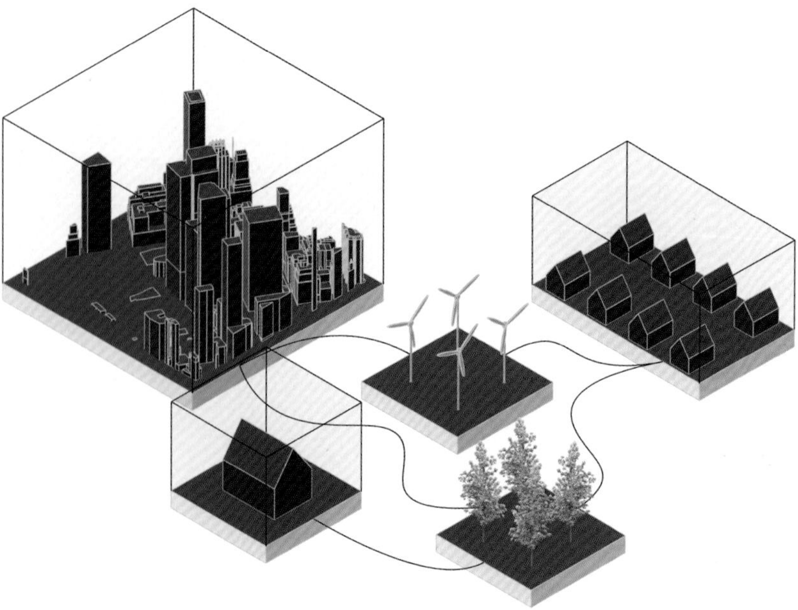

c

that brings to light the collaborative practice, participatory design, online communities, and sharing economy of CAD files and various other records. The question that remains is how technologies like encryption and digital watermarking facilitate workability for creators under the "paracopyright law" **9**. Why are they desirable to creators? The issues of authorship that arise in the Digital Age may lack the protections of ownership, especially when the virtual exchange of objects supersedes the traditional means and normative use of protocols and value propositions.

The Principal of Ownership in Law and Economics Applied to Architecture

Consequences of Ownership

The custom in the architectural profession is for the architect, and not the client, to retain ownership of drawings and plans. **10** Within the basic interpretation of architectural works, ownership is thus determined by the contracts established between client and architect. However, the larger consequences of the contemporary debate over ownership of digital versus real property often lead to negotiations among multiple participants and multiple owners. In 1990, *Section 102 of the United States Copyright Act* was amended so that the artistic copyright of works of architecture made after 1990 would extend for the life of the author plus 70 years. As Otero-Pailo, points out in *On Architecture and Authorship*, the Copyright Act has important implications for the life of recent buildings since those designed after 1990 are more likely than older buildings to be subject to conservative preservation interventions given that the original designs of the latter lack such copyright protection. And while critical and experimental preservation is moving away from 19th-century ideas about originality and authorship in architecture, copyright law is reinforcing the idea of a single, original author. Legally, buildings are preserved for the public good, which is why private property activists have traditionally been opposed to preservation and portray it as a violent government "takeover" of private property, although it is merely a form of regulation.

The critiques of the 1960s and the 1970s, structuralist and post-structuralist, revealed that architecture is more than a building and part of a larger discourse. **11** This is evident in the many dialogues purporting that the building is of less significance to architecture than is a movement. It is also what sparked the critique of the role of *architect-author*. This movement subsequently reinforced the traditional perception of the *architect as author*, whereby the architect who stamped or signed the building was regarded as the author. Accordingly, the *creative agency* and larger participation of the collective, or the designers who worked as creative agents on the architecture, were disregarded. The notion of the architect was singular, not participatory. The formation of the traditional architect as the sole creator thus diminished the importance of ownership in the multi-agent model **12** of design. Since the late 1990s and early 2000s, the multi-agent designer–and the multi-authored design–have grown more prevalent in the parametric and algorithm-based forms of computational architecture, as the role of designers, in particular, and the computational methods that they employ have gained momentum. **13**

The discourse on collective ownership in the practice of architectural open-platform design is currently garnering greater interest. Open-platform forums purport to offer open access, thereby expanding collective ownership. Founded by Jose Sanchez in 2011, *Plethora* is a digital educational project that advocates for online computational training in digital tools and techniques for architectural use. The *(c)ode-(c)ollective*, likewise inaugurated in 2011, is a *"Digital Learning + Script + Code Collective forum for Grasshopper, Rhino, Parametric Modeling, and other digital media and tooling"* that poses as an educational and developing archive site for formulating the critical utility of digital design. These types of open-platform forums–and many others–offer the transfer of online exchange between various means of collective participation on architectural education, but also - and most critically -provide a sense of ownership and communal authorship through their mode of creation. Other online platforms, such as *OpenSim* **14** and *Git Hub* **15** are more traditional in the computer science community, but are also heavily used by architects and computational designers who help build coding languages in the digital world of computational architectural design.

Ownership in Relation to Collective Works in Law

According to law *17 of U.S. Code § 201* (ownership of copyright), ownership, in the driest sense of the law, can be broken down into four accounts. **16** However, the creator of a copyrighted work does not always own the copyright. In some cases, other persons or entities do. There are also rules governing copyright ownership when two or more people create the work. Finally, copyright owners can assign rights to the copyright to other people, particularly for the purpose of marketing the protected work. The factors pertaining to ownership in copyright, include: a) initial ownership **17**; b) works made for hire **18**; c) contribution to collective works **19**; d) transfer of ownership **20**; and e) involuntary transfer **21**. The rest of this chapter is devoted to the "contribution to collective works" as it relates to ownership rights.

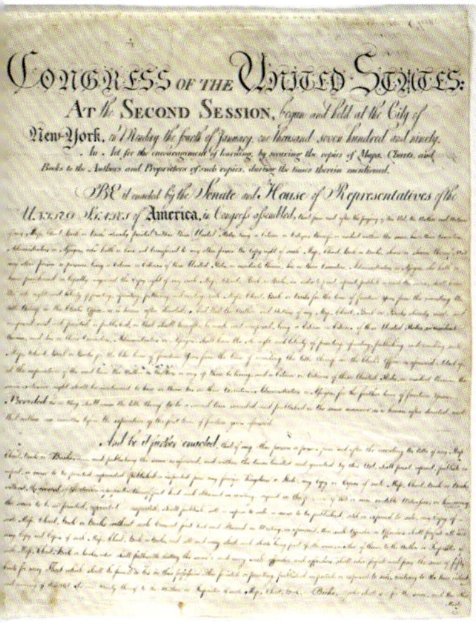

Congress of the United States:
At the Second Session, begun and held at the City of New-York, on Monday the fourth of January, one thousand seven hundred and ninety.
An Act for the encouragement of learning, by securing the copies of Maps, Charts, and Books to the Authors and Proprietors of such copies, during the times therein mentioned.
Be it enacted by the Senate and House of Representatives of the United States of America, in Congress assembled, [illegible]

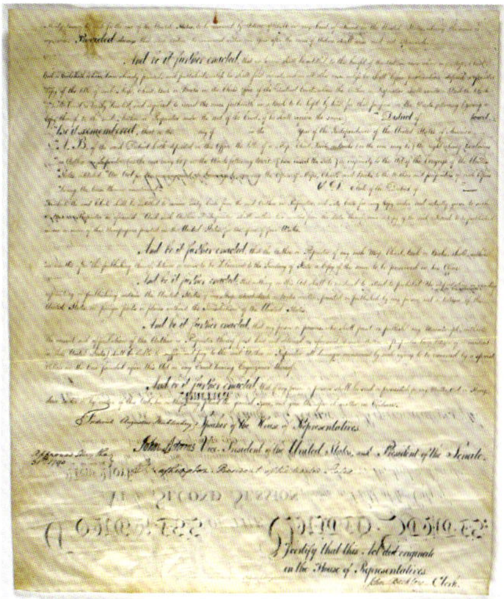

[illegible]
Speaker of the House of Representatives
Vice President of the United States, and President of the Senate
I certify that this Act did originate in the House of Representatives
Clerk.

d

Historically, the *Copyright Act of 1790* was a two-page article enacted by the Senate and House of Representatives of the Congress of the United State, and issued on May 31st, 1790. The original article was passed to protect creators, or "authors," for "any map, chart, book or books, written, printed, or published" (Section 5, Copyright Act of 1790). Between 1790 and 1991, the two-page article grew to a doctrine of several hundred pages, which by 2015, had seen over twenty attempts at reform.

The current Copyright Law of the United States—hereafter, the "Copyright Act"—is intended to encourage the creation of art and culture by rewarding authors and artists with a set of exclusive rights. **22** While granting them the exclusive right to make and sell copies of their works, it also provides individuals the right to creative derivative works, and to perform or display these works publicly, using the original version of the work(s). **23** According to the U.S. Supreme Court, a plaintiff suing for copyright infringement has to show "(1) ownership of a valid copyright, and (2) copying of constituent elements of the work that are original."

Ongoing innovations in the international artistic arena call for a robust discussion on the relevance, purpose, and effective circumvention of copyright laws. The art market relies heavily on software and open-source dispositions as it presides over the advancement and interchange of digital media and technology (including CAD and 3D printing, among other digital tools). Copyright law should be regarded as a means of advancing digital media in the ability for creators to innovate their fields, or else be complemented by technological measures administered by the Copyright Office that work in tandem with these. Any such dealings require a better understanding of technological advancement for the sake of protecting the appropriation of arts and open-source software.

Digital tools should be looked on as a means of enhancing—but not replacing or surpassing—the creator's power to intervene in the intellectual or critical analytical process from concept to reality. While the fabrication process can be limited by the techniques and tools applied to a given product, the ability to examine and think critically about an iterative process of physical experimentation should transcend the pure creative process. The current Copyright law limits the experimental and iterative processes of creative prototyping or versioning, the testing of multiple materials, as well as the creator's ability to formulate a coherent technical and design methodology that could be further refined and developed, in both physical and theoretical terms.

Networked Systems / Commons

The Internet has reshaped communication, but more importantly, it has also transformed how society gathers data and processes information. Therefore, to move copyright law into the digital millennium, the Copyright office must take into consideration the ethical and equitable measures needed to protect the use of advanced technology, in relation to the appropriation of the visual, design, and sound arts.

If copyright is to advance the creative process in the sciences and the arts, then it must be able to identify the source of creation and design, along with the designer through whom the information included in the metadata is distributed, much as information is distributed by a label in a museum; The alternative is to include only enough information to enable the identification and endorsement of the original creator. Architects should adapt to tagging their work with meta-data, similar to the current practice of tagging digital songs and movies in the entertainment industry, **24** as in the case of *Digital Rights Management* (DRM)-protected music. **25**

William Terry Fisher, the *Wilmer Hale Professor of Intellectual Property Law* at the Harvard Law School and faculty director of the *Berkman Klein Center for Internet and Society*, has proposed the use of digital fingerprinting in combination with a royalty, or fee-based system and encrypted information as an alternative method of compensation. **26** If the legal protection measures in the law of copyright prove incapable of ensuring the distribution of creations over the internet or in a digital format, the reform of the legal intellectual property and copyright system should promote the ability of traceable metadata in creative works to serve as an ethical and equitable manner of rewarding creators and owners of copyrighted materials.

The May/June 2013 edition of the *Foreign Affairs* Journal published an article by Kenneth Cukier and Viktor Mayer Schoenberger that describes three ways of understanding and approaching the rise of big data. **27** The general attack method is: 1) to understand, collect, and use a great deal of data rather than settle for small amounts or samples; 2) to show preference for highly curated and pristine data, instead of accepting sloppiness and tolerating the inaccuracy that benefits the vast amount of data, which outweighs the cost of using smaller amounts; 3) to stop the quest to discover the cause of things and instead accept correlations. Whether the approaches mentioned here is the only approach, the larger issue of the developmental understanding between *gathered* data and *useable* data remains in the stage of *beta* interpretation. These opinions have truly become the underlying issues of open-sourced software, even to crowd-sourced projects.

Behavioral economics have allegedly shown that humans are conditioned to see causes even where none exist. **28** Benkler reveals that when organizing production, free software projects do not rely on markets or managerial hierarchies, while Suber insists that the development of open access would allow consumers to better adapt and share perfect copies of creations at virtually no cost by offering variety. **29** Programmers generally do not participate in projects because their boss tells them to do so. This eliminates the need for any discussion of market-based, firm-based, and/or hybrid economic models. However, the plus point of participatory, collaborative freeware is the basic and radical challenge that it proposes. This therefore posits the rational question: if the actor is not motivated by profit, then what progressive motive should they have? The progressive motive could be altruism, however, the development of communal trust is often a devised cause.

Our contemporary understanding of the network environment of a radically decentralized ownership network is an interpretation of non-proprietary system, It is based on sharing resources and outputs among widely distributed, loosely connected individuals who cooperate with each other, without relying on either market signals or managerial commands. Whereas the basis of Benkler's *commons-based peer production*, is a radical new modality of organizational production suggesting an asymmetrical purpose of "the owner" and their relationship to the commons. This can include the relationship between who uses the commons, and what could one do within the commons. This pushes the discussion on necessary parameters to ask a) whether the system is open to anyone or solely to a defined group, and b) whether the commons system is regulated or unregulated. **30**

Ultimately, the regulated or unregulated system also permits for certain socio-political interventions, whereby a regulated approach will always have a hierarchy of system management, which controls the access between certain layers of information. This brings into question the ability to control ownership over and user interface between the different layers of information sold to individuals who "buy into" a crowd-sourced project. Meanwhile, the concern of unregulated systems is to outright avoid having joint product appropriation by a single party, where participants in a traceable or licensed system should be required to retain copyrights of their contributions to the model. Their ability to do so, however, would allow users to license the distribution, reuse, or perhaps further exploration of the crowd-sourced project (design).

References

1 Nicholas Negroponte. *Being Digital*, "The Typology of a Shrinking Planet," p. 178. Vintage Books. 1995.

2 Armen Albert Alchian, *Property Rights and Economic Behavior*, ed. by Daniel K. Benjamin (Indianapolis, IN: Liberty Fund, c2006), p. 35. Retrieved from: http://lccn.loc.gov/2005044683

3 Banner, Stuart. *American Property - A History of How, Why, and What We Own*. Harvard University Press. 2011.

4 Benkler, Yochai, *The Wealth of Networks: How Social Production Transforms Markets and Freedoms*. New Haven, Yale University Press. 2006. pp 62 - 63

5 Armen Albert Alchian, *Property Rights and Economic Behavior*, ed. by Daniel K. Benjamin (Indianapolis, IN: Liberty Fund, c2006), p. 35. Retrieved from: http://lccn.loc.gov/2005044683

6 David Adjaye, Nikolaus Hirsch, and Jorge Otero-Pailos, "On Architecture and Authorship: A Conversation," Places Journal (October 2011). Retrieved from: https://placesjournal.org/article/on-architecture-and-authorship-a-conversation

7 Karen I. Vaughn, "John Locke and the Labor Theory of Value," *Journal of Libertarian Studies* 2. No 4 (1978): pp 311.

8 Prosumer: a prospective consumer involved in the design, manufacture, or development of a product or service. The term is also once popularized by economist and author, Don Tapscott. Retrieved from: http://dontapscott.com/tag/prosumer/ *See also* Susan Gunelius, "The Shift from CONsumers to PROsumers," *Forbes* 3 (July 2010). Retrieved from: http://www.forbes.com/sites/work-in-progress/2010/07/03/the-shift-from-consumers-to-prosumers/"

9 Paracopyright Law: a term derived from Diane Zimmerman's paper on Authorship without Ownership, in which she highlights the laws, such as the Digital Millennium Copyright Act (DMCA) Pub. L. No. 105-304,112 Stat. 2863 (1998) (codified as amended at 17 U.S.C. §§ 1201-1205 (Supp. 1998). *amended* by 17 U.S.C.A., §§ 1201-1204 (West Supp. 2000)) that augment traditional copyright, but do not actually offer direct rights in protected expression. For example: the DMCA helps copyright owners by protecting their ability to encrypt works so that copying them is more difficult. Adding to the list are Creative Commons and their attribution rights, which pertain to the use of creators and online users for rights distributed through the Internet.

10 Authorship as previously addressed in art and architecture:
Carpo, Mario. *The Alphabet and the Algorithm* / Mario Carpo. Cambridge, Mass. : MIT Press, c2011.
Mario writes about *Authorship* -- The early modern pursuit of identical reproduction through the authorial obsession of Alberti, into the digital turn of the 1990s. Similarly tackled in the *Architecture in the Age of Printing* (MIT Press, 2001), Carpo in the *Alphabet* argues the desire to reproduce effortless variability in production

and authorship due to the technological advancements and abilities arrived by automated system, generative forms, and algorithms offered by the modern computational innovations.

Benjamin, Walter. *The Work of Art in the Age of Mechanical Reproduction*, 1936
Benjamin writes extensively about the copy and the reproduction due to the industrial revolution, an examination of the changed experience of art in modern capitalist society, where mechanical reproduction is not only possible but expected. The essay further speaks on explorations on media and theories of reproduction in the visual arts of the machine age.

Authorship as addressed by legal definition:
"The product of creative expression, especially literature, music, art, and graphic designs, is referred to as work of authorship. Copyright protects a work of authorship if it fulfills three criteria. First is that the work should be original and should not be a copy of such original. Secondly, the work should be presented in a fixed medium, such as a computer disk, a canvas, or a paper. Finally, there should be some creativity involved in the work's creation; however the amount of creativity required depends on the particular work. Work of authorship is also termed as creative work." Retrieved from: http://definitions.uslegal.com/w/work-of-authorship/

11 Jorge Otero-Pailos, "On Architecture and Authorship: A Conversation," *Places Journal* (October 2011). Retrieved from: https://placesjournal.org/article/on-architecture-and-authorship-a-conversation

12 A multi-agent system (M.A.S.) is a computerized system composed of multiple interacting intelligent agents within an environment. Multi-agent systems can be used to solve problems that are difficult or impossible for an individual agent or a monolithic system to solve.

13 Patrik Schumacher concludes by arguing that advances in crowd and multi-agent modeling techniques provide designers with a powerful new tool for shaping how users interact with environments. October 2012. Video retrieved from: http://sma.sciarc.edu/subclip/patrik-schumacher-parametric-semiology-clip_7732/ Text retrieved from: http://www.patrikschumacher.com/Texts/Parametricism%20Order_Semiology.html

14 OpenSimulator is an open source multi-platform, multi-user 3D application server. It can be used to create a virtual environment (or world) which can be accessed through a variety of clients, on multiple protocols. It also has an optional facility (the Hypergrid) to allow users to visit other OpenSimulator installations across the web from their 'home' OpenSimulator installation. In this way, it is the basis of a nascent distributed Metaverse. Retrieved from: http://opensimulator.org/wiki/Main_Page

15 GitHub is where great software is built. With more than 10 million people, GitHub is a community where developers can easily discover, reuse, and contribute to more than 24 million projects using an industry standard workflow. Retrieved from: https://github.com/about

16 The Copyright Act of 1976 grants a number of exclusive rights to copyright owners, including the:
• *Reproduction right* -- the right to make copies of a protected work
• *Distribution right* -- the right to sell or otherwise distribute copies to the public
• *Right to create adaptations* -- the right to prepare new works based on the protected work (called derivative works), and
• *Performance and display rights* -- the rights to perform a protected work or to display a work in public.

17 17 U.S. Code § 201 (a) Initial Ownership – *Copyright in a work protected under this title vests initially in the author or authors of the work. The authors of a joint work are co-owners of copyright in the work.* Accessed May 1, 2014: http://www.law.cornell.edu/uscode/text/17/201

17 U.S. Code § 201 (b) Works Made for Hire – *In the case of a work made for hire, the employer or other person for whom the work was prepared is considered the author for purposes of this title, and, unless the parties have expressly agreed otherwise in a written instrument signed by them, owns all of the rights comprised in the copyright.* Accessed May 1, 2014: http://www.law.cornell.edu/uscode/text/17/201

17 U.S. Code § 201 (c) Contributions to Collective Works – *Copyright in each separate contribution to a collective work is distinct from copyright in the collective work as a whole, and vests initially in the author of the contribution. In the absence of an express transfer of the copyright or of any rights under it, the owner of copyright in the collective work is presumed to have acquired only the privilege of reproducing and distributing the contribution as part of that particular collective work, any revision of that collective work, and any later collective work in the same series.* Accessed May 1, 2014: http://www.law.cornell.edu/uscode/text/17/201

17 U.S. Code § 201 (d) Transfer of Ownership –
(1) The ownership of a copyright may be transferred in whole or in part by any means of conveyance or by operation of law, and may be bequeathed by will or pass as personal property by the applicable laws of intestate succession.
(2) Any of the exclusive rights comprised in a copyright, including any subdivision of any of the rights specified by section 106, may be transferred as provided by clause (1) and owned separately. The owner of any particular exclusive right is entitled, to the extent of that right, to all of the protection and remedies accorded to the

copyright owner by this title. Accessed May 1, 2014: http://www.law.cornell.edu/uscode/text/17/201

17 U.S. Code § 201 (e) Involuntary Transfer – *When an individual author's ownership of a copyright, or of any of the exclusive rights under a copyright, has not previously been transferred voluntarily by that individual author, no action by any governmental body or other official or organization purporting to seize, expropriate, transfer, or exercise rights of ownership with respect to the copyright, or any of the exclusive rights under a copyright, shall be given effect under this title, except as provided under title 11.* Accessed May 1, 2014: http://www.law.cornell.edu/uscode/text/17/201

To promote the Progress of Science and useful Arts, by securing for limited Times to Authors and Inventors the exclusive Right to their respective Writings and Discoveries. *Article 1, Section 8, Clause 8.*

18 17 U.S.C. ß 106 (2002) *("The owner of copyright ... has the exclusive rights ... : (1) to reproduce the copyrighted work in copies or phonorecords; [and] (2) to prepare derivative works based upon the copyrighted work.").*

19 Fisher, William W. 2004. *Promises to keep: Technology, law, and the future of entertainment.* Stanford, Calif.: Stanford Law and Politics. *Chapter 6: An Alternative Compensation System*, p.199-258

20 Gasser, Urs, Palfrey, John. 2007. *Case-Study: DRM-Protected Music Interoperability and e-innovation.* Berkman Publication Series. Harvard University. Sponsored by Microsoft.

21 Fisher, William W. 2004. *Promises to keep: Technology, law, and the future of entertainment.* Stanford, Calif.: Stanford Law and Politics. *Chapter 6: An Alternative Compensation System*, p.203

22 Cukier, Kenneth / Mayer-Schoenberger, Viktor. *Foreign Affairs Journal*, May/June 2013 issue, p. 28 - 40. *The Rise of Big-Data: How it's changing the way we think about the World*

23 Benkler, Yochai. 2006. *The wealth of networks: How social production transforms markets and freedom.* New Haven: Yale University Press. Chapter 3, p. 59 - 90.

24 Fisher, William W. 2004. *Promises to keep: Technology, law, and the future of entertainment.* Stanford, Calif.: Stanford Law and Politics. *Chapter 6: An Alternative Compensation System*, p.199-258

25 Gasser, Urs, Palfrey, John. 2007. *Case-Study: DRM-Protected Music Interoperability and e-innovation.* Berkman Publication Series. Harvard University. Sponsored by Microsoft.

26 Fisher, William W. 2004. *Promises to keep: Technology, law, and the future of entertainment.* Stanford, Calif.: Stanford Law and Politics. *Chapter 6: An Alternative Compensation System*, p.203

27 Cukier, Kenneth / Mayer-Schoenberger, Viktor. *Foreign Affairs Journal*, May/June 2013 issue, p. 28 - 40. *The Rise of Big-Data: How it's changing the way we think about the World*

28 Yochai Benkler, *The Wealth of Networks: How Social Production Transforms Markets and Freedom* (New Haven: Yale University Press, 2006), Chapter 3, pp. 59 - 90.

29 Peter. Suber, *Open Access*, MIT Press Essential Knowledge Series (*****2013), Chapter 3, *Varieties*, pp. 49 -75. Email interview with Peter Suber accessed on May 5, 2014. Please contact author for transcript.

30 Yochai Benkler, *The Wealth of Networks: How Social Production Transforms Markets and Freedom* (New Haven: Yale University Press, 2006), Chapter 3, pp. 59 - 90.

Image Credits

a Confined Phygital Property - Yarzar Hlaing & Wendy W Fok

b Networked Urbanity - Yarzar Hlaing & Wendy W Fok

c Connected Isolation - Yarzar Hlaing & Wendy W Fok

d 1790 Artifact - Copyright Act of 1790. Image courtesy of Library of Congress. 2015

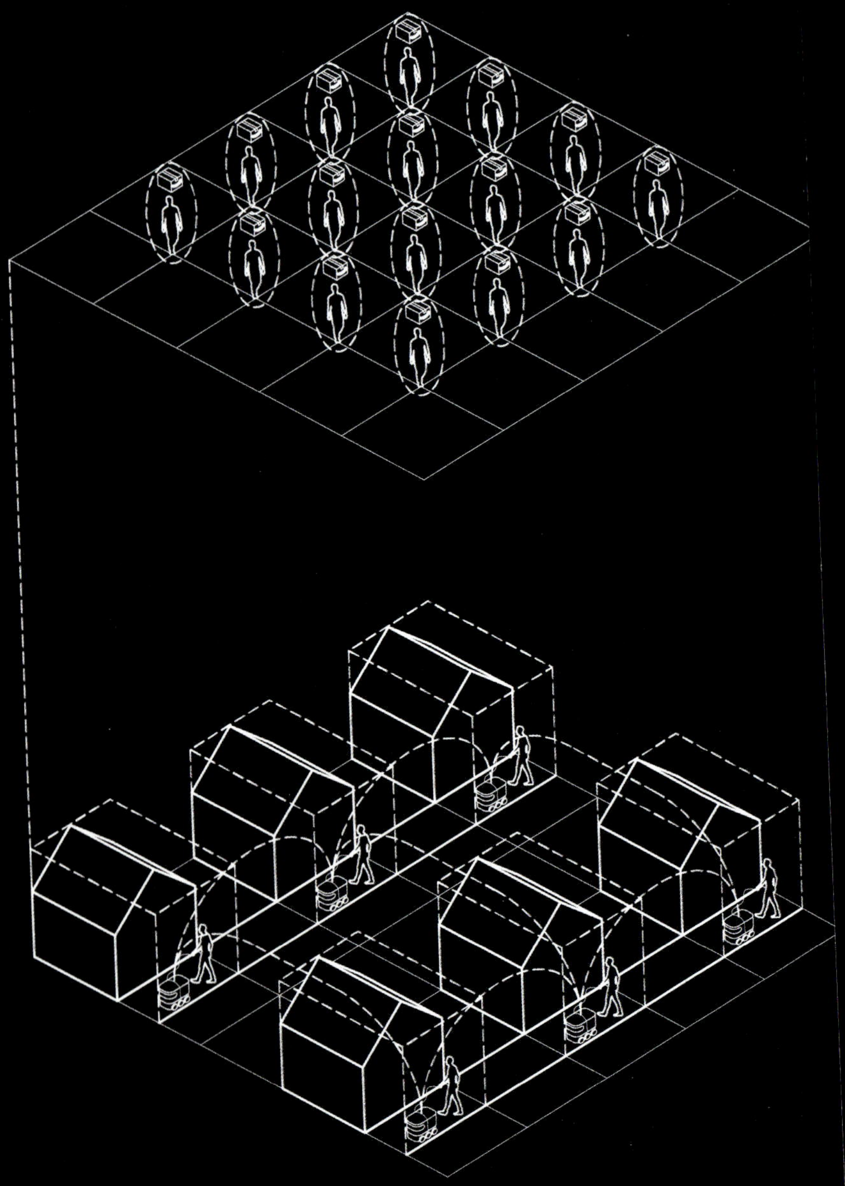

Things Left Unsaid

An Interview with Saskia Sassen by Wendy W Fok and Biayna Bogosian

This was part of a series for the *17th Venice Architecture Biennale*, titled *"How Will We Live Together"* based on Hashim Sarkis' curated theme. Or, is it more appropriate to ask how will we not live together – especially with the post-pandemic considerations.

This is a series of interviews with a number of scholars, practitioners, innovators, policy makers, and creatives to put forward several questions and concerns regarding the relationship of data and the future of our cities.

It's also about the people living in the cities such as citizens, how people curate the cities, in the context of cultural and social impact and how individuals build our cities in terms of architects, urban planners, policy makers, and innovators.

WF *I think there's a lot of work that's influenced on the definition of cities, and how you see cities. Do you feel like the definitions of cities have evolved since the beginning of your career, and how has that changed the post pandemic city to you, perhaps?*

Cities, of course, have existed long before we had empires and all kinds of other things–I mean there are millennia that some cities have endured, so to speak, it seems to me that in our current epoch there are several modes in which cities are problematic or can be fantastic, and so I'm sort of interested in these different modes.

A city like New York for instance, or any very large city, at some point that city ceases to be of support, of help, to especially the poorer classes because they are the ones who will have to take trips to get to their jobs, that will take them two hours or more. We have now a group of cities in the world that are simply too big – they are not too big for the entrepreneurs, they are not too big for the rich, they are too big for the poor, because the poor are the ones that live at the edges of those cities and that hence, they never sleep enough, they get up at four AM, etc., etc. And so that is sort of one way of looking at the city. There are clearly many other ways, other ways have to do with what are the qualities of how we built, are we abusing mother nature when we build some cities, are we trying to enable poor people, are we trying to concentrate only on the rich because they are the ones that have the money, and they produce the nice beautiful buildings?

You have an extraordinary range and the one result of all of that is that every city is a bit different. It's not like a car where you can have multiple models of the same car -- no. Every city is a bit different now, there are many things that cities share, but the amazing point is really not that sharing, it is the differences, and the differences play partly -only partly -- via the poverty versus rich vector. But that's just one. There are many other vectors.

For instance, the Dutch, half of that country is below sea level. Well for them to build a city that is below sea level is a completely different story from what it is, let's say in New York. So, when you really move into the zone of major cities you begin to see number one–a lot of things that are very similar. Number two–the challenges. Every city seems to have its own version of a challenge, something that is difficult, something that must, be dominated, or arranged, or saved, or whatever. And that of course keeps a certain kind of energy in a city, because otherwise you could just say why do these cities have such long lives? Much longer lives than all kinds of very powerful actors across our long, long histories.

WF *You refer to cities as complex yet incomplete systems, and in the past decades in your writings you have advocated for open-source approaches and hackability as a method to begin to understand and work with this complexity in order to construct new cities. Can you speak about the role of data in this conversation, and how you could suggest that architects, policy makers, innovators, begin to better strategize for the future of our cities?*

SS In our current period, given the knowledge that we have acquired, given the experiences which we have seen in other words, the fact that certain types of cement, certain types of stones, certain types etc. etc. are not good, whereas others might be just at least a bit better. So, you have a whole new complex. I would think that the last twenty years or so has really launched a new epoch because we have too much knowledge now.

For instance, I did an analysis for Japan of what were the variety of elements that they could use in building. And in Japan they are very, very, serious about how they build because they have very little. It's basically a huge rock, and so they have very little space, and they have a very large population. The space that is available that is not pure rock is actually extremely protected. So, one of the things that I found in that process of researching that, was the varieties of materials that they use, compared to the United States for instance where they have a very–when all is said and done–mostly a very limited range of types of materials.

In Japan they have made extraordinary things, they have man-made materials. They haven't just gone to some wood and cut wood – no, no. They made these materials. In other words, a whole set of innovations that then presents itself as something that can be of use to support a tree and all kinds of other things that have to do with natural conditions. And that is something for instance that in the United States we haven't really seen. Now there are a few very fancy setups that are doing that but Japan has been way, way, ahead of the United States. There is really an enormously strong difference. They're a good comparison apparatus to see. And then the motivation on the part of the Japanese to use whatever Mother Nature has given us to develop high quality instruments that they can use, instruments of all sorts–I mean instruments in a very broad sense. It could be for building, it could be for making vases, or a very broad spectrum.

Japan is very overpopulated, there is, of course, there's always a risk of water etc. So, they have had to develop in order to survive kinds of knowledge that in the United States almost nobody thinks of or knows about. The construction economy that we have in the United States is a bit brutal. Not all of it, clearly, but it is not particularly refined, with exceptions of very expensive modes of building.

B B *Thank you so much Professor Sassen for highlighting issues of cities and management. Another question before we move away from the questions of cities is, do you think that there are kind of ways of leveraging privacy issues, or there's a public literacy on that that could be part of this conversation within cities?*

S S This is increasingly happening. I am not sure as to what it is that has raised these set of issues in this current period of ours, the only simple answer that I have is that the new generations, the youth, in other words you not me–I'm old generation–the new generations have a kind of knowledge and a kind of awareness that they must be knowledgeable and that they must be aware of all kinds of things. Let's say when I was young, it simply didn't enter the picture, and nor did it enter the picture for our parents, so we lived in a zone of innocence.

Today, in any big city, you begin to notice all the things that are in play, and you stand back and you say wow, when is this all going to collapse, or how are you going to survive, etc. So it really is a new epoch and again, you know, we have long histories with many different epochs, but with complex systems it is not easy to detect that you have entered a new system, that you have entered a new epoch. And that is in itself a very interesting proposition, and we don't quite notice that, we don't see it.

When you begin to, at my age, to see – you see the epochs. You begin to see epochs and an epoch can live off yet another epoch, but ultimately, they are changing, they are changing elements.

And, nowadays we know with all the tech apparatus that it is like an explosion, in terms of what does it mean to have change.

Saskia Sassen is the Robert S. Lynd Professor of Sociology at Columbia University and a Member of its Committee on Global Thought, which she chaired from 2009 till 2015. She is a student of cities, immigration, and states in the world economy, with inequality, gendering and digitization three key variables running though her work. Born in the Netherlands, she grew up in Argentina and Italy, studied in France, was raised in five languages, and began her professional life in the United States.

She is the author of eight books and the editor or co-editor of three books. Together, her authored books are translated in over twenty languages. She has received many awards and honors, among them twelve doctor honoris causa, multiple named lectures, the 2013 Principe de Asturias Prize in the Social Sciences, election as a Foreign Member of the Royal Academy of the Sciences of the Netherlands, and made a Chevalier de l'Ordre des Arts et Lettres by the French government.

In each of the four major completed projects that comprise her 30 years of research, Sassen starts with a thesis that posits the unexpected and the counterintuitive in order to cut through established "truths." These projects engendered four major books. There are also a few smaller books and about 40 academic articles in peer-reviewed journals.

Scan the icon to view
dynamic content

egastructures and Infrastructures

The Internet as Megastructure?

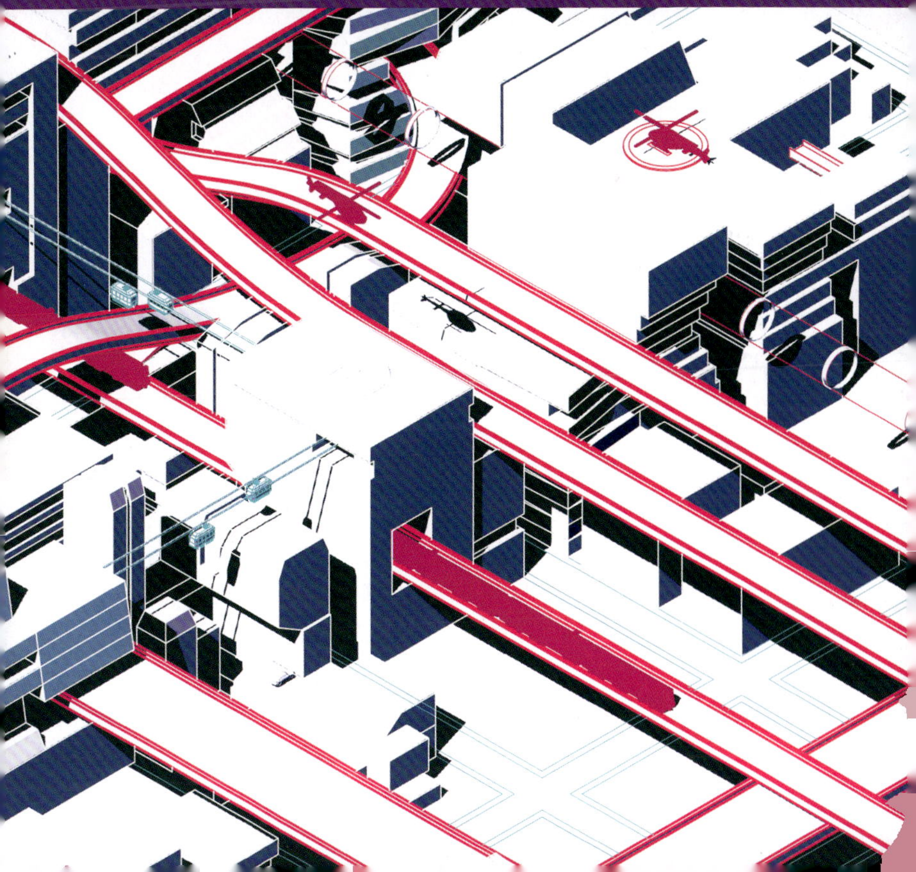

2.

> "Today's discontiguous megastructures, such as the supply chains that eventuate into a mobile phone, are as equally totalizing as their grandparents were, but are based on an adaptive modularity that makes them more resilient – and also less accountable."
>
> \- Benjamin Bratton, *The New Normal*

1964 is considered the *Megayear*. It was the year, in which, according to Reyner Banham, Fumihiko Maki coined the term "megastructure" in his *Investigations in Collective Form* [1]. *Mega* most likely derives from "megaton," that is, from atomic weaponry, as Wilcox proposes in his *Bibliography*, while "structure" is used here in the sense of "infrastructure." Curiously, the term has spawned variations, and Maki (along with Masato Otaka) and various *Metabolists* have interpreted megastructure as both "compositional form" and "monumentality of form."

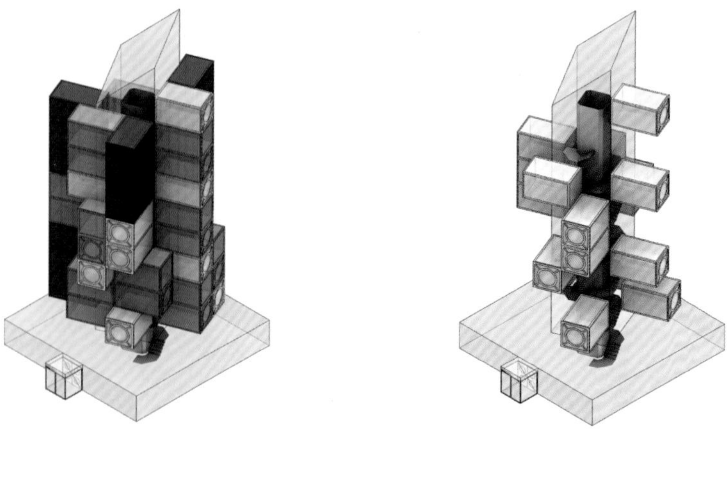

a

In 1976, the same year that Banham published *Megastructure: Urban Future of the Recent Past,* the *Random House Dictionary* defined "megastructure," as a noun meaning "a complex of huge, usually high-rise buildings for many purposes, such as apartments, offices, stores, theatres, athletic facilities, etc.," [2] and "infrastructure" as "the basic, underlying framework or features of something, esp. of a technological kind, as the military installations, communication, and transport facilities, etc., of a country or organization."

In 2022, the foremost US tech companies invested in the internet and its privatized expansion are corporations and conglomerates such as *Google* (Alphabet), *Microsoft*, *Facebook* (Meta), *Twitter*, *Amazon*, *Cloudflare*, and *Yahoo* (2016). In the late 2010s and early 2020s [3], significant Chinese actors and state-owned companies, such as *Huawei Marine*, rapidly expanded around the investment and build-u of submarine internet cable structures.

These submarine internet cables, which crawl the depths of the ocean, are what we call the digital infrastructure—or substructures—that connect networked societies from continent to continent and across oceans. Their construction takes a dramatic and climatic toll on the marine life as it requires dredging and damaging the seabed. Yet, these same megastructures are what allow the trade

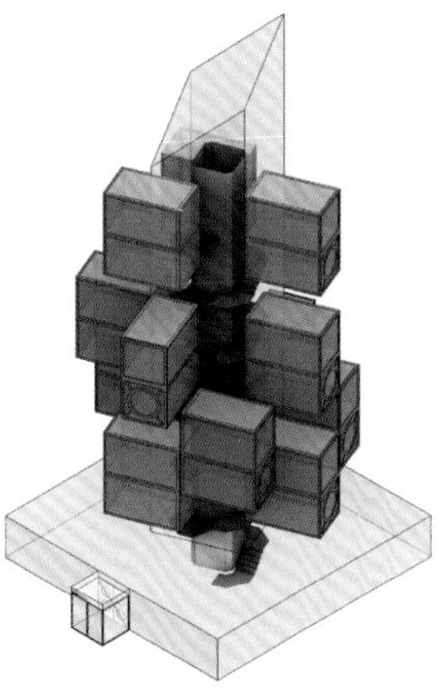

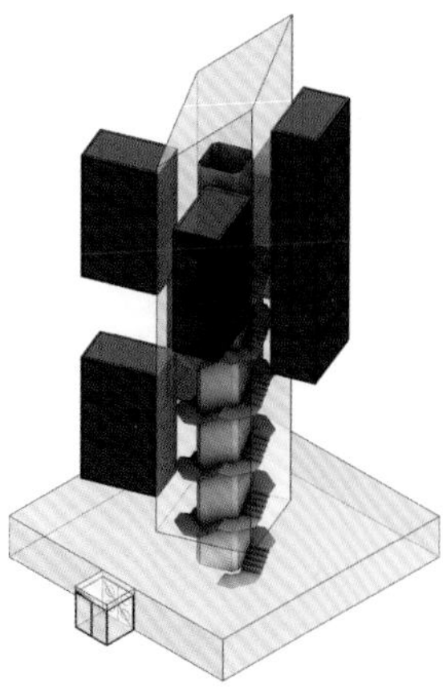

Scan the icon to view dynamic content

and supply chains of architecture and construction industries to conduct their various formulations.

As we proceed into the world of Web 3.0 and phygital (physical and digital) space, it is difficult not to wonder how various democracies will continue to hold and freely distribute information, and which logistic channels will distribute our raw materials, especially if digital technologies and data infrastructures continue to be soft powered and built by private corporations and select nation-states. Since the internet and data distribution vary from country to country, information on digital governance is still a widely debated topic and one bound up with the 'western' interpretation of the internet.

Kenzo Tange's *Tokyo Bay* or *Boston Harbor* can be regarded as megastructures or architectural infrastructures. This chapter will examine the complexity of these two terms and their relation to the phygital. Henceforth, both terms will be misinterpreted and playfully interrogated throughout the book in order to exhaust the nature of *how we are living together* (challenging the topic of Hashim Sarkis' brief of the *17th La Biennale di Venezia of architecture*) today in a world of digital property and data infrastructures that compound our daily lives.

Birth of Megastructures as Architectural Infrastructures

> Since the nineteenth century, infrastructure has been overtly used as a model resulting in the amplification of systems of movement, distribution, and control. While the proliferation of these systems has necessarily been attendant to modernization, they are rarely questioned or seen as anything other than discrete components of a hierarchy no greater than its parts.
>
> - Jesse Reiser & Nanako Umemoto **4**

Dissatisfaction with the status quo pushed experimental architectural collectives and individuals, such as *Archigram*, The *Metabolists*, *Ant Farm*, Reyner Banham, Paul Rudolph, Fumihiko Maki, et al., to dream about alternative urban scenarios that flew in

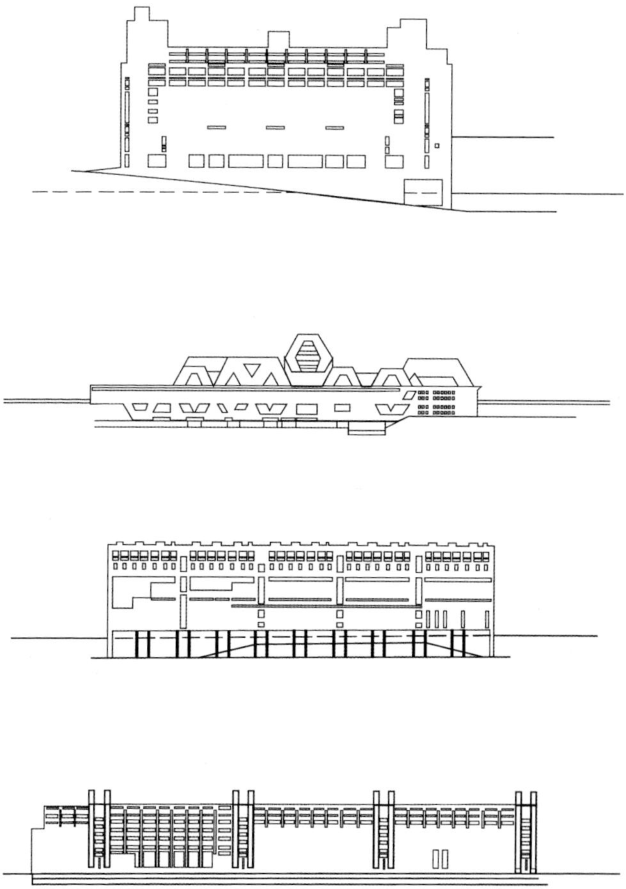

b

the face of the superficial formalism and dull suburban tendencies of the Modernist architecture of their time. Projects such as The *Plug-In City*, The *Walking City*, or The *Instant City*, suggested a nomadic way of life and, more importantly, a liberation from the modernist solution of suburbia. **5**

Were Reyner Banham alive in 2022, would he consider the Internet a megastructure? Do data centers fall into the category of megastructure or infrastructure? Or, in terms of architecture, are they simply dreamy theories of fluff?

Between 1960 and 1974, *Archigram* made over 900 drawings, among them the plan for Peter Cook's "*Plug-in City*." This provocative project consisted of a hypothetical fantasy city with modular residential units that "plugged in" to a central infrastructural mega machine. The *Plug-in City* was not, in fact, a city, but a constantly evolving megastructure that incorporated residences, transportation, and other essential services, all of which were movable by giant cranes. **6**

Though never built, the project and ideas behind it provoked debates. Combining architecture, technology, and society, *Plug-In City* offered a fascinating new approach to urbanism, reversing traditional perceptions of infrastructure's role within the city.

Persistent precedents and the concerns of modernism lay at the heart of *Plug-In City's* theoretical impulse, which was not limited to collective living, the integration of transportation, and the accommodation of rapid change in the urban environment. In *Archigram: Architecture Without Architecture*, Simon Sadler suggests that "The aesthetic of incompleteness, apparent throughout the Plug-In scheme and more marked than in megastructural precedents, may have derived from the construction sites of the building boom that followed the economic reconstruction of Europe."

Archigram (whose name combines the words "architecture" and "telegram") was founded at London's Architecture Association in 1960 by six architects and designers: Peter Cook, Warren Chalk, Ron Herron, Dennis Crompton, Michael Webb, and David Greene. In 1961, *Archigram* (an eponymous publication) was born as a single sheet magazine filled with poems and sketches.

As David Greene wrote in the first issue, it was meant as a platform for the voices of a young generation of architects and artists:

> A new generation of architecture must arise with forms and spaces which seem to reject the precepts of "Modern" yet in fact retains those precepts. We have chosen to bypass the decaying Bauhaus image which is an insult to functionalism.

Archigram's visions did, in fact, succeed in inspiring a new generation of architects and architecture. Among these were Renzo Piano and Richard Rogers, a dynamic duo that contributed to the built form of megastructures that fall into the classical category of infrastructural architecture. Their monumental visions of architecture and urbanism in the 1970s continue to contribute to the integrated smart infrastructural cities and megastructures being built today.

Building Physical Infrastructures for Digital Goods

We are choosing data over people. Data centers and the collection of information has exacerbated the architectural definition of the machine landscape. When we build more data centers, we are choosing a specific speculative future of how to design the urban landscape of digital storage.

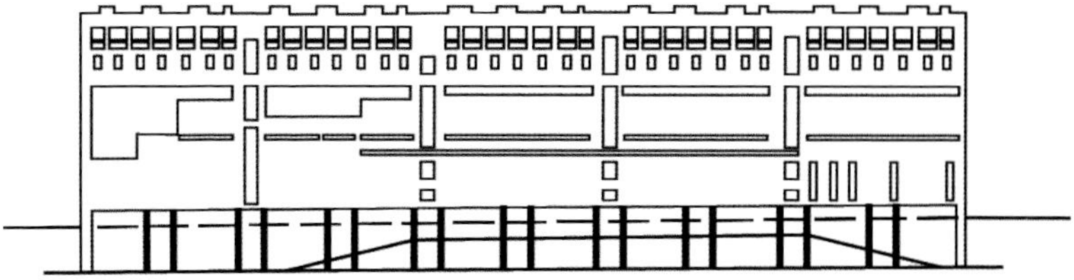

C

Any individual that pays a visit either to warehouses with shipping containers used to store physical goods or raw materials meant to be loaded at the docks of port cities, or to industrial towns that host data centers, will experience the vast machine-like visions of starkly inhuman buildings that host our data.

Every time a city government offers *Amazon, Facebook,* or other technology consortium an opportunity to build warehouses (for storing either physical goods or digital data), it is choosing machine over man.

As Sarah Williams points out in *Data Action*, "in American and European contexts, private companies currently hold and are set to hold exponentially more data about cities, their populations, and their communities." This also means that more physical space will be needed as these private consortiums and nation-states continue to generate and store data.

Although data consumption and sustainability may seem to lie at competing ends of the spectrum, momentum is shifting towards greener, more sustainable forms of cloud computing. Consumers are increasingly demanding that companies take a proactive role in reducing their emissions and are putting the spotlight on big tech companies and cloud providers to address the issue.

Before diving deeper into the storage and monumentality of data storage, we must understand the history of the internet, how it has been impacted by the direct path of trade and supply chains, and how we've gotten here.

How the internet was created and how it affects our built environment

The ancient Chinese *Silk Road* provided those countries along its route the groundwork for an early networked system that impacted global trade and the exchange of resources. Established when the Han Dynasty in China officially opened trade with the West in 130 B.C.E., the *Silk Road* remained in use until 1453 C.E. Historians regard it as an early version of the cyclical supply chain that connects Asian, African, Arab, and European nations. Dominated in the four principal continents, it excluded North and South America.

d

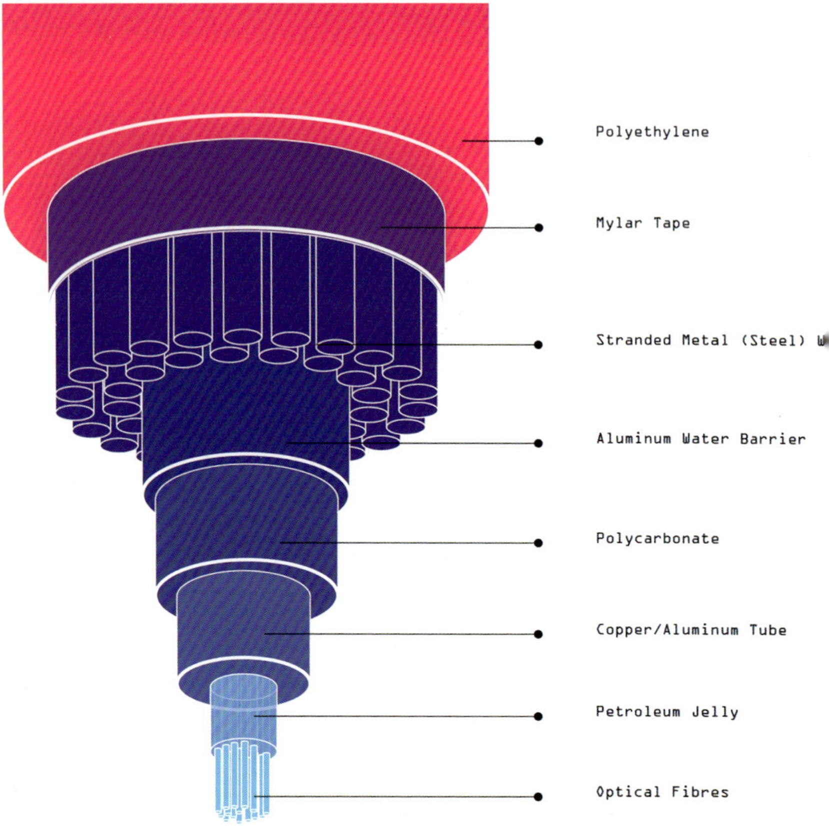

e

Just as the ancient *Silk Road* can be perceived as the trade and supply-chain of an early, physically macro-networked society, so too the Internet can be viewed as a data supply-chain and distributor of digital goods.

Before the internet, there was *ARPANET*, a United States (US) military experiment built in the 1960s. A precursor to the modern internet, *ARPANET* was an academic project funded by the *Advance Research Projects Agency*, a branch of the US military known for funding ambitious research projects with no immediate commercial or military applications. Although the *ARPANET* grew in the 1970s and 1980s, it became the "Internet" only in 1984.

At the time of its origin, *ARPANET* was a centralized system managed solely by the US military. Its network operators realized that if it continued to grow, it would become unmanageable. Thus in 1984, the US military expanded the network into a decentralized "network of networks."

It was not until 1992 that the *NSFNET* T3 Network, funded by the National Science Network, came to serve as the first backbone of the internet. Arguably, 1986 was the key year in which the TCP/IP-based network called *NSFNET*, which was linked to supercomputing centers, became available to researchers, but it was only in 1993 that the internet became a global network. **7**

The Chinese megastructural hold of Soft-Power

Submarine cables are predominantly owned and operated by consortiums of telecommunication companies and carriers that join together to pay for these huge projects. The cables use fiber-optics technology to transmit the information through encoded waves of light transmitted by lasers across thin glass at up to 200-terabits per second. This information is the basis of the data that is stored between data centers and in machine landscapes across the world.

Cable construction has increased over the past few years, and the bulk of these megastructures has been constructed since 2017. In that year alone, the cables grew by over 100,000 kilometers, which was more than they did in all three years prior.

Meanwhile, China's *belt road initiative* (BRI) is acting as both the new digital silk road as well as a physical infrastructural system that encompasses an expansive network of ports, hubs, and key landmarks that stretch beyond the old silk road. First conceived in 2013 by China, the main nation-state soft-power holder of the Internet and submarine-cable infrastructure, the BRI holds a stake in both land and marine trade as well as supply-chain power, and controls manufacturing networks and channels between China, North and Northeastern Africa, parts of Europe, and deep into Eurasian trade routes. The BRI is a global infrastructure development strategy used by the Chinese government to invest in nearly 70 countries and international organizations.

Google (Alphabet), *Facebook (Meta)*, *Amazon*, and *Microsoft*, which have been investing in larger networks of submarine cables since 2016, expanded the reach of their cloud-based providers during the COVID-19 pandemic. Today, these four companies either own or lease more than half (> 50%) of the undersea cable capacity, with China (as a nation-state) lagging just barely behind. China's *Huawei Marine*, a joint 2008 venture and partnership between the Chinese firm *Huawei* (51% ownership) and the UK's *Global Marine Systems* (40%)–is active around the world, but has a particular interest in the internet and data colonialism of Africa. *Huawei Marine* has been responsible for building the major infrastructural digital connections in many cities in Northeast Africa

Scan the icon to view dynamic content

and, due to the nature of the partnership, other African nation-states. Consequently, China has become the relative relationship builder of digital networks. Since the reign of Deng Shao Ping, China has become a force in the global distribution of both physical manufacturing and digital power.

The quiet and soft-power approach to constructing a massive data infrastructural network has now become even more indeterminate. The submarine cable network, constructed by companies funded by China, American private conglomerates, as well as corporate collaborations, brings to the forefront questions and concerns about the future of information and who owns it.

f

Outer space is governed by marine law. In the US, the Federal Communications Commission (FCC) regulates interstate and international communications via radio, television, wire, satellite, and cable in all 50 states, the District of Columbia, and US Territories. At the time of this book's publication (2022), the entire internet infrastructure in the US and much of it in other countries, was provided and owned by the private sector and/or Chinese funded ventures **8**, or a multi-stakeholder non-profit known as the *Internet Corporation for Assigned Names and Numbers* (ICANN). ICANN was created by the *US Department of Commerce* in 1998 and was given a government contract to manage the internet. Its

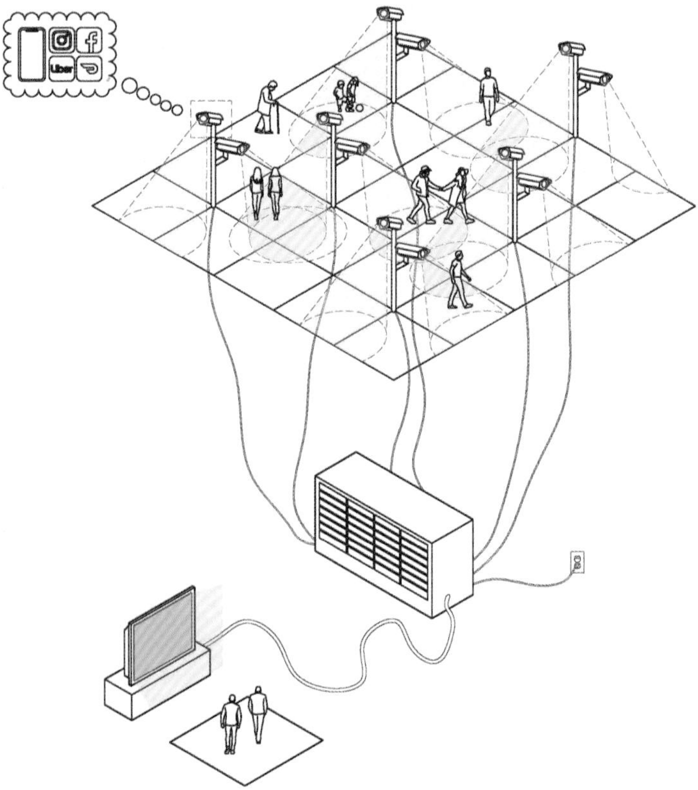

g

foundational system was meant to assist in the government's long-term goal of offering international players, namely, corporations and individual internet users, a multinational organization and ownership of *domain name systems* (DNS).

The question that remains is who owns these internets, and who holds the power to their informational assets. As submarine cables have a long history of surveillance, and the security of their infrastructure has been called into question at their ports, landing sites, and the nexuses at which they connect and splice into multiple cables under the ocean, we architects need to ask how these encryption systems are actually run. Their physical management as well as the digital software that controls this management are prime targets of hackers and intelligence agencies. **9**

Megastructures, Machine Landscapes, and the Digital Domestic

Whereas Le Corbusier designed his buildings according to the scale and proportions of the human body **10**, the concept and physical structure of a data center is based on that of a machine the purpose of which is storage, efficiency, and optimization, and which uses an excruciating amount of energy that accelerates climate change.

As Liam Young observes, the *"data centers of the networked world are the extraordinary material consequences of our ever-digital shelves."* **11** I would expand on this to say that in the world of Web 3.0, the data center is an architectural typology on a megastructural scale that defines the realities of both the digital and physical age. Sensorially speaking, data centers are loud due to the amount of coolant required to operate the massive structures. They are also hot to the touch, as they offset a great deal of heat while operating the storage capacities of trillions of data passing through on an average day.

I would further argue that policy should enable architects to limit its construction based on how the data centers interact with its relationship to information exchanged on the Internet, and should be measured as energy used for input and output.

Yet somehow, they remain a form of "invisible architecture" that users rarely notice or engage with. Like the edge cities of brown field sites or industrial ports, data center landscapes are machine landscapes of the uncanny, usually located far from the public, sometimes for security, sometimes for aesthetic reasons.

There is a certain truth to the perception of data centers in suburban landscapes as stark, machine-lined landscapes of industrial storage that offer little to no human access, consume power and huge quantities of water coolant, and are full of internal hallways that glow blue and green as data hums and processes through fiber-optics.

In reality, we are surrounded by data centers on a daily basis. Sometimes, we may not even realize it. In metropolitan cities, many data centers are masked to look like conventional architecture. This brings up the uncanny nature of our new digital domestic life and our growing familiarity with the eerie nature of automation.

So, if data centers are not meant for human access, for whom are they intended? Even Google admitted in 2018 that they are accessible to "*maybe one of the less than one percent of Google employees authorized to ever to set foot into a data center. If so, you'll first get your identity verified at the campus security gate,*

h

then undergo security screening at building reception, then pass through a secure exterior corridor, and ultimately go through a multifactor access control process involving lenticular badges and biometrics."

From an anthropological perspective, the urban megastructure of data centers brings up the issues of community, census, demographics, and population. Who should be living amid the machine hum of data centers? How would our sense of neighborhood change if our neighbors were non-human, but simply white picket-fenced homes made to look like any other, yet housing only information?

Veiled as a mundane commercial real estate office building in the heart of the Financial District in Downtown Los Angeles is *One Wilshire*, a building that boasts utility and power as well as 24/7/365 security. Yet this vital structure, developers claim, is the premier communications hub of the Pacific Rim. The property, which serves some of the dominant players in global communication and data centers, is managed by the Hines. Designed by *Skidmore, Owings & Merrill* (SOM), and completed in 1966, it underwent a major renovation that consisted chiefly of telecommunication network upgrades in 1992. Today, its website commits to its marketing as *"one of the most densely connected buildings in the world."*

i

The invisibility of data storage in our day-to-day lives often makes us forget the reality that data (a digital informational commodity) requires storage. There is a limit to the amount of information that each device, microchip, or cloud can store. The "cloud," a term that simplifies the technological realities of data storage, is actually a systems infrastructure that is part of a larger network of data centers that deliver the everyday information decentralized amongst a regulated system of machines that live within our urban landscape.

In the Netherlands, for example, data centers use an average of 1 million cubic meters of water per year, the equivalent of 19,230 one-person households. Yet Google's data center in Eemshaven, the Netherlands (Holland) – very much a machine landscape–sits idyllically in a landscape amongst windfarms, green pastures, blue skies, and ultimately, an information warehouse. **12**

In 2021, there were reports that data centers might cause water shortages for residents of northern Holland. While this claim was disputed by the local government, it has raised concerns about the impact of water consumption by ever-growing data centers on our warming climate. Can sustainability and technology thrive together?

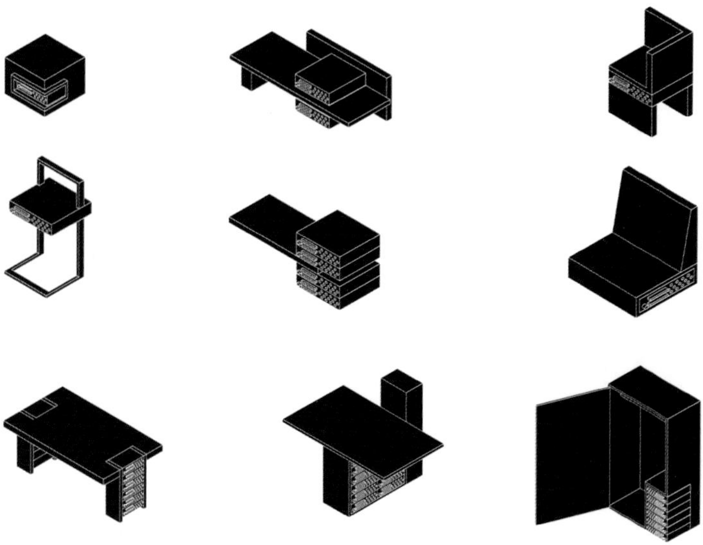

j

Our reliance on tech to power businesses and our daily lives will inevitably increase our data processing needs. Yet data and machine landscapes are neither identifiable nor idyllic, and can easily be viewed as hostile to human cohabitation. If data and information become the raw materials (such as wood and fuel) that builds out the nature of which we live, will architects become solely designers who facilitate the functionality of industrial complexes? What if we were to engage with the data centers in their purity, as objects in our interior spaces and integrated into our structural framework on a daily basis?

Digital Domesticity

This section is co-authored with Rachel Pendleton

Emerging technologies and capital ventures are paving the way for new domestic relationships and experiences. The conditions in which American suburbia was birthed have changed dramatically, yet remnants of 1950s views of domesticity or community are still detectable. Urban planning has gotten smarter, and more and more emphasis has been placed on community, integration, ecological concerns, and quality of life. Yet what may have gotten lost in intelligent urban planning initiatives is the condition of the house, and the feedback loop between the domestic scales of house and neighborhood.

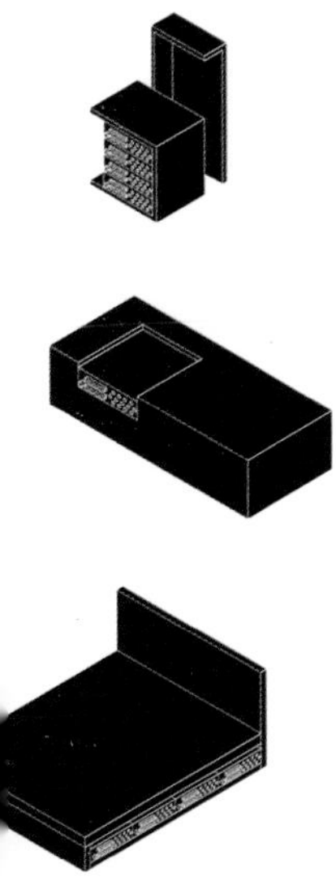

American suburban life is built into a rich history that engages with urban relationships and challenges. The invention of suburbia in the 1950s relied heavily on marketing and imaging techniques that appealed to white families and presented a new model of what the family and its house should look like. The construction of homes for non-white, non-nuclear families was neither accommodated nor desired in these new complexes. Suburbs also had a broad ecological impact. They were designed to encourage social conformity through the monotony of similar houses, streets, and cul-de-sacs. They made sameness desirable, excluding anyone or anything that did not fit into their ideal. Reacting against these shortcomings, housing and urban planning models of the 1970s introduced new ways of living that further integrated many aspects of urban life. Cities like Columbia, MD, Irvine, CA, and Woodland, TX, for example, were planned on a neighborhood

INDUSTRIAL ROBOT TIMELINE

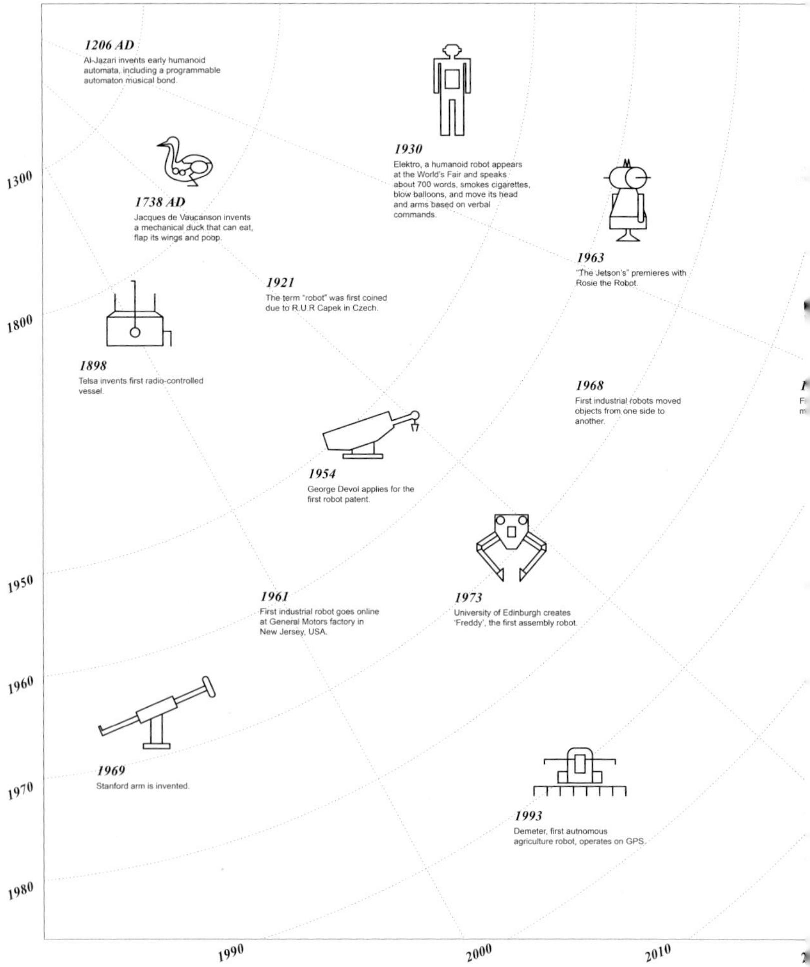

scale and designed to appeal to the nostalgia for small towns, while engaging with environmental concerns and providing shopping, schools, employment, and other amenities.

Yet despite all these changes, the scale of our cities once again need a new model of living. Meanwhile, the way we conduct our lives in the city needs to be refashioned and re-thought. Today's technological solutions are rapidly changing how we live and operate in the domestic sphere.

Google *Nest*, Amazon *Alexa*, Philip *Lights*, the *Gita* Robot, *Ring*, and Amazon *Scout* are just a few of the encroaching technologies currently entering our homes. Daily life is becoming hyper-connected in advanced ways that allow us to control our environments and access information. As never before, our living systems have reached a high level of integration that expands what we can achieve or control in our domestic space from in or outside. I can watch what is going on in my neighborhood from my phone through *Ring* cameras, and while at work, I can use my phone to control the temperature and lighting of my home. Such technologies are making life more accessible and adding to what our domestic spaces can do.

It is crucial that we start speculating about the appearance of our present or future–especially with reference to past efforts–so that we can leverage good qualities and exclude bad ones from our urban environments. Yet, as we rapidly grow more dependent on technology, will the old inequalities stay put? If our domestic and suburban spaces turn into technologically savvy systems, will they exclude people who cannot afford certain devices? Is such a future utopic or dystopic?

Digital suburbanity?

The rise of suburbia in the United States drastically changed the fabric of urban environments. Exerting political, social, and economic influence, the imagery of suburbia became integral to the nation's culture. Movies and TV series such as *Edward Scissorhands, Wandavision,* and *The Truman Show*, hold a critical lens to the ideal standard of living upheld by suburbia and the social structures represented by it. The *fakeness* of Seaside, Florida, served as the perfect backdrop for *The Truman Show*. Yet beneath the perfection promised in this picturesque suburban life, new planning methods were being realized. Public transportation, diversity of land use, and walkability introduced new ways to think about the community and plan social utopias.

Thanks to media's representation and critique of American standards, urban designers began thinking about how to counter the monotony and social conformity of suburban life. In "Planning Lessons from Three U.S. Towns of the 1960s and 1970s," Ann Forsyth discusses Columbia, MD, Irvine, CA, and Woodland, TX as case studies of innovative design techniques that provide insight into more comprehensive and supportive ways of living. Columbia, with a population of 100,000, consists of a town center with nine surrounding villages. Unlike suburbia, which is highly segregated, this planning tactic was an attempt to create a racially and economically integrated space. Relieving pressure from inner-city areas, a diverse population was given the opportunity to leave urban areas and find all the amenities it needed in a more suburban setting. Woodland TX, which has a population of 55,000, has centered its planning tactics on ecological issues. The town includes natural drainage systems that limit runoff, protect the water systems, and recharge aquifers. The use of nature, such as trees, facilitates as a façade to mask the development of its infrastructural monstrosity, to conceal the appearance and harsh monotony of the structures. The development of Woodland was funded by the *Title IV* and *Title VII* federal programs. It stands as an example of a community that prioritized ecological factors over strictly human habitation, and, in stark contrast to earlier suburban development that took no consideration of environmental impact, but instead sprawled as far as possible and privileged human growth.

While urban planning gradually adapted to new ideas about community, nature, and economy, additional factors must now be introduced to the way in which we design the places in which we live. Are these towns suited to a digitally intertwined manner of living? Given Amazon *Scout* and other delivery methods, will there come a time when we don't leave our homes and have everything we need delivered to us? This may seem like a wild prognosis, but there are, in fact, fewer and fewer reasons to leave our dwellings. And, with the advancement of at-home comforts and tools such as *Nest* and *Ring*, we may never want to.

Domestic Technocracies?

Current and developing domestic smart technologies are changing the functions and relationships of the domestic environment. Our most private and inner lives are now far more public than we can even realize. In *"Privacy and Publicity in the Age of Social Media,"* Beatriz Colomina argues that today's technologies are recentering the spatial priorities of everyday life. As she explains, *"Social life takes place in the streets or even the living room, but in the car, the bathroom, on the toilet–and above all in bed, floating alone without bedroom, house, or city. The bed has become the other spaces of our homes, what does that mean for the way we live? Will domestic architecture neglect the design of all outlying spaces?"* Colomina's questions urge us to understand the current conditions of our hyperconnected lives: if social media, phones, laptops, and other domestic tools are already making our domestic lives public, then we can expect this trend will only increase with our never-ending desire for new technologies.

It is also worth noting that our media-centric, interconnected, public-private homes are being manipulated and designed by forces greater than our own desires for convenience and accessibility. The capital interests of companies like Amazon and Google are actively shaping our home environments through new inventions that introduce yet other ways for us to rethink the ways in which we live. For example, Google *Nest* allows people to closely monitor their home environments and modify temperature by room. It can also control home cameras, doorbells, as well as alarms, smoke, and CO2 detectors, all of which can be linked to a Google account.

Similarly, *Ring* uses indoor and outdoor cameras to closely monitor homes, detect motion, and alert their owners to trespassers or visitors. The devices will sends notifications and footage to their smartphone, and allow them to speak to such strangers or neighbors through their phones. The system is interconnected with Amazon *Alexa*. The ways in which such devices make our homes more comfortable and secure is notable. They assist our smartphones in extending and maintaining the environment and space of our houses and and allow us to watch over them even when we are away. This requires us to rely on and place a great deal of trust in companies like Amazon and Google, which have the power to store and track our data even when it relates to our intimate domestic lives. Within the parameters of the capitalist frameworks, the digital domestic poses a risk to our individuality and privacy. All this may exhaust or further strengthen the organization of American society, including the social order that determines the specific way in which our domestic scales are organized.

Otherness

American suburbia enforces rigid social, gender, racial, and class structures. The suburbanization of the country has placed marginalized groups into spatial and social conditions of otherness that determine their roles in society. Women belong in the kitchen as housewives, for example, while people of color have been left behind in cities, where they are largely excluded from home ownership. Suburbia was built on racist and classist ideals that led to separate housing for people who did not fit the model of the white, heterosexual American nuclear family.

Is the rise of smart home technologies deepening the risk of such exclusionary housing? Perhaps, or perhaps not. The benefit of the hyper-connected domestic space is that it grants life a certain ease. It is especially helpful for the aging population, as it empowers the elderly and makes them less dependent on others. It could even encourage the decentralization of healthcare, bringing medical assistance to homes, and alleviating the need for senior housing facilities.

In "*The Implications of Smart Home Technologies*," Fisk writes, that "the promotion of smart technologies by statutory agencies would be, therefore, an essential prerequisite to the empowerment and social inclusion of many older people who are already disadvantaged by virtue of physical or sensory impairments, their limited wealth, and their marginalization in economic, tenurial, and geographical terms." **13** The "empowerment" brought by technologies is an important consideration. The term suggests *utility* and *ease of living* based on smart home technologies such as Amazon *Alexa, Nest, Ring,* etc., that offer the user accessibility and empowerment. Fisk's statement can be extended to marginalized populations beyond the aging. So, for example, we might ask whether the accessibility of digital domestic tools could ease the constraints of gender roles in the household? Could houses become less gendered and heterosexually oriented?

There are ways in which smart home technologies could relieve the pressure that commonly falls on household members who identify as female and who continue to find themselves in certain domestic positions due to gendered standards. Amazon *Alexa* makes it easier to order items like diapers, toilet paper, and other necessities on a subscription basis, which alleviates household duties. Amazon *Scout*, in turn, can retrieve packages from Amazon facilities and deliver them to the front door. Philip *lights* can be controlled from a smartphone without the inconvenience of rising from one's couch. Relieved from such domestic duties, will women be able to claim new social positions? Will the ease of domestic tasks be distributed to all members of the household, regardless of gender? While there may not yet be a clear answer to these questions, we can speculate by looking back at earlier domestic technologies.

Margaret Schütte-Lihotzky's *Frankfurt Kitchen* was a progressive invention of the 1920s that was meant to bring efficiency and functionality to domestic space, assist women in terms of workflow, and reduce their time in the kitchen. Its design made cooking and cleaning the space easier and quicker and gave women more time to spend with her family or doing activities beyond their domestic duties. Nonetheless, it also brought the risk of spatial confinement as it isolated women from the rest of the home and trapped them in kitchen duties.

The *Frankfurt Kitchen* can help us understand what will happen with new domestic technologies and their impact on gender relations in the household . The ease of household tasks afforded by systems like *Alexa*, *Nest*, or *Ring*, will provide little full-time relief from rigid domestic gender roles. A stay-at-home mother may now be able to save time by using her devices to have groceries or other household items delivered to her home or

Amazon Scout to retrieve packages, but such assistance does not provide full liberation from gendered domestic duties. Despite the convenience and high-tech advances of such household aids, the highly gendered roles of motherhood could remain in place. In fact, due to the lightening of their load, women and mothers may grow further isolated and receive less assistance in or relief from their duties. The fact that Amazon and Google systems are helping them cope with their workload may well reinforce the belief that a stay-at-home mother is an easy job.

I

A great deal of risk and danger comes with our technological tools and the control that they and the companies that make them hold over us. They breach our privacy is breached, turning us into mere data points in a billionaire's pocket. As Fisk warns us, "*There is a danger [...] that while the credentials of organizations undertaking or promoting the smart home initiatives may be sound, technologies could be used in ways that underpin or consolidate ageist, disablist, and oppressive service frameworks.*" **14** His remark points to the close relationship between society and technology. Since our devices play such a significant part in our lives, they can uphold, damage, enforce, or change social structures. As Fisk points out, the danger lies in the possibility that the very agency that they bestow on aging members of society can just as easily lead to marginalization and otherness and thus exclude and discriminate against them.

In "*What 'Normal' Dwelling Looks Like: The History of Home Technologies*," Chelsea Schelly argues that home technologies do foster dependence and isolation. Our reliance on them puts us in the danger that Frisk warns against as this reliance is what grants them control over our social structures. As Schelly notes, "*Technology and society are co-constituted; technologies not only shape societies, but also the ways of being, thinking, and knowing embraced and practiced by individuals within a society.*" **15** According to this assessment, people are malleable beings, a fact that grants technological advancements further control over how we live. What Schelly is addressing here is the human susceptibility to influence and to falling victim to new products and the latent features of technological smartness. It is crucial that we understand and address the intertwinement of society and technology. Inasmuch as the digital domestic comes with new opportunities and a different understanding of our intimate households, we must be critical of its implications, good and bad, on our social structures.

Deconstructing the Megastructural Landscape of Data Centers

By investigating the impact of technologies on the domestic scale, we can begin to understand how our future living environments may change and adapt. Indeed, the digital domestic is upon us, if not already here; it encroaches on our lives and is changing the ways in which we operate. While our future may seem daunting, there remains an opportunity to create a more inclusive and equitable domestic space that will enable accessibility and ease of living.

We have a chance to accept the *digital domestic* as a way of accessing the perfect, hyper-connected, spaces of our home. By critiquing capitalist agendas, we can begin to extract a digital domestic that avoids false narratives and security and confirms human freedom and willpower on the intimate household scale, and thus enables us to dismantle and engage with new social and technological structures.

Reframed and a reminder: *if Reyner Banham was still alive, would he consider the digital domestic households (or its microcosms of interior data centers) megastructures?*

One fact remains: the storage and transmission of data within the megastructural machine landscape of data centers has an impact on climatic change–from macro issues that surround water consumption to micro issues of power and energy, whose maintenance requires natural gas and fossil fuels. If we do not start regulating them now, the transfer and storage of digital information will cause serious environmental damage in the near future. **16**

In 2021, *COP26* ended without addressing the explicit nature of tighter regulations on the exponentially growing cloud-computing industry.

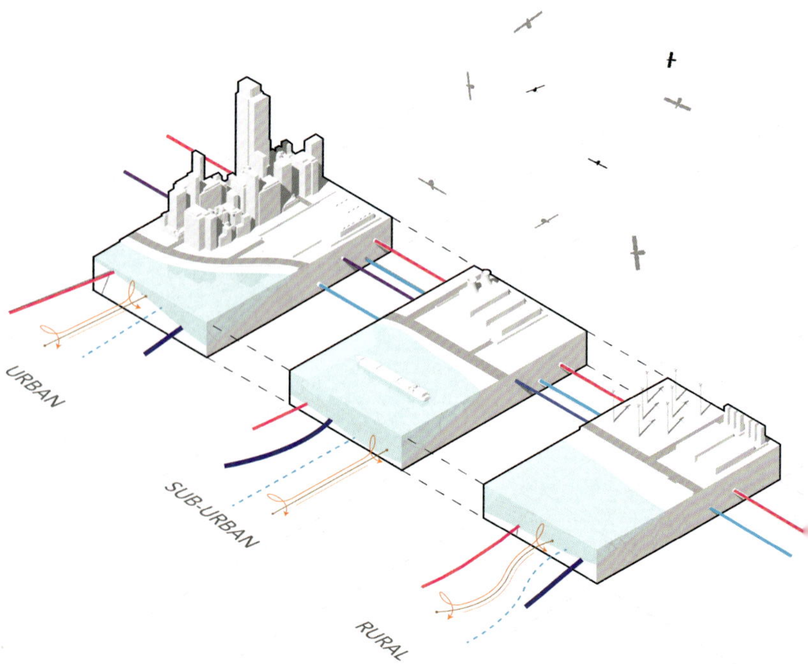

m

With the average adult spending 4.2 hours per day on smartphone apps in 2020, human reliance on technology has increased even more than we ever thought possible. Platform urbanism is providing daily conveniences, from ordering food online to video conferencing with friends and family abroad or binge-watching the latest series. Today, data consumption is no longer a trend, but an integral part of everyday life.

Tech consortiums will build more data infrastructure as businesses continue to consume more data than ever. And as the data hunger of the private and public sector grows, life on earth will come closer to dying. Although the transition to the cloud promised to solve many of our data overload problems, data centers are now producing the same number of emissions as is the global airline industry. Each individual in a developed country, in fact, is responsible for the emission of the equivalent of six one-way flights between Paris and New York.

While it is impossible to repair the damage caused by raw materials extracted from the earth to build new construction in a hard-to-regulate industry, architects could focus on building data centers and adjacent buildings that are better for the environment. Renewing and retrofitting buildings for the use of data storage or granting new uses to older buildings could help limit greenhouse gas emissions caused by new material consumption and fabrication.

Uptime Institute's 2021 *Global Data Center Survey*, reports the stark parallel realities of data and power consumption. According to Andrea Hak, the electricity and water resources needed to keep data centers cool are often not accounted for or tracked. The same goes for the e-waste created by the need to continuously replace servers. **17**

Although some tech consortiums, such as Google–which worked with the *Ellen MacArthur Foundation* in 2018 in order to showcase its effort to create a circular economy and reuse e-waste at the Lenoir, NC, and 13 other data centers around the world **18** – have made something of an effort at sustainability, most have publicly claimed to be "carbon neutral" without the public's understanding of the real costs. Many countries and tech consortiums offset their sustainability goals on paper by purchasing *Renewable Energy*

Certificates (RECs) that serve as a band-aid for the problems caused by these companies' emissions, but are hardly long-term solutions.

Architects and policy makers need to work more closely together to understand the lack of transparency in the RECs. Without universal reporting standards, neither citizens nor designers can understand how much energy is being used to power data centers, or, more importantly, what percentage of it comes from purchasing REC offsets.

Information has become the new currency of the economy of exchange. Data has increased at an exponential rate at which designers are generating designs. Information and data should be used as a foundational and organizational growth strategy for the future of architectural and design practice. In the past three decades, the transference, sale, and distribution of data as well as the process of controlling information have become the normative means by which tech companies such as *Google, Yahoo, Adobe, Autodesk, Dropbox, Box*, among many other startups, dominate equitable exchange. As many software companies move to cloud license their software, and the construction industry migrates closer to a tech platform model, architects and designers who work with CAD-based models and process technical information with consultants on a daily basis, will have to consider this a means of enquiry. Therefore, an open system of practice should be introduced to the practice of architecture, engineering, and construction.

References

1 Banham, Reyner, 'Megayear 1964', *Megastructure: Urban Futures of the Recent Past*, Chapter 4, Page 76, Monacelli Press (2020). Original 1976.

2 Random House Revised Edition Dictionary, 1976

3 Brake, Doug, 'Submarine Cables: Critical Infrastructure for Global Communications', ITIF (Information Technology and Innovation Foundation) Policy Report, April 2019

4 Jesse Reiser & Nanako Umemoto, 'On Infrastructural Urbanism (1998)', *Projects and their Consequences*, Pg 216 - 217, Princeton Architectural Press, 2019

5 Sadler, Simon, '*Archigram: Architecture without Architecture*', and Merin, Gili, 'AD Classics: The Plug-In City / Peter Cook, Archigram', *ArchDaily*

6 Gili Merin. "AD Classics: The Plug-In City / Peter Cook, Archigram " 10 Jul 2013. ArchDaily. <https://www.archdaily.com/399329/ad-classics-the-plug-in-city-peter-cook-archigram> ISSN 0719-8884

7 Stariano, Adam, 'How the Internet Travels Across Oceans', *New York Times* (March 2019), and Brake, Doug, 'Submarine Cables: Critical Infrastructure for Global Communications', ITIF (Information Technology and Innovation Foundation) Policy Report, April 2019

8 Baral, Susmita, 'Who controls the internet? US Government hands over Control to ICANN', *IBTimes*, October 3, 2016

9 Swire, Peter, 'Online Privacy and ISPs', Institute of Information and Security & Privacy at Georgia Tech (Feb 2016); Bressie, Kent, 'Government Surveillance, Hacking, and Network Security: what can submarine cable operates and their customers do?', *SubOptic* (2016): Emerging Subsea Networks

10 Young, Liam, *'Architecture without People', The New Normal*, Edited by Benjamin Bratton, Nicolay Boyadjiev, Nick Axel, Strelka Institute & Park Books Press, 2020

11 Young, Liam, *'Architecture without People', The New Normal*, Edited by Benjamin Bratton, Nicolay Boyadjiev, Nick Axel, Strelka Institute & Park Books Press, 2020

12 Mayer, Vicki (2019) "The Second Coming: Google and Internet Infrastructure" *Culture Machine* Vol 18. The Nature of Data Centers https://culturemachine.net/vol-18-the-nature-of-data-centers/the-second-coming/

13 Fisk, Malcom J., "The Implications of Smart Home Technologies," *Inclusive Housing in an Ageing Society: Innovative Approaches*, edited by Sheila M. Peace and Caroline Holland, 1st ed., Bristol University Press, 2001, pp. 101–24, https://doi.org/10.2307/j.ctt1t895gc.10

14 Fisk, Malcom J., Page 107

15 Schelly, Chelsea, What 'Normal' *Dwelling Looks Like: The History of Home Technologies, Dwelling Resistance: Living with Alternative Technologies in America*, Page 12, Rutgers University Press, 2017

16 Hak, Andrea, 'Data centers could cause series environmental damage – if we don't regulate them now: taking a deeper look at the data economy', *The Next Web*, 2021

17 Hak, Andrea, 'Data centers could cause series environmental damage – if we don't regulate them now: taking a deeper look at the data economy', *The Next Web*, 2021

18 'Once is Never Enough', Environment Projects March 2018, Circular economy of Google data centers. Google Sustainability, URL: https://sustainability.google/progress/projects/circular-economy/

Image Credits

a Redrawn Hybridized Capsule Tower - Jessica Marquez & Beiry Duran

b Redrawn Megastructure Silhouettes - Mary Reyner Banham, Wendy W Fok, & Jessica Marquez

c Redrawn Megastructure Silhouettes (Pompidou) - Mary Reyner Banham, Wendy W Fok, & Jessica Marquez

d How does Digital affect Real Property - Yarzar Hlaing & Wendy W Fok

e Internet Submarine Fiber Cable Diagram - JJ Jin & Wendy W Fok

f Data Center Map (2022) - Yarzar Hlaing & Wendy W Fok

g Mass Social Surveillance - Rachel Pendleton & Wendy W Fok

h One Wilshire (Los Angeles) - Wendy W Fok

i Google Data Center (Eemshaven, Netherlands) - Google Images

j Embedded Domestic Infrastructure - Yvonne Fu & Wendy W Fok

k Industrial Robotics Timeline - Wendy W Fok & Yarzar Hlaing

l Interior of Google Data Center (Eemshaven, Netherlands) - Google Images

m Infrastructural Connectedness (Urban, Suburban, Rural) - Wendy W Fok & JJ Jin

n Submarine Internet Cables (Interactive Map) - Wendy W Fok

o LinkNYC Patent Drawing - Isa Dabrowski

p Light Pollution and City Energy Facts - Isa Dabrowski & Wendy W Fok

n

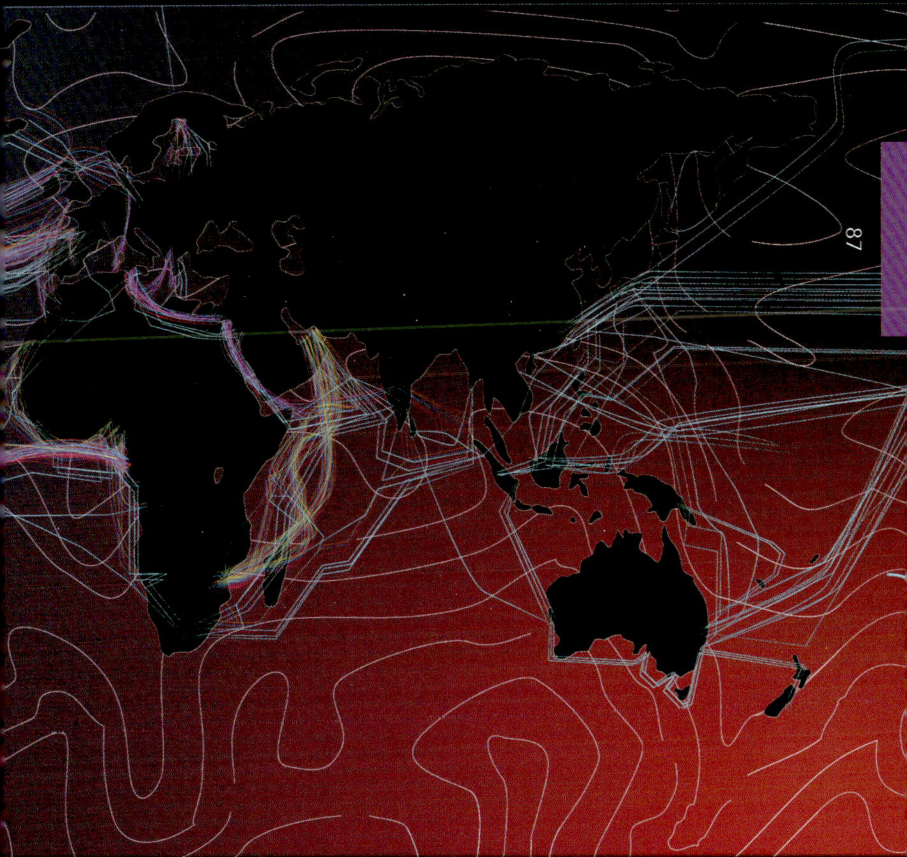

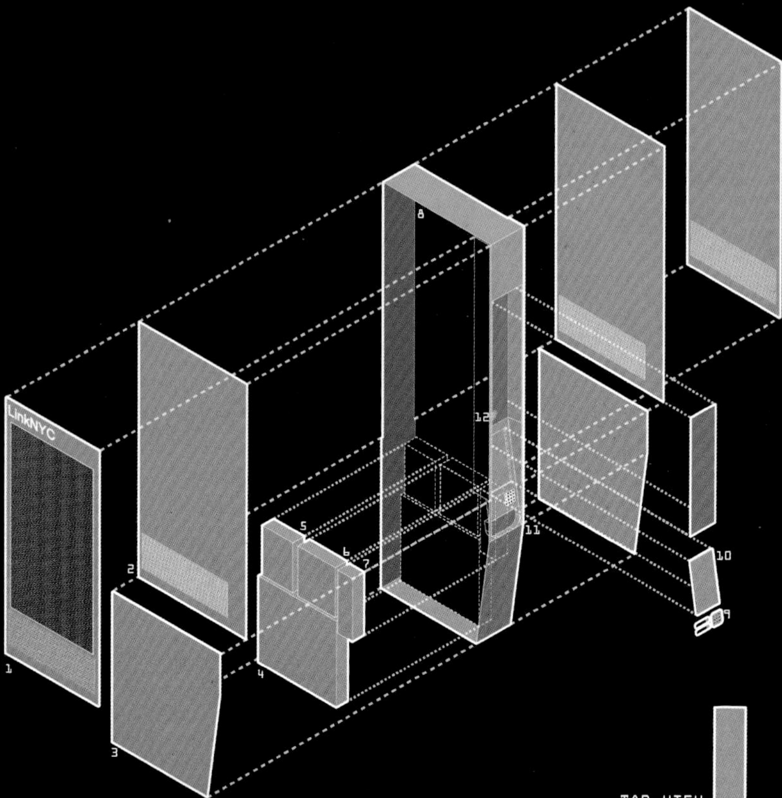

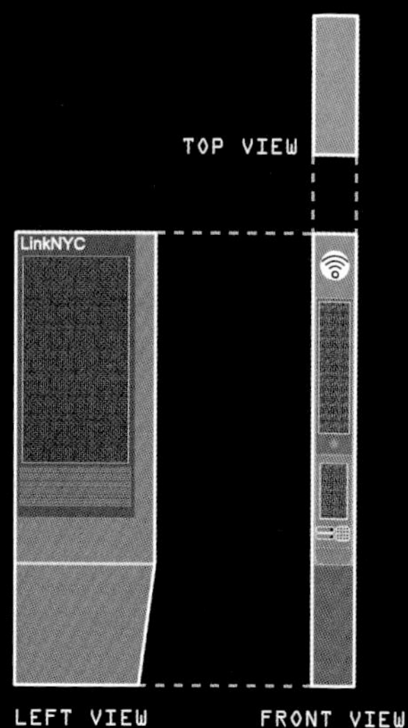

SPECIFICATIONS

1. ADVERTISEMENT SCREEN
2. VENTILATION PANEL WITH WIRING CONDUITS
3. ELECTRICAL PANEL COVER
4. FIBER CONNECTION
5. NETWORK SWITCH
6. NETWORK BAY
7. BATTERY
8. HOUSING UNITS
9. KEY PAD
10. TABLET
11. HEADPHONE JACK AND CHARGING PORT
12. SPEAKER ASSISTANCE

Free Public Wi-Fi as Street Furniture: LinkNYC in the City of New York 2014-2016

Minerva Tantoco

It is estimated that in the City of New York that 22% of residents to don't have access to broadband connectivity to the internet. As more private and public services, such as job searches, educational resources, health information, and access to government benefits are increasingly available online, those who do not have access are left behind the digital divide. One of the key goals of the "Smart and Equitable" City Strategy was to design new approaches to providing this utility to more New Yorkers. One of the programs begun by the previous administration, offered an opportunity to put free Wi-Fi on City streets as part of the requirement to replace the payphones. Why not combine the end of an expiring contract with a new approach to publicly available connectivity?

LinkNYC, which was the fastest free municipal wi-fi network when it was launched in 2016, was a groundbreaking initiative for the City of New York. These LinkNYC kiosks were to replace the City's 12,000 outdated payphones with sleek kiosks that boasted up to gigabit-speed secure Wi-Fi, wheelchair-accessible tablets, and charging.

It started in the Spring of 2013, when the previous Mayor Mike Bloomberg announced a competition "Reinvent Payphones" as a call for designs and request for proposals to replace the payphones, whose 15-year contract was set to expire the following year at the end of 2014. When I was appointed the first-ever Chief Technology Officer (CTO) of the City of New York in September 2014, I learned about the results of the contest from the previous year, and the December 31st deadline. The proposals which were a result of the public RFP in which the public was able to cast a vote for their favorite. By September a new administration under Mayor de Blasio chose LinkNYC, a consortium of four companies which submitted a proposal as a group, the CityBridge Consortium. The City had the top three RFP responses and needed to select the winner and get the contract approved in 10 weeks.

The existing payphones, which had been contracted through a concession agreement 15 years earlier, were largely in disuse. They were considered eyesores, with paper advertising wrapped on the outside, and mostly non-working phones inside. The booths were blocking the view of street level businesses, and were often used as trash receptacles and a place to hide. In contracts, the winning design offered and Android tablet on which to make free phone calls. It was ADA-compliant, with a wheelchair height tactile keypad, a dedicated 911 button for emergency calls, a cell phone charge, integrated lighting, and a two-sided digital display which would offer a rotating set of advertisements and could display location-based public alert messages. Inside, a new and powerful radio which could provide up to Gigabit speed free Wi-Fi at distances of up to 400 feet. The winning contract was awarded and approved by the New York City Franchises and Concessions, just under the deadline in December 2014.

LinkNYC then began the design and construction process for the kiosks themselves, and across several City agencies, the Department of Transportation, the Department of IT and Telecommunications, and the new Mayor's Office of Technology and Innovation (the Office of the CTO), worked through the installation, street construction, and most difficult, the conduits for internet access to where the existing payphones stood. The first LinkNYC was activated on February 2016 and the first phone call was made to 311.

The response to the LinkNYC was mixed. Some privacy activists were concerned about the security of the wi-fi. There was HotSpot 2.0 level security and encrypted communication, but it was possible to opt out of the encryption. There were concerns about whether the distribution of the kiosks was evenly spread throughout the five boroughs. Although the payphone footprint they were meant to replace was not even distributed and focused mainly in commercial areas of the city, some new installations in Staten Island (where there were very few payphones) we agreed to. Gigabit Centers in each borough were also agreed to be built in each of the five boroughs, to put internet access in community centers, with internet access to be provided by LinkNYC. One of the first of these opened in Harlem in February 2022.

In the early days of the Links, as they were activated throughout 2016, created concern about the Links as an unwanted gathering place. Some users were playing music and having dance parties. The Links volume setting was changed and eventually turned off in the evening. Using the phone would require a headphone after a certain hour. Others in the community objected to attracting the homeless to the kiosks to use the chargers and the wi-fi. During 2019, there were several incidents of vandalization of these devices.

Over time, the LinkNYC kiosks seem to have become a familiar part of the City streetscape. New applications on the tablets allow users to register to vote or access City services via the tablets. The photo below as taken in January 2022, where a woman in a wheelchair was filling out a form at the kiosk, while her child stands beside her. Over a million internet sessions have been provided for free from these kiosks, which were paid for by the advertising on them. This model reflected the same concession as the original payphones, but for the digital age.

The LinkNYC kiosks did not "solve" the digital divide. They were part of a larger plan to design and negotiate additional free wi-fi in other public areas, including public housing, libraries, and schools. The current federal level investment in infrastructure will likely enable a much larger expansion of publicly available wi-fi.

The kiosks inspired important dialogue on the role of community input, digital privacy, and the nature of public-private partnerships in the digital world. The agreement with LinkNYC included a

CityBridge privacy policy written in 2015, but which allowed for later updates as regulations change. It requires opt-in consent in order to receive marketing information. Compared with similar free wi-fi in airports, the LinkNYC hotspots provided more security, encrypted sessions, and an agreement not to sell personally identifiable information to third parties.

The kiosks could later install environmental sensors for pollution. The cameras may NOT be used for facial recognition or track movement, but they may be used for video calls should the user wish to use them. These changes would require community input and City approval.

Although questions remain about LinkNYC, overall, they provide a much-needed public service which is used by the residents who need it most. It is an example of how "tech for good" can provide much-needed internet access, though a creative re-use of urban infrastructure, community input through public proposals, and a strong design process.

Minerva Tantoco has spent over 30 years in innovation, is the founder of two startups, and is a pioneer in mobile technology,.She has also served as Senior Product Manager at Palm, Chief Technology Officer at Merrill Lynch and UBS, and holds four US patents on intelligent workflow. Minerva Tantoco most recently served as New York City's first-ever Chief Technology Officer (CTO). Appointed in 2014, Tantoco directed the Mayor's Office of Technology and Innovation. As CTO, Tantoco launched groundbreaking initiatives in smart city policy and government tech, such as LinkNYC, CSforAll, Neighborhoods.NYC, the first-ever IoT Guidelines for New York City, and NYC's Smart+Equitable City Strategy. Based on her efforts, New York City was named "2016 Best Smart City" at the Global Smart City Awards. Tantoco was named 2016 Distinguished Fellow, Bard College, Athena Center for Leadership Studies. Tantoco serves on the Board of the New York Hall of Science (nysci.org), and as Board Member, New York Tech Alliance (nytm.org). Ms. Tantoco is currently an entrepreneur and investor, and is a frequent speaker on AI, blockchain, and IoT.

Scan the icon to view
dynamic content

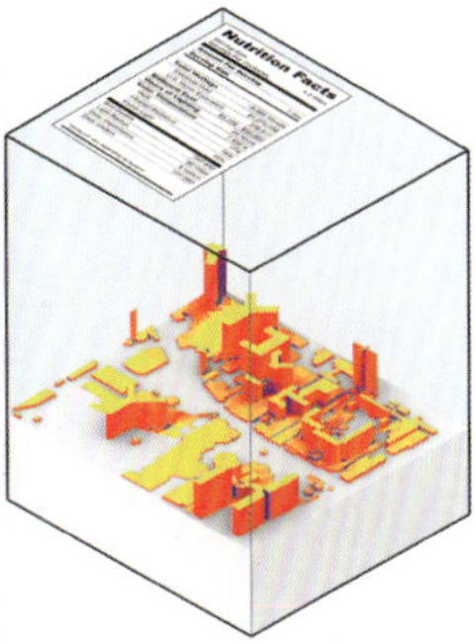

Nutrition Facts

Serving Size	4.2 Miles
Servings Per Container	
Amount Per Serving	
Serving Size	1 day
Total Wattage	~8,000 Mwatts
Electrical Cost	$1,270,056
U.S. Home Equivalent	276,817
Billboard Cost	$5,000 - $50,000
Hours of Lighting	24 hours
Color Temperature	7,500 K
Heat	17%
Infrared Radiation	76%
Visible Light	15%
Bird Deaths	247-630
Light Radius	40 miles
Daily Impressions	.9 million
Daily Visitors	107,000

*Values will vary depending on location.

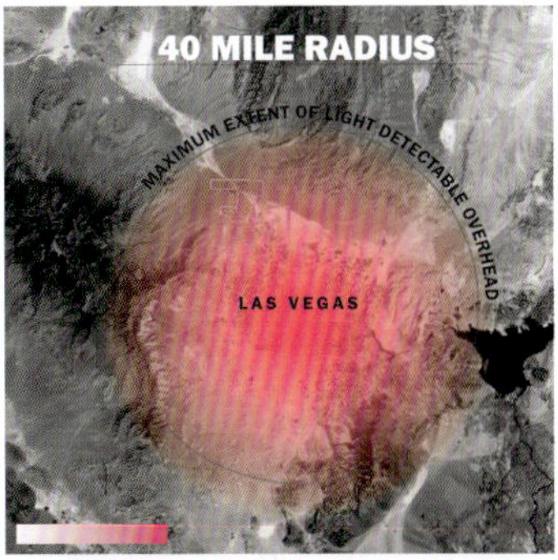

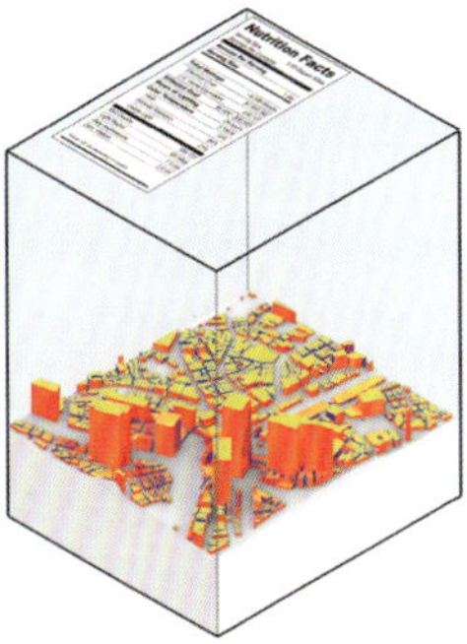

Nutrition Facts

Serving Size	5.83 Square Miles
Servings Per Container	
Amount Per Serving	
Serving Size	1 day
Total Wattage	~9,056 Mwatts
Electrical Cost	$1,963,362
U.S. Home Equivalent	416,117
Billboard Cost	$5,000 - $50,000
Hours of Lighting	24 hours
Color Temperature	7,700 K
Heat	14%
Infrared Radiation	84%
Visible Light	21%
Bird Deaths	304-720
Light Radius	85 miles
Daily Impressions	7.5 mil
Daily Visitors	2.4 mil

*Values will vary depending on location.

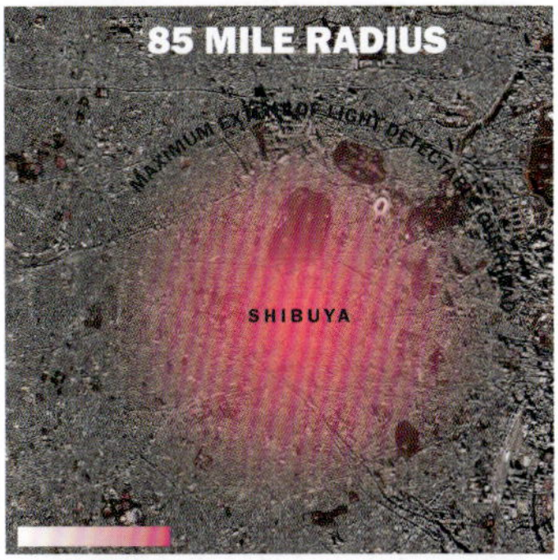

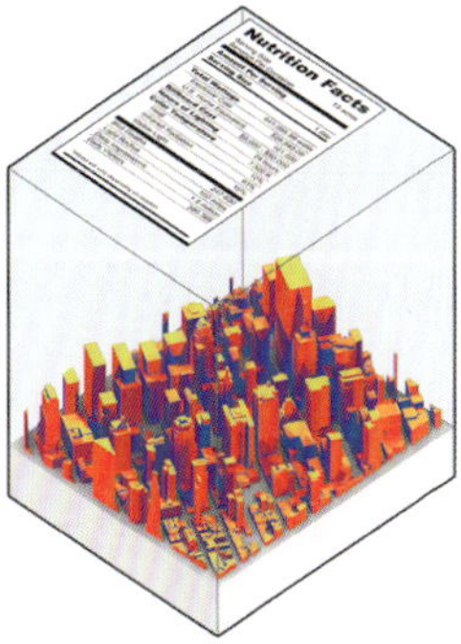

Nutrition Facts

Serving Size	13 acres
Servings Per Container	
Amount Per Serving	
Serving Size	1 day
Total Wattage	441,095.89 watts
Electrical Cost	$26,645.08
U.S. Home Equivalent	161,000
Billboard Cost	$5,000 - $50,000
Hours of Lighting	24 hours
Color Temperature	7,500 K
Heat	12%
Infrared Radiation	83%
Visible Light	15%
Bird Deaths	247-630
Light Radius	100 miles
Daily Impressions	1.5 million
Daily Visitors	390,368

*Values will vary depending on location.

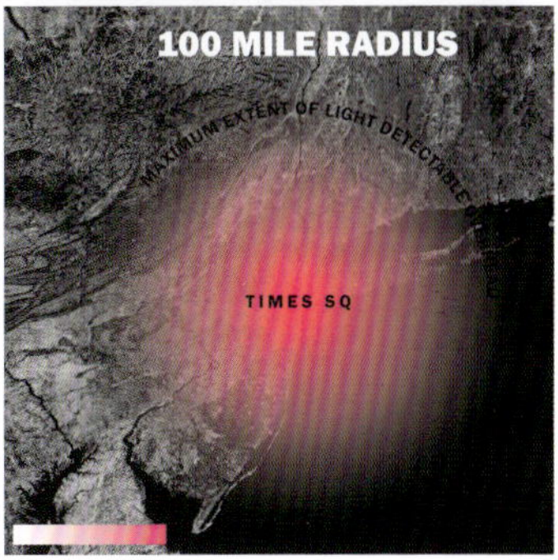

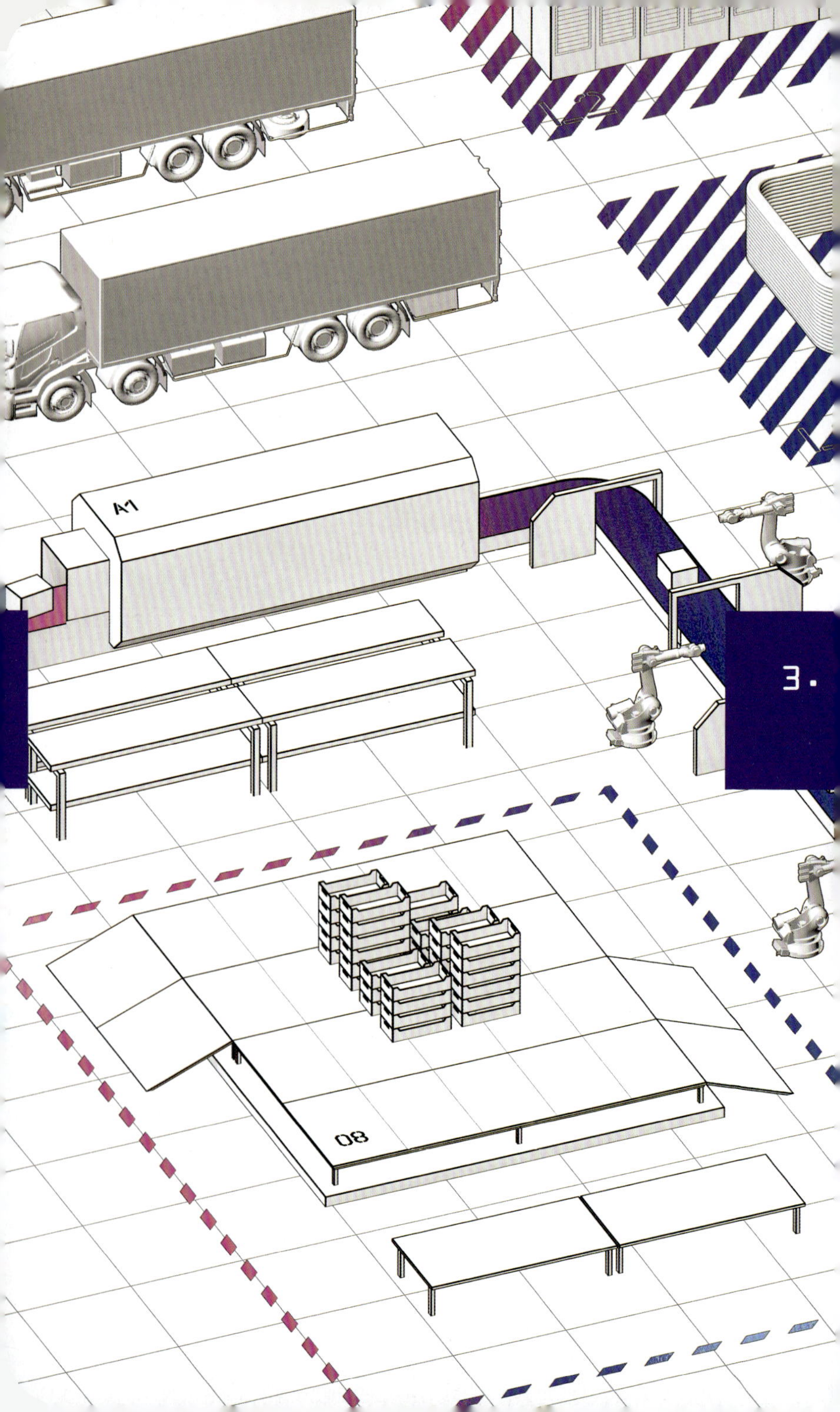

A1
08
3.

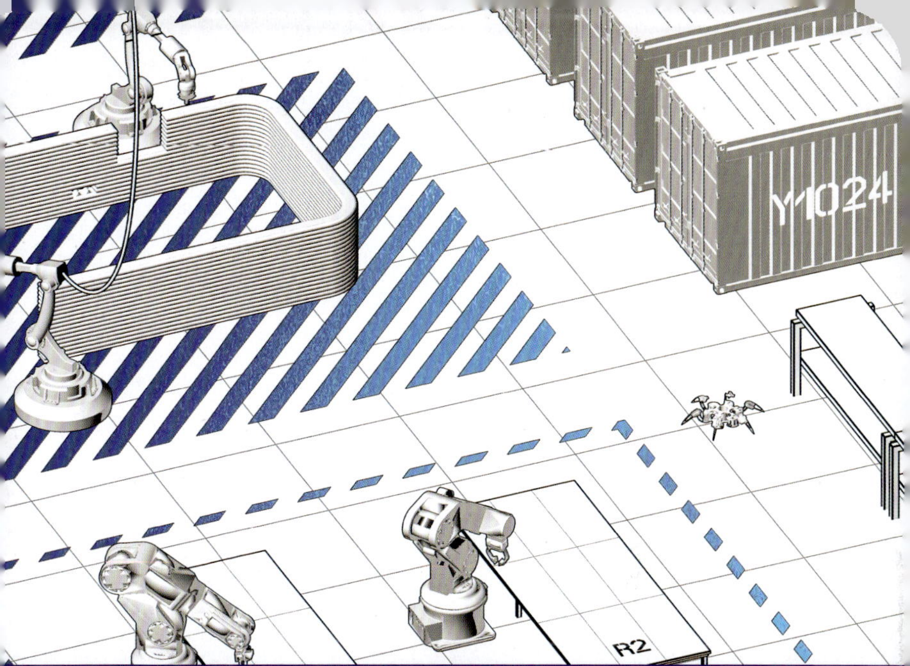

omation / Software / Manufacturing

Can Architecture Be Licensed as Commodity?

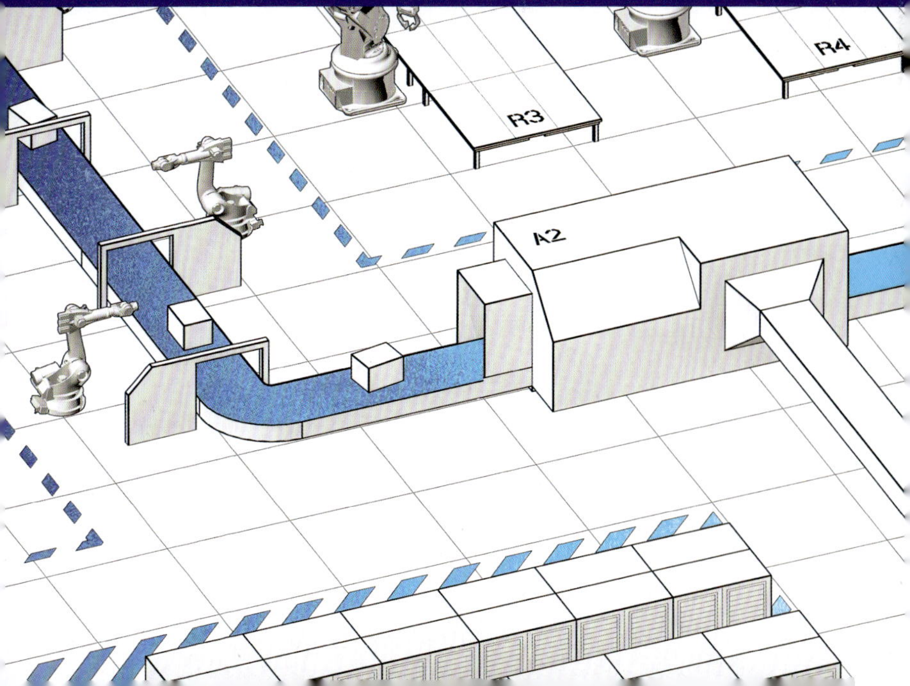

3.

> "A new, a vast, and a powerful language is developed for the future use of analysis, in which to wield its truths so that these may become of more speedy and accurate practical application for the purposes of mankind than the means hitherto in our possession have rendered possible."
>
> - Ada Lovelace

As advancements in robotics, automation technologies, and manufacturing capabilities have emerged, so too have questions on what effects these may have on the workforce, especially in terms of the expansion of construction abilities in architecture, where recent trends such as coding, programming, and both algorithmic and parametric modeling owe much to computer science. Although these questions have been asked about American economic development in general, the current scope and pace of new technological advancement adds more dimensions to these familiar conversations.

a

b

Questions addressed in this chapter include: 1) Will traditional industrialized workforces adapt to new automated technologies? 2) Will robotic technologies displace laborers? 3) What benefits may be expected from the widespread deployment of these technologies?; 4) Could architecture come to be viewed as a commodity? and 5) If its commodification is inevitable, then, what insights can the field gain from computer science and software licensing?

With US President Joe Biden's $1.5 trillion dollar infrastructure bill approval in 2022, the questions remain on whether new systems of exchange and automation will provide a more robust system of infrastructural network that provides for the problematic regional and global supply-chain.

This chapter will begin with a brief history of robotic development, looking primarily at automation's impact on traditional fields, such as industrial manufacturing. It will then present examples of how these new technologies may affect labor forces once considered impervious to advancements in robotic technologies, and examine their macroeconomic effect as a rapidly advancing and potentially labor-disrupting technology. It will conclude by discussing the principles of decentralized ownership, and potential models of licensing and royalties as economic interest to architecture, and question whether architecture could be commodification as a product.

Design as Commodity
The Value of Robotics, Technology, and the Labor Force

The Development of Robotics

According to research firm *Forrester*, 25 million jobs will be eliminated by technology by 2027 **1**. The implications of robotics replacing workers has been a concern since the invention of the first industrial robot patent, the *Unimate*, filed in 1954 by George Devol. Should we be fearful of our new robotic workforce? This chapter looks at the technological development of robotics and mechanization and what that means for contemporary labor forces and the future of conventional human work.

The word "*robot*" was coined in 1920. Its earliest documented use in mainstream culture was in the title, "R.U.R.," or *Rosumovi Univerzální Roboti* (Rossum's Universal Robots) **2**, of a science-fiction drama staged that year by Czech playwright Karel Čapek. The next decade saw *Elektro* **3**, a humanoid robot that appeared at the 1939 New York World's Fair. Elektro could speak approximately seven hundred words, smoke cigarettes, blow balloons, and move its head and arms in response to verbal commands. Its introduction forced people to view the coexistence of robotics and humanity as a distinct possibility.

The earliest robots were fixed machines capable of manufacturing tasks that facilitated mass production without the need of human assistance. Among these was George Devol's *Unimate*, commissioned by General Electric. However, it was the invention of the microcomputer-controlled industrial robot, *ASEA IRB 6* **4**, in 1973 that provided the key to automotive innovation and the development of material handling, packing, transportation, polishing, welding, and grading. These advancements foreshadowed contemporary robots' ability to perform beyond mundane, task-based roles that is incentivized solely by labor gains.

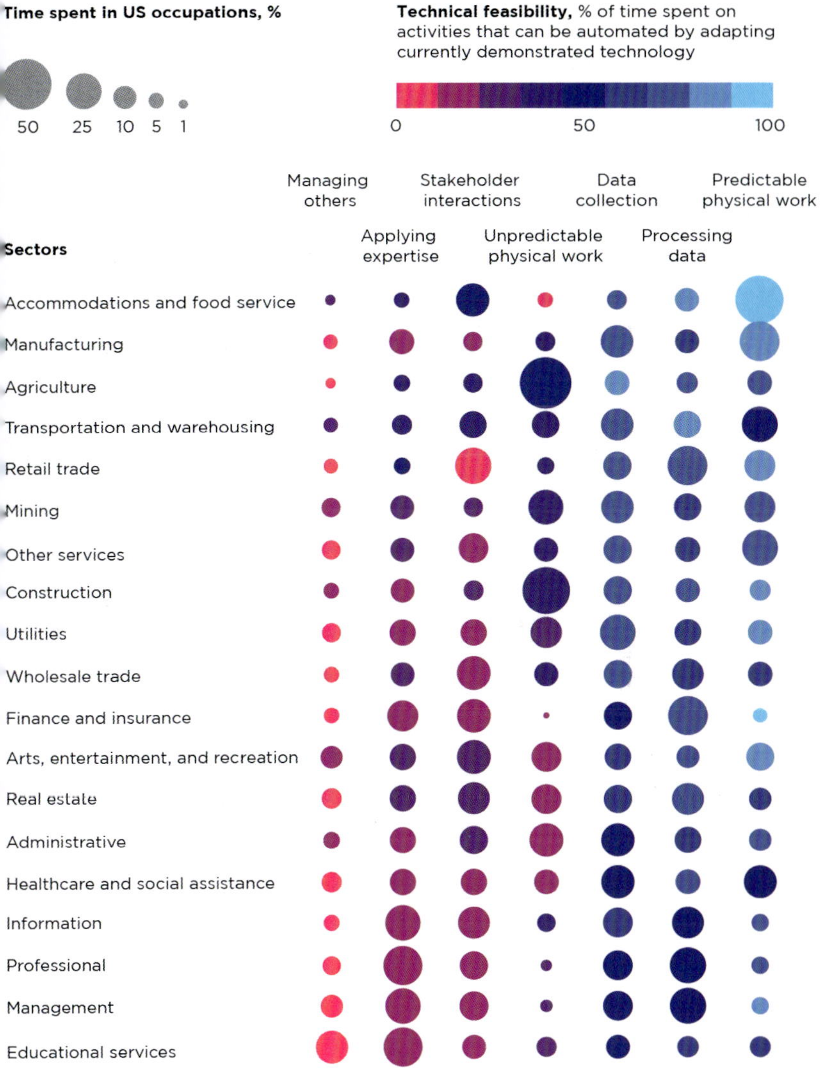
Time spent in US occupations, %
50
25
10
5
1
Technical feasibility, % of time spent on activities that can be automated by adapting currently demonstrated technology
0
50
100
Managing others
Applying expertise
Stakeholder interactions
Unpredictable physical work
Data collection
Processing data
Predictable physical work
Sectors
Accommodations and food service
Manufacturing
Agriculture
Transportation and warehousing
Retail trade
Mining
Other services
Construction
Utilities
Wholesale trade
Finance and insurance
Arts, entertainment, and recreation
Real estate
Administrative
Healthcare and social assistance
Information
Professional
Management
Educational services

C

Designed and innovated by Björn Weichbrodt, the *ASEA IRB 6* was the first industrial robot series that allowed for movement on 5 axes and a lift capacity of 6 kilograms. Equipped with Intel's first chipset, it was the first fully electronically driven and microprocessor-controlled robot. **5**

The mandate driving many of the automation engineers designing robotic machines lay in Isaac Asimov's *Three Laws of Robotics*. Introduced in 1942 in his short story, "Runaround," **6** the three laws continue to be observed today:

> – *A robot may not injure a human being or, through inaction, allow a human being to come to harm.*
> – *A robot must obey the orders given to it by human beings, except where such orders would conflict with the First Law.*
> – *A robot must protect its own existence as long as such protection does not conflict with the First or Second Law.* **7**

Robotics and its use in manufacturing are hardly new; nor are the moral and economic questions surrounding innovation. Robotics has enabled the manufacturing industry to increase the speed of production and delegated low-skill labor to machines. According to the *IEEE Spectrum*, the IFR Statistical *Department of World Robotics* **8**, and the *Second Machine Age* **9**, the rise of robots offsets costs, increases productivity, but may cause structural changes that ultimately harm human employment.

The grandfather innovators behind automation and robotics in architecture, construction, and engineering are Fabio Gramazio and Matthias Kohler at Research ETH Zurich, which has probed the possibilities of designing and fabricating buildings with digital automation beyond the classical forms of 5-axes production **10**. *Gramazio and Kohler* are historically referenced in forefront of automation in the robotics fabrication due to excessive funding from the Swiss research institute, but also due to their focus, foresight, and rigor of how architecture could use automation to push the boundaries of building, both onsite and offsite. Whether with flying or stationary robots, the core mission of *Gramazio and Kohler* Research is to innovate robotics within architecture by exploring the capabilities of architecture in relation to production, some may argue that *Gramazio and Kohler* has institutionalized the

d

e

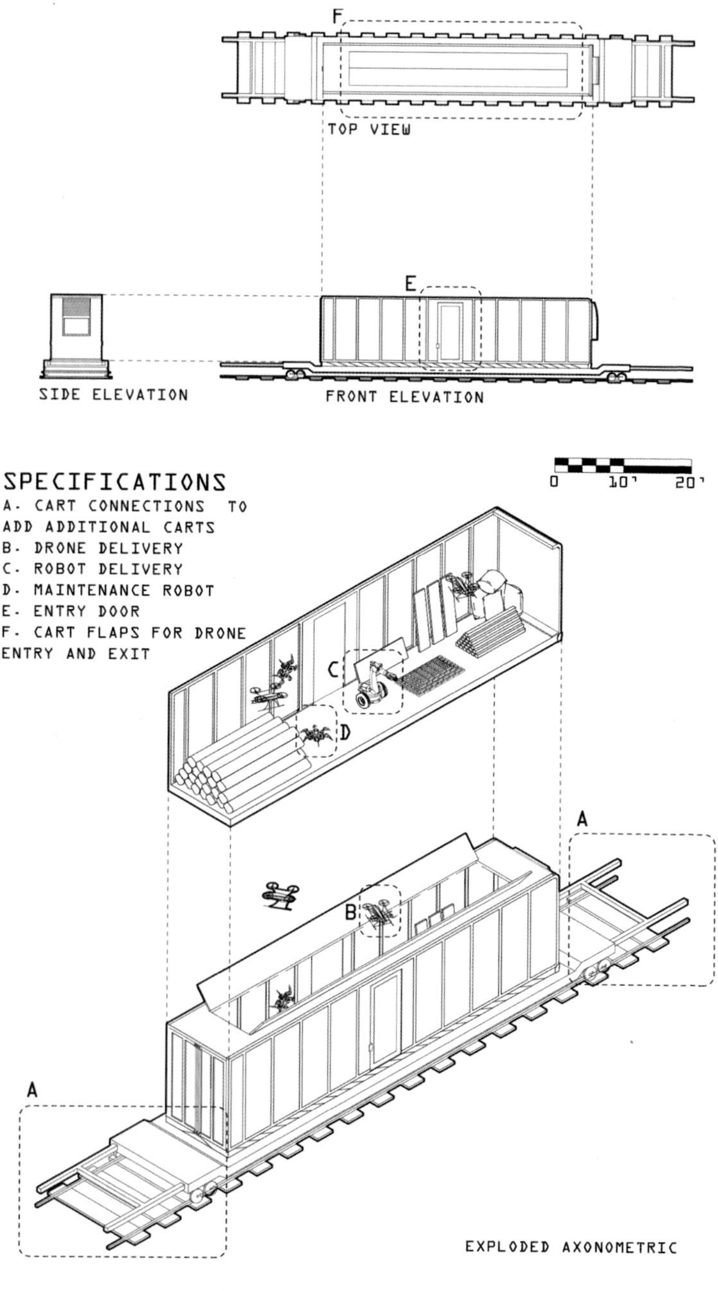
F
TOP VIEW
E
SIDE ELEVATION
FRONT ELEVATION
0 10' 20'
SPECIFICATIONS
A. CART CONNECTIONS TO ADD ADDITIONAL CARTS
B. DRONE DELIVERY
C. ROBOT DELIVERY
D. MAINTENANCE ROBOT
E. ENTRY DOOR
F. CART FLAPS FOR DRONE ENTRY AND EXIT
C
D
A
B
A
EXPLODED AXONOMETRIC

f

practice of robotics in architecture, and have led way to seeding other architects into pushing deeper to innovate the space. **11**

As noted on its website, *"The Robotic Fabrication Laboratory (RFL) is set up as a worldwide unique environment that allows for internationally leading research in the field of robotic fabrication in architecture and construction. It is as an integral part of the new building for the Institute of Technology in Architecture (ITA), located on the Science City Campus of the ETH Zurich."*

BrickDesign, another robotics research project, has developed a powerful software package that enables architects, planners, and engineers to design with a large set of discrete elements. It thus grants designers the power to fully exploit the design potential inherent in novel and innovative robotic fabrication processes. So, for example, the robot allows the architect to position each brick. Such computer-controlled fabrication allows for the realization of highly informed building elements in ways that are both economical and efficient, while demonstrating that novel fabrication technologies require novel design tools.

In my opinion, research of automation is meant to encourage practical experimentation and prototypes to facilitate the discussion of the future of robotics in the global practice, which is increasingly reliant on computational technology. Such as in the case of *BrickDesign*, its objective is to navigate production and labor within computational design to better understand the transformative state of digital fabrication, while examining the force of labor and production that permits value-added productivity and transparency in technological and legal advances in digital design. Architecture, as a practice, with its limitations to onsite production and construction will require better protocol and adaptation to developing better labor practices, and imaginably automation could assist in a renewed ability to engage with safety and human limitations.

Manufacturing the Architectural Commodity
Robotics and Labor, Automation as Megastructure

> "Manufacturing towns in the 1800s relied on coal-powered steam for power. Inflexible, dirty, and noxious, heavy industrial activity was better suited to large, compact, central locations with proximity to railheads and harbors for oil and coal... Since 90 percent of the nation's rural dwellers had no electricity in the late 1920s, electricity provided means for mechanization and automation."
>
> – Pierre Bélanger **12**

Renzo Piano and Richard Rogers may have considered the *Centre George Pompidou* as a derivative of the 1960s *Fun Factory* by Cedric Price. But, in a manner of speaking, the megastructure architectural dreams of the 1960s and 1970s by Banham, Rudolph, Friedman, the Metabolists, Ant Farm, et al, is now being reconceptualized by the technology giant Amazon.

Since shifting its business model to logistics and distribution, by negotiating and incorporating long-term leases with regional city governors of warehouses in strategically chosen port hubs and cities, Amazon, has been changing the game of having one of the farthest outreaches of digital cloud infrastructure and physical storage distribution. Amazon and other larger technology giants are realizing and dominating the reconstruction of the megastructure city structure, by using automation and robotics as a framework for future infrastructure urbanism in American cities.

In August 2021, Amazon applied to a design and utility patent that incorporated a fully automated drone and manufacturing shipping container modular that is also transportable through freight rail. The system is detailed in design, but also pushes the larger needle of merging the world of automation, distribution, and megastructure vision of launching workforce that is limited to robots (reference image f).

Beyond the concept of the manufacturing towns of the 1800s, and warehousing, the extension of using a fully automated system of distribution logistics, and manufacturing 'on the go', while carrier freight trains are heading from one side of the country to other plays hard on the US President Joe Biden's $1.5 trillion infrastructure bill, signed on March 2022. **13**

The robots discussed here thus far offer a mere snapshot of how technological advances in mechanization continue to advance and replace human labor. With smarter, faster, and more efficient robots emerging every day, humankind must look critically at whether the intellectual and technical capacity of robotics will soon displace segments of the labor force.

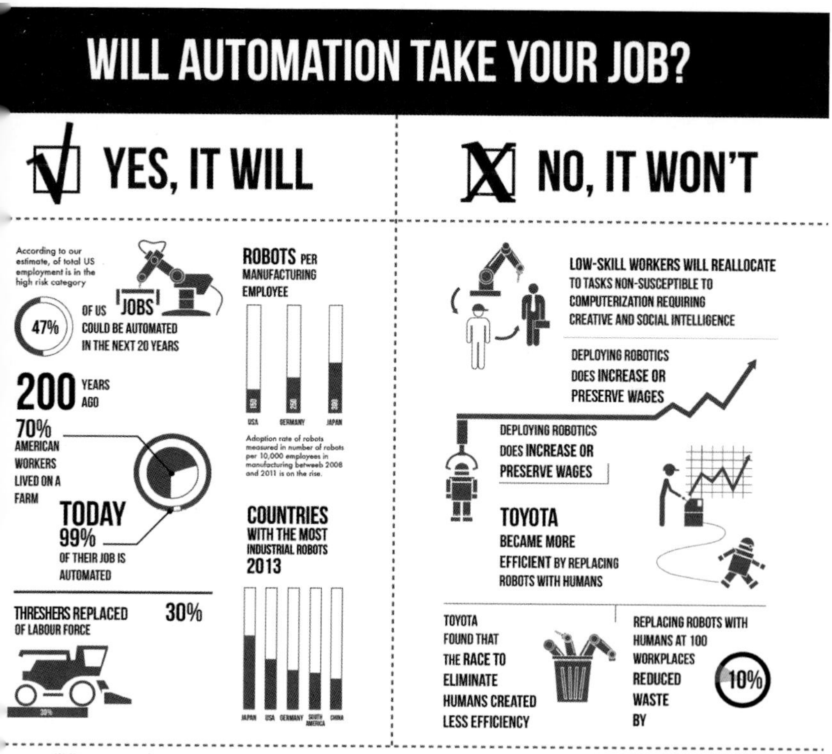

IMAGE CREDIT: WENDY W FOK | NATALIE RODRIGUEZ-GORIS (2014) // INFORMATION SOURCE: IFG | NEW YORKER | WORLD ROBOTICS | SCIENTIFIC AMERICAN | THE ROBOT REPORT | NATIONAL JOURNAL

A. Explaining the Pace of Growth in Robotics

Much of the recent growth in robotics derives from exponential advances in digital technologies. Moore's law–that computing power doubles roughly every eighteen months–has held true for approximately forty years. **14** The primary driver of this exponential growth has been designers' ability of designers to innovate and deploy newer and faster microprocessors at regular intervals. . **15** Industry leaders believe that future design optimizations will uphold the validity of Moore's law for at least another decade. **16**

Moore's law drives robotics growth because when diverse non-digital technologies are digitized, they improve exponentially. **17** Furthermore, the fact that multiple technologies come to share a common digital platform leads to the possibility of recombination; non-rival digital goods with a nearly zero marginal cost of duplication can easily be combined into new technologies, thus generating an ever larger combinatorial array of potential innovations. **18** In other words, digital products can easily and cheaply be used as building blocks for new products, either by combining existing digital products or by grafting digital technology onto an existing non-digital product. For example, many of the robots developed today would be unable to function had their sensors (e.g., cameras and microphones) not been converted from analog into cheaper digital forms and thus made to provide data in a common format that can easily be copied and processed by digital microprocessors.

B. Past Effects of Technological Growth on Labor

Since exponential growth and recombination in robotics is expected to continue soon, what will be its impact on labor? Tension between technological innovation in the workplace and fears of mechanization disrupting the workforce is a recurring historical problem. Past large-scale technological innovations, such as the automated loom, steam power, and electricity invariably displaced labor as they entered the marketplace. Such displacement sometimes led to violent physical retaliation against the technology in question, as in the case of "*General Ned Ludd*" and his followers. Historically speaking, *Luddites* drew their numbers from textile workers during Britain's Industrial Revolution. They protested the introduction of machines that threatened to make their jobs obsolete. Today the term *'luddite'* continues to be used for those opposed to new technology. In the long run, however, technological changes have not significantly altered labor's market share relative to capital. Despite the massive automation brought about by industrial mechanization throughout the twentieth century, new technologies provided Americans with more jobs each decade. In fact, growing mechanization is widely believed to have increased worker productivity and corresponding GDP growth for the past 200 years. **19**

This increase in productivity can be explained by the fact that labor-displacing technologies lower production costs, which leads to greater output demand, which, in turn, raises the demand for labor. **20** Of note, the labor demanded is generally not equal to that displaced; however, new technologies tend to create new opportunities and thus create jobs that complement them. Thus, as a technology is being introduced, we can expect an initial but temporary period of unemployment, followed by labor adapting to it and the opportunities it offers. The Da Vinci surgical robot, **21** for example, may reduce the demand for nurses or for surgeons with exceptionally fine motor control. However, the introduction of such a machine creates jobs for those who can repair or maintain it as well as for individuals who want to be surgeons but lack the motor control required to handle a scalpel.

The idea that automating technologies are net job creators helped overcome initial skepticism **22** and eventually became the prevailing economic view, supported in large part by the history of the industrial and electrical revolutions and the fact that employment has risen alongside labor productivity for much of the 20th century. **23**

C. Why This Time Might Be Different

While efficiency and production continued to increase through and past the turn of the twentieth century, the disastrous effects of the "Great Recession" combined with ever greater technological, robotic, and AI capabilities **24** to shake up the notion of technology as labor-disruptor-cum-job-creator. Today, some experts in the field as well as economists are concerned that advances in robotics may lead to structural unemployment. **25** The following sections will

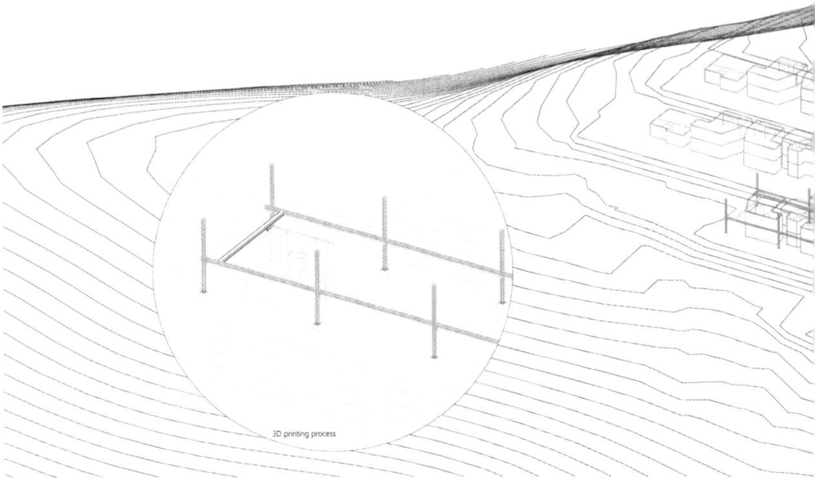

h

delve more deeply into the economic theory between automation as an inelastic good and the growing labor and technological gap that will affect the AEC industry thanks to advances in automation and robotics.

i. Inelastic Goods

First, cheaper production costs do not necessarily lead to greater demand for the product in question. Products for which demand is inelastic may see no increase in demand even if their production costs drop. **26** For example, if kitchen salt was to become cheaper, it is unlikely that many additional units would be purchased; salt is a necessity and consumers therefore purchase it as such. Thus, for inelastic goods, labor-displacing production improvement may not generate a corresponding rise in demand that would fuel further employment. The common counter to this argument is that the savings gained on inelastic goods are instead spent elsewhere in the market, as in the AEC industry, so that aggregate demand across the economy rises enough to create new jobs. **27**

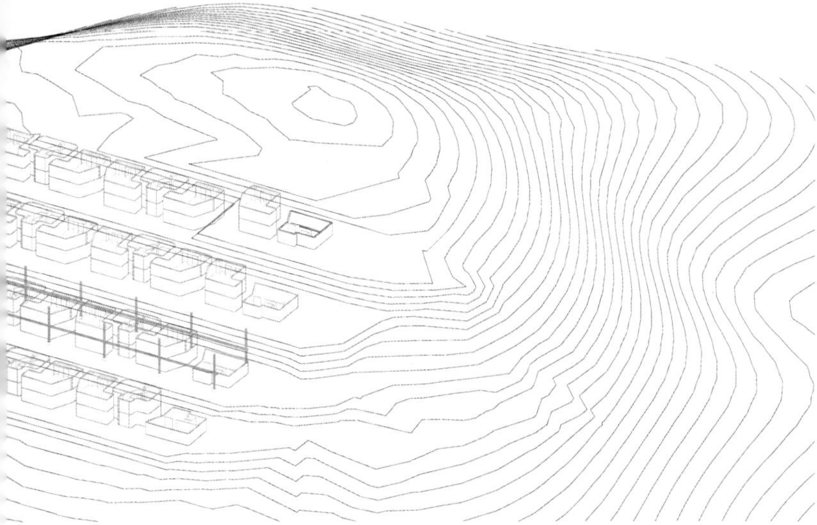

ii. Growing Technological/Labor Gap

Second, in the standard scenario, any displaced labor must wait for a decrease in production costs and consequent uptick in demand that will drive new employment. If technology jumps ahead again during this lag period, then the displaced labor may not have time to adjust to the first change before the second one occurs. For instance, a cab driver may lose his job due to the advent of self-driving cars and thus decide to enroll in an automotive maintenance program. If, during the time that he is in training, a new technology enabling automated diagnosis and repair is

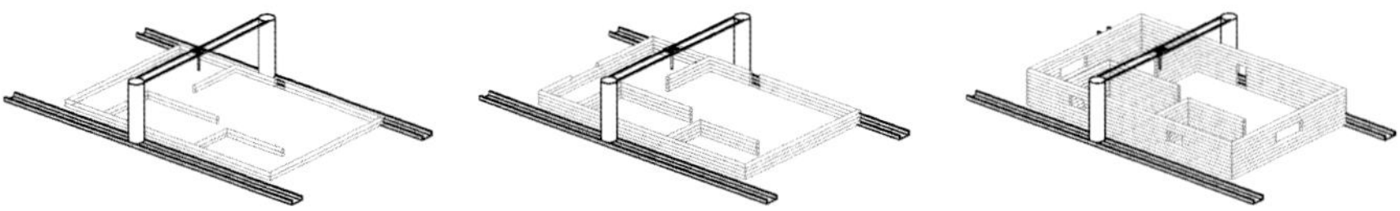

i

deployed, the cab driver will be forced out of his new technology-complementing job thanks to an additional technological advance. Given the exponential growth of robotics and other digital technologies, the gap between automating technologies and displaced labor that cannot adapt quickly enough to complement the new technology may grow ever wider. **28** Erik Byrnjolfsson and Andrew McAfee have come up with an optimistic solution to this "gap" by promoting the integration of labor with technology to advance creative and knowledge-based professions instead of a "*race against the machine*" that pits labor against technology in an unwinnable battle for highly routine, arithmetic work. **29**

iii. Digital Technologies in Robotics Create a Wealth Spread

Finally, there is no guarantee that complementary work will arise or that it will pay as much as a displaced laborer's previous job. Context is key, and statistically, not all numbers are relevant to the field of architecture, and not all automation will develop the same impacts on every industry. It is important to understand that statistics are generally skewed away from architecture and construction industries that require a lot of onsite work and low skill labor. This is supported by the fact that median wages no longer track productivity despite the fact that productivity and the GDP have seen a hand-in-hand upward trajectory over the past decades. **30** The laborer is not capturing the benefit of the production growth that drives GDP upward. Traditionally, two-thirds of national income has flowed to salaries and wages, while one-third has gone to owners of capital as dividends and capital gains. But that ratio is decreasing as today's laborer captures only 60% of the profits.30 Between 1983 and 2009, most of wealth increase in America accrued to the top 20% of households. The remaining four-fifths of the population saw a net decrease in wealth in that same period. By contrast, the top 5% saw an increase of over 80%, and the top 1%, of over 40%. **31**

Automation will disrupt architecture, engineering, and construction, but not in the immediate future. The technological improvements that enable onsite construction with customized robots pose major challenges, as Andrew Witt discovered during *Geometrica*, a robotics research project led by the *Harvard Graduate School of Design* in partnership with an engineering company in New

Mexico. As Daneila Rus, Professor of Electrical Engineering and Computer Science and Director of the *Computer Science and Artificial Intelligence Laboratory* at the *Massachusetts Institute of Technology* (MIT) has pointed out, there are still, *"significant gaps between where robots are today and the promise of a future era of "pervasive robotics,"* when robots will be integrated into the fabric of daily life, becoming as common as computers and smartphones are today, performing many specialized tasks, and often operating side by side with humans. Current research aims to improve the way robots are made, how they move themselves and manipulate objects, how they reason, how they perceive their environments, and how they cooperate with one another and with humans."

According to basic economic theory, one reason for the phenomenon described above lies in automation's ability to replace labor with capital. Those who own capital are investing in automation technologies, while the creation of complementary labor creation has slowed down. **32** In short, job creation is not keeping pace with investment in automation. Although it is possible that this is the normal capitalization attendant to any technological change and that labor has simply not caught up, several unique features of the digital goods present in these automation technologies suggest that this is not the case.

Architectural Consultation Agency

Servicing the needs of the larger industry

According to Andrew Witt (partner of *Certain Measures*, Professor of Practice at *Harvard Graduate School of Design*, and 'alum' of over a decade of working with *Gehry Technologies* (GT) before they sold to *Trimble*), *Digital Project* (DP), is designed both as a service and training package within the larger umbrella of *Gehry Technologies*. The idea of DP was to provide a product, through several levels of service provisions, including and not limited to enterprise service and consultation service. As most industry parties are more interested in solution-based services, it is often the case where the GTeam offers need solutions rather than the product. Therefore, the solution for a problem is mostly for the consultation. In a way, the broader problem to be addressed is the ability to sell solutions rather than products.

Whereby, the GT approach became a consulting company, talking about solutions, and meeting a business objective, with the clients who are interested in delivering the product, that is tied into a marketing strategy for a larger goal. GT, in terms of an architecture and software-based company, thus is unique in both a product and a service, as it is a complete package. Companies, such as *Zaha Hadid Architects* (ZHA), that is led by some of the world's most difficult and curvilinear architectural buildings, are offered the software of Digital Project, but also the training from the individuals from the GTeam to work in-house with the ZHA, based on their $10,000 per commercial license. Economics of the two are very different, and the refinement is very difficult.

Working through the mentorship of Prof Andrew Witt helped me put into perspective and recognize how he develop prototypes of commercial research for GTeam (now *Trimble Connect*), to become the current iteration of a cloud-based 3D platform. Witt's focus was on acquisition talks and positions for the GTeam, including bin-share, and brought in the WebGL talent. Evolving role of product development, market validation, and corporate level on how to develop the elements within the business, Witt has been critical in promoting and developing the initial nimble GTeam to 130 plus people, by the end of 2014. The ambition of the GTeam was to make the company have as large of an impact as possible, through a company structure that is established as a series of research 'regions', whereby each 'region' developed very specific task for the larger umbrella of the Gehry Technologies corporate office.

Although optimistic of the software and service-based model of GT, Witt now has commenced on a new venture called, *Certain Measures*. Part service based, part solution based, but fully digitally and computationally focused, *Certain Measures*, works closer to the model of a software company start-up, and looks to challenge the future of the AEC industry through innovative solutions, that establishes partnerships with the client, rather than just focusing on a top-down premise of creating solutions for the client. Even though Witt is skeptical of the sharing economy, and critically considers the future of ownership models, Witt thinks ultimately profitable sharing economy ownership models are focused only to a concentrated few, and may not be applicable to all assets and digital properties. Witt has carefully highlighted that, "3D models are depreciating asset, perhaps as a shelf life". At the end of it all, Witt would like Certain Measures to become a broad impact company, where designers can work everywhere, but also question, how does the design company evolve? What is a design company? In the words of Witt, *"(w)e are not interested in looking at what is the future of a software company, but we would like to create a future of a design company. Airbnb, Pinterest, Gillette, Microsoft. Indie artist with Pop-goals."*

Ownership sharing has different types of financial models, and ultimately, the broker for the various types of physical property, usually has the strong hold on the digital assets that are shared amongst various users. The owners of the physical properties, such as real estate *(Airbnb)* and cars *(Uber)*, at the end of the day, benefit the most. New wealth of the owners of the assets are transferred, but the users are still at a disadvantage. There are transaction costs that are often generated through a depreciating asset. Perhaps the assets between digital file transfers, currently, are different for car share versus property share, but the future of digital file sharing within the AEC industry needs to focus on how automation and manufacturing, especially for on-demand manufacturing such as companies like *Protolabs* and *Shapeways*, will gauge the depreciating value of the distributed digital property, and when the value of ownership becomes beneficial to which party.

How does Architecture Benefit from Automation, Decentralized Software, and Platforms?

First, unlike producers of traditional physical goods, *capital-substituting* (monetary substitutes) producers of digital goods can offer their products to a vastly expanded global audience -- with the help of modern communications networks. Distribution costs of market expansion are almost zero because digital goods are *non-rival* (goods that have no competition) and may be copied with limited costs and indefinitely. However, producers are no longer insulated from competition by communications and transportation costs. Consumers, in turn, are given a larger universe of products with low costs of switching between them. They predictably choose the best product available, even if the second-best product is only marginally worse than the best one. The result is a "winner-take-all" or "superstar" economic system in which a relatively small number of well-capitalized individuals and smart, lucky top performers reap most of the benefits. 33 Consequently, a disproportionately small portion of the population harvests most of the benefits, while everyone else receives a smaller slice of a bigger pie.

Notably, these phenomena – costless copying, non-rival goods, and global communications networks - were not present in the major historical analogues to the current digital technology revolution. Further, economic data lends this theory of a winner-take-all economy some credence. If the non-rival, costless nature of exponentially and combinatorically growing technologies leads to a situation where only a few benefits, then one should expect that the profits can be shared – instead of a standard bell-shaped wealth distribution curve corresponding to a middle class. We should see a power curve in which the majority of wealth is concentrated in a small number of individuals. 34 This spread in wealth, clearly observable in the past few decades, 35 will only be exacerbated as the rate of return on capital continues to be significantly higher than general economic growth and income. 36

It may be that even if wages shrink or stagnate and unemployment rises, the benefits of increased automation outweigh the costs. In other words, automating technologies provide some social bounty that is received by all, even if not everyone sees an increase in traditional measures of wealth. For instance, the benefits of a travelling worker to be able to text, email, or video conference with family may produce a benefit that outweighs the fact that her job pays less than it would in a world of robotics and digital technology.

The primary difficulty of this hypothesis is that it attempts to perform a cost-benefit analysis with intangible benefits. As such, some economists have attempted to quantify the amorphous benefits provided by new technologies. Typically, this quantification is framed as a consumer surplus. Benefits are defined as the difference between what the consumer would have had to pay for a service absent some enabling technology and what the consumer had to pay for the service given the technology. 37

Economists similarly point out that the increasingly digital, information-centric focus of the current economy requires alternative measures of productivity, wealth, and economic growth. They thus favor modifying traditional measures such as the GDP to more accurately capture the welfare increases provided by the bounty effect. **38** Although such projects are underway, **39** only Bhutan has included some measurement of intangible well-being in its GDP calculation. **40**

In sum, as reported by Daniela Rus (MIT), in the August 2015 *Foreign Affairs Magazine "The Robots are Coming"* issue on the future of work and robots, increased automation due to robotics currently appears to be having a detrimental effect on labor. Although two hundred years of experience indicate that this unemployment may be transitory, key aspects of digital technologies (Mason, 2015) **41** suggest that their effects on labor may not comport with historical analogues. Structural unemployment may indeed result, particularly if exacerbated by a greater flow of wealth to capital holders.

In my opinion, however, the AEC industry will highly benefit with the assistance of robotics and automation, which has better precision and ability of operating heavier machinery and digital tooling. Designers and architects will start to develop new modes of interaction design and experiences, while maintaining the ability of creative thinking, systematic comprehension, and imagination. As positively indicated by Rus, *"(b)y working together, robots and humans can augment and complement each other's skills"*. As architecture becomes more autonomous, it may remove the physical body and human interaction and experience. However, if humans start to co-habituate more with the labor supplementation aspect of robotics and automation, new forms of innovation could be developed by humans. While, basic labor and low-skilled jobs will be diminished, the next questions to consider within this new, uncharted landscape, is: what happens to those who are no longer able to find work? What happens to those who will reap the benefits of robotics production? What will people do with their new jobless lives?

These are the peculiar questions we will continue to evolve as human when paired with the machine landscape.

Would the growing adoption of artificial intelligence, driven by automation and software based on license distribution, through the promises made by luddites benefit the population at large, or would manufacturing through automation be detrimental to the job displacements, in labor sectors where robotics has already replaced human labor, and would inequality of technical education based on software engineering practices become the future blue-collar job.

If incentive-based initiatives are based on software programmers (the creators of the codes), then designers and architects could potentially again focus on the development of designs focused with the tooling of technologies, rather than become their own tool generators.

The software industry for architecture continues a slow growth in the development of the regular CAD software giants, such as *Autodesk* and *Dassault Systemes* – previously, before being sold to *Trimble*, also by *Gehry Technologies* (GT). If software programs were treated as forms of commodity, they would utilize user experience as the currency and programs like AutoCAD, Rhino, and Maya would be considered strong candidates from the software development perspective. But these programs are limited within the user interface and user experience environment. Ironically, these applications are less engaged with the built environment, than creating tools that architects could use to produce the product of architecture.

On the other hand, since 2010, *Adobe*, *Snap*, and now *Meta* (previously, *Facebook*) has been entering the phygital space in developing a different kind of phygital property exchange. Most of these platforms are focused on entertainment, incorporating AR, VR, and XR, but realistically, engages with the world of architecture that is not necessarily including the dialogues with architects. If Bernard Rudofsky wrote *Architecture without Architects*, in the sense that cybernetics would be overcrowded in the world of the unspecified definition of platforms, then non-architecture companies like *Wayfair* and *IKEA* are in the forefront of developing AR applications (apps) and XR platforms that directly engage with the field of architecture and interior architectures. More importantly, interactive and game designers, not architects, are designing these applications for the world that engages with architecture.

The resulting concern is whether the software development companies would produce equally user-friendly experiences and whether the software could be distributed on a level where users themselves could operate on an open source or open innovation level. Large software consortiums would limit their users from altering their software, due to licensure issues, while users who would like to improve their interface want to customize their experiences. These two operations are currently working in parallel with each other, and they are seemingly working against each other. Subscription-based cloud licensure also limits the distribution of experimental software, unless the platform is digitally grounded. *Rhinoceros3D*, on the other hand, is a much smaller software company owned by *McNeel*, which offers users a channel for direct feedback to their developers; more often than not, their suggestions are integrated into newer versions of the *Rhinoceros3D* upgrades.

In 2016, I predicted that built environment will only continue into the world of *Virtual Reality* (VR) and *Augmented Reality* (AR) in the world of Web 2.0. My prediction stood strong to the hypothesis, and now in 2022 in the world of Web 3.0, the question remains whether automation and robotics supply-chains, 3D portable scanning and 3D printing, and democratized programming within integrated software design processes should be, or would be, made accessible to the larger public. Would these concepts remain niche, or would these systems be widely distributed? If teams of corporate consortiums allowed versions of their software to be shared in the field of AEC – like in the case of *Spark* by Autodesk, *Snap*, amongst many others – there could be a greater open policy discussion about improving design competition of bridging architectural software design and the built environment. Perhaps, even with a decentralized form of public interaction.

References

1 Passy, Jacob. *"This Is How Many U.S. Jobs Robots Will Create over the next 10 Years." MarketWatch*. Wall Street Journal, 09 Apr. 2017. Web.

2 Adam Roberts, *The History of Science Fiction* pg. 168 (2006).

3 The Middleton Family at the New York World's Fair (Audio Productions Inc. & Westinghouse Electric Company 1939). The film shows *Elektro*, the Smoking Moto Man, from an exhibit at the 1939 New York World's Fair. This robot, created by Westinghouse, is an amazing technological feat for that era.

4 Brian Rooks, *Thirty Years in Robotics*, in Special Report: Robotics (ABB Review 2005), available at http://www05.abb.com/global/scot/scot271.nsf/veritydisplay/ef27d6c7e1c59be1c1256fc500385aed/$file/ABB%20SP%201-05_72dpi.pdf

5 Björn Weichbrodt, *The Story Behind the First Commercial Electrical Robot*, ABB, http://www.abb.us/product/ap/seitp327/14ec74a2a8c5dcfdc1257648003df18c.aspx.

6 Issac Ashimov, *Runaround*, in I, Robot (1950). "Runaround" is notable for featuring the first explicit appearance of the Three Laws of Robotics.

7 Id. at 85.

8 *Service Robot Statistics: 2014 Service Robots*, International Federation of Robotics, http://www.ifr.org/service-robots/statistics/.

9 Erik Brynjolfsson & Andrew McFee, The Second Machine Age, (2014) (hereinafter Second Machine Age).

10 Matthias Kohler, Fabio Gramazio & Jan Willmann, The Robotic Touch: How Robots Change Architecture (2014).

11 *About*, Gramazio & Kohler Research, http://gramaziokohler.arch.ethz.ch/index.php?lang=e&this_page=about&this_page_old=&this_type=&this_year=&this_id= (last visited December 11, 2014).

12 Bélanger, Pierre. "Redefining Infrastructure". *Ecological Urbanism*. Edited by Mohsen Mostavi and Gareth Dorethy. Lars Muller Publishing. Harvard University Graduate School of Design. 2010.

13 David R.S. Cumming, Stephen B. Furber, and Douglas J. Paul, *Beyond Moore's Law*, pg. 372 Philosophical Transactions of the Royal Soc'y pg. 376, 376 (2014).

14 Robert Schaller, *Moore's Law: Past, Present, and Future*, 34 IEEE Spectrum 52, 53 (1997).

15 Rachel Courtland, *The Status of Moore's Law: It's Complicated*, IEEE Spectrum (Oct. 28, 2013), http://spectrum.ieee.org/semiconductors/devices/the-status-of-moores-law-its-complicated (explaining that the push to achieve greater density forces engineers to ignore potential design optimizations that can be harvested later), Jeremy Gleeland, *Moore's Law: 'We See No End in Sight', Says Intel's Pat Gelsinger*, Sys-Con Media (May 1, 2008), http://java.sys- con.com/node/557154 (stating that previous physical limitations have been worked around, that current limitations are being worked around by introducing non-silicon impurities to chip substrates as a performance boost, and that Moore's law is expected to hold until 2029).

16 Erik Brynjolffson and Andrew McAfee. *The Second Machine Age: Work, Progress, and Prosperity in a Time of Brilliant Technologies*, 48 (W.W. Norton & Co. 2014) (hereinafter Second Machine Age).

17 Martin Weitzman, Recombinant Growth, 113 Quarterly Journal of Economics 331, 333.

18 Steven E. Jones, Against Technology: From Luddites to Neo-Luddism 47 (Routledge, 2006).

19 Second Machine Age at 173.

20 supra section III.A.

21 David Ricardo, On the Principles of Political Economy and Taxation, 31.3 (John Murray ed., 3rd ed., 1817), available at http://www.econlib.org/library/Ricardo/ricP.html ("I am convinced, that the substitution of machinery for human labour, is often very injurious to the interests of the class of labourers.").

22 Second Machine Age at 97.

23 discussion of current robotics capabilities, supra pages III.A.

24 Paul Krugman, *Degrees and Dollars*, The New York Times, (March 6, 2011), Web. http://www.nytimes.com/2011/03/07/opinion/07krugman.html?_r=0; see also *Robots and Social Justice: The Distributive Consequences of Automation*, The Economist, (Mar. 8, 2011), Web. http://www.economist.com/blogs/democracyinamerica/2011/03/robots_and_social_justice; *Labour Markets: The Robot Menace*, The Economist (Mar. 1, 2013), Web. http://www.economist.com/blogs/freeexchange/2013/03/labour-markets.

25 Second Machine Age at 174.

26 Second Machine Age at 174.

27 Wassily Leontief, *Technological Advance, Economic Growth, and the Distribution of Income*, Chapter. 9 Population and Development Review pg. 403, 403 (1983).

28 Eric Brynjolfsson and Andrew McAfee, *Race Against the Machine: How the Digital Revolution is Accelerating Innovation, Driving Productivity, and Irreversibly Transforming Employment and the Economy*, Kindle Location 808 (Digital Frontier Press, Kindle ed. 2011) (*hereinafter* Race).

29 Race Against the Machine at Kindle Location 1860.

30 Noah Smith, *The End of Labor: How to Protect Workers From the Rise of Robots*, The Atlantic (Jan. 14, 2013 10:15 AM), http://www.theatlantic.com/business/archive/2013/01/the-end-of-labor-how-to-protect-workers-from-the-rise- of-robots/267135/.

31 Race Against the Machine at Kindle Locations 500-503.

32 Steve Musil, *Foxconn Reportedly Installing Robots to Replace Workers*, CNET (Nov. 13, 2012 9:25 PM), http://www.cnet.com/news/foxconn-reportedly-installing-robots-to-replace-workers/.

33 Iannella, Renato. "On-line Trading of Rights-Enabled Learning Objects". International Journal of Electronic Commerce. Volume 8, 2004 - Issue 4. 2004. Page 99 - 113. Web: http://www.tandfonline.com/doi/citedby/10.1080/10864415.2004.11044309?scroll=top&needAccess=true

34 Gilbert-Knight, Ariel. "Making Sense of Software Licensing." Making Sense of Software Licensing. Techsoup, 9 Mar. 2012. Web. 24 Jan. 2017.

35 Second Machine Age at 152-55.

36 Drew Delsiver, *5 Facts about Economic Inequality*, Pew Research Center (Jan. 7, 2014), Web. http://www.pewresearch.org/fact-tank/2014/01/07/5-facts-about-economic-inequality/.

37 Thomas Piketty & Arthur Goldhammer, *Capital in the Twenty-first Century.* pg 571. Belknap Press of Harvard University Press, (2014)

38 Second Machine Age at 108, 111.

39 Joseph Stiglitz, Amartya Sen, and John-Paul Fitoussi, *Report by the Commission of Economic Performance and Social Progress*, Council on Foreign Relations (Sep. 2009), http://www.stiglitz-sen-fitoussi.fr/documents/rapport_anglais.pdf.

40 Gardiner Harris, *Index of Happiness? Bhutan's New Leader Prefers More Concrete Goals*, The New York Times (Oct. 4, 2013), http://www.nytimes.com/2013/10/05/world/asia/index-of-happiness-bhutans-new-leader-prefers-more- concrete-goals.html (noting that although Bhutan has used a gross national happiness index, it has elected to move toward unidirectional GDP measurements due to industrialization and a desire to increase standards of living).

41 Mason, Paul. "*The End of Capitalism Has Begun.*" The End of Capitalism Has Begun. Economics. The Guardian, 17 July 2015. Web. Retrieved from: http://www.theguardian.com/books/2015/jul/17/postcapitalism-end-of-capitalism-begun

Image Credits

a Wikipedia - Capek (Public Domain). Information Source: Roberts, Adam (2006). The History of Science Fiction. New York, NY: PALGRAVE MACMILLAN. p. 168.

b Unimate Robot by George Devol, 1954 - 1961. Image Information: people.inf.elte.hu.

c Automation is technically feasible for many types of activities in industry sectors, but some activities can be more affected than others. Original Information and Image source: McKinsey and Company (2017)
Redrawn by: JJ Jin & Wendy W Fok (2022)

d Gramazio & Kohler - *Aerial Constructions* (2010 - 2015).
Image Source: http://public.media.smithsonianmag.com/legacy_blog/Gramazio-Kohler-1.jpg

e Gramazio & Kohler *BrickDesign*, (2011 - 2012).

f Amazon Patent Drone Distribution - Isabelle 'Iza' Dabrowski (2022)

g Will Automation Take Your Job? - Wendy W Fok & Natalie Rodriguez-Goris (2014).

Information Source: PDF electric & supply company | IFG | New Yorker | World Robotics | Scientific American | The Robot Report | National Journal

h & i Diagram of 3D printing Modular Cities and Housing, Karina Garcia

j Robotics Data Connectivity - Yarzar Hlaing & Wendy W Fok

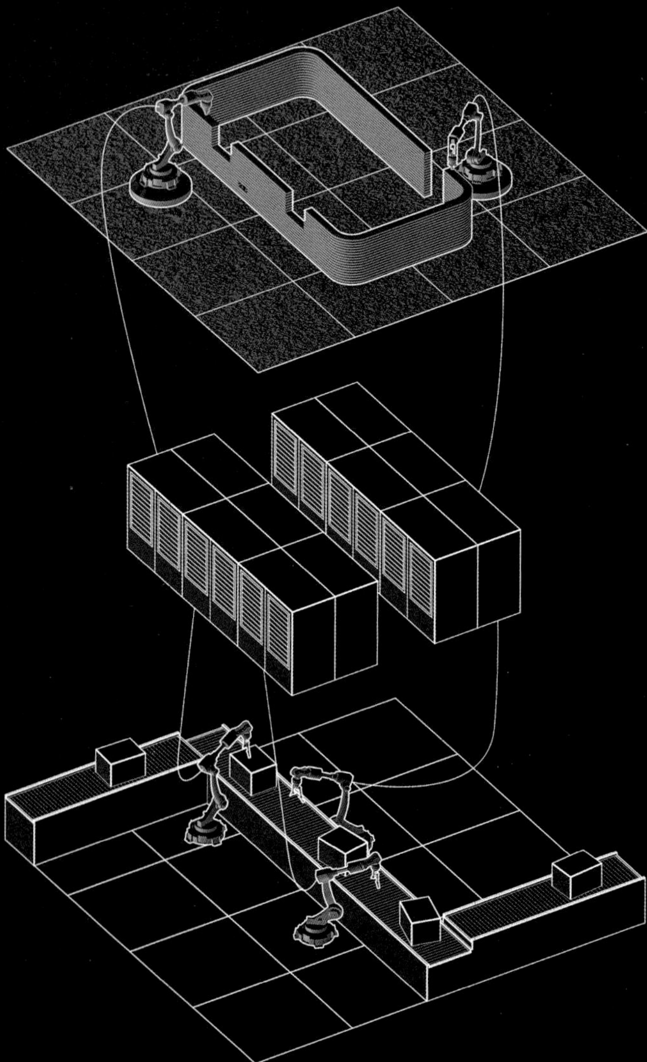

j

Defabricating Architecture: AI, Disassembly, and Radical Reuse

Andrew Witt

Architects have often looked to automated tools for design and fabrication—robotic and CNC fabrication as well as advanced software—as panaceas for frustrating limitations of control. With the proper design and assembly automation, surely architects would no longer be beholden to the onerous and unpredictable vicissitudes of human construction, and they could at last realize their most fantastic visions. In the first decade of this century, the file to factory dream of frictionless and perfectly precise architecture seemed tantalizingly at hand, perhaps even inevitable. Robots could assemble complex walls and entire buildings could be 3D printed with infinite detail. With the advent of CNC processes, the Renaissance ideal of the master builder—an architect capable of informed and coordinated control of every aspect of the building project—seemed an apt avatar for a new age of integrated construction.

Yet, in the 20 years or so since the advent of CNC and robotic construction and the resurrection of the master builder, those dreams have proved elusive. To be sure, technologies like BIM have enabled more fluid connections between architects and downstream makers, and the architectural imagination has been enriched immensely from the new formal possibilities of these processes. Prototypes for 3D printed structures abound. A periodic and almost cyclic enthusiasm for off-site construction regularly resurfaces. Yet scaling these methods for broad application remains stubbornly difficult. The world is not awash in parametric brick walls, construction has not been disrupted to the extent imagined, and the architect's role remains largely unchanged. The collapse of ambitious and lavishly funded construction automation enterprises such as Katerra, only the latest attempt at vertical integration of construction, has called into question how impactful such processes may ultimately be. More traditional practices of construction not only persist but vastly predominate. Even more fundamentally, there is deep ambivalence around the sustainability of new construction, however automated, in a world of finite resources. Judicious material and process choices can make an impact on the material and energy use of new buildings, yet from an ecological perspective the basic calculus of new construction is irreducibly expensive. In fact, to some extent, architecture as it is currently practiced is predicated on an assumption of inexhaustible demand for new building, and thus inexhaustible raw materials. Aside from the irresistible ecological pressure, shifting economic and social trends further encourage a shift toward more circular thinking. The population growth of developed nations is decelerating and may soon reverse. Demand for buildings with new uses may continue but with a shrinking population, and many may soon be abandoned. Already processes of deindustrialization and shrinking cities are leaving considerable building stock to decay while building demand lies elsewhere. Is there a way to correct this mismatch between architectural ambition and global need?

Recent developments around AI and machine learning prompt architects again to reflexively plumb these innovations for formal novelty and to raise hopes of a radically restructured design and building culture. Yet perhaps they also hold the key to shifting architecture from its focus on new construction toward a more holistic view of material cycles and sources. Instead of applying these revolutionary technologies to make new buildings, why not use them to unmake old ones intelligently? Why not use the power of pattern recognition and AI to reverse engineer existing buildings in such a way that they can be sustainably deconstructed and reused? Instead of surgical and precise assembly, why not use them to drive circular reassembly?

New technologies could transform the reuse of deconstructed building materials, and even enable a more scalable approach to deconstruction. Design for disassembly, already in common use in product design, has been slow to impact architecture and construction. Moreover with the relatively small percentage of building stock replaced each year, it could well take a century before such practices made a significant impact. But with AI-enabled tools that could optically scan and generate deconstruction plans of existing buildings, architecture could be intelligently disassembled regardless of how it was originally constructed. Robotic tools could assist in this careful demolition. Digital technologies could also confront challenges of material reuse. Historically, a major obstacle to material reuse from demolition was the laborious and uncertain process of regrading reclaimed materials in a reliable way. Yet today, advances in machine vision, AI classification, and tomographic scanning could be used the regrade materials with unprecedented precision. Automation, once a tool of endless production, could be the key to ending the cycle of limitless material use in architecture.

Despite its aspirations for disciplinary autonomy, architecture must wrestle with economic, environmental, and social trends beyond itself. As those trends move in urgent and unprecedented directions, they call into existential question the assumption of endless new building. Technologies turned toward automated dis- and re-assembly may offer a way not only to close the loop on construction materials but also to open new avenues of creative research in part by seeing existing architecture as a resource to literally be mined, taxonomized, and radically reimagined. The master builder is dead. Long live the master re-builder!

Andrew Witt is an Associate Professor of Practice in Architecture at the *Harvard Graduate School of Design*, teaching and researching on the relationship of geometry and machines to perception, design, construction, and culture. Trained as both an architect and mathematician, he has a particular interest in a technically synthetic and logically rigorous approach to form. Witt is also co-founder, with Tobias Nolte, of *Certain Measures*, a Boston/Berlin-based design and technology studio that combines imagination and evidence for systemic and scalable approaches to spatial problems.

Scan the icon to view dynamic content

4. Access, Permission, and D

How Is Arc

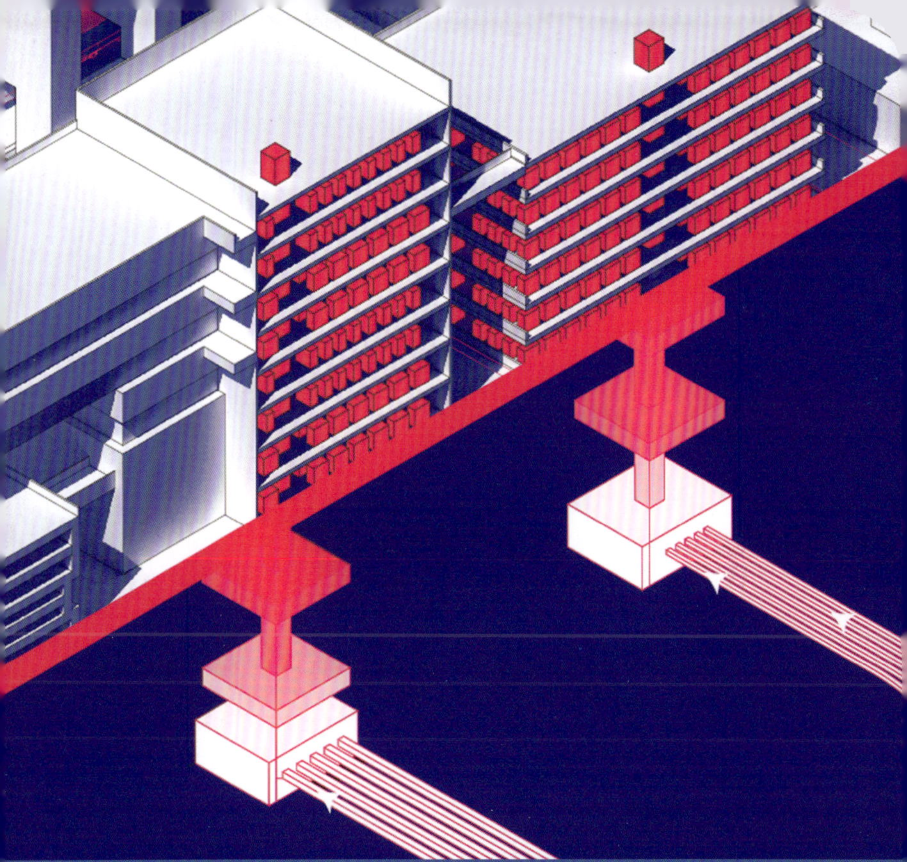

ibution of Design in Architecture

ure Affected by Blockchains and Digital Exchange?

4.

> "In the physical world, ownership actually fences people out. It precludes others from enjoying what you can own. Digital Space, however, is expansive. It's home to the infinite, instantaneous, and exponential. NFTs offer a system of ownership that reflects this expansiveness."
>
> - Kayvon Tehranian, Founder of *With Foundation*

Big data is on the rise. More organizations are storing, processing, and extracting value from data of all forms and sizes. The importance of political data and its value grew exponentially between the period of 2016 and 2020 during the US presidential elections. with the discovery of Cambridge Analytica's data rigging surrounding electoral strategy. *Cambridge Analytica* (CA) is a private company that combines data mining and data analysis with strategic communication for the electoral process. Founded in 2013 as a big-data offshoot of its British parent company, SCL Group, with the objective of participating in American politics, CA claimed it could predict the political leanings of every American adult.

Data has shifted the way we navigate the world, but also the way we think of owning its distribution. If data can be predictive, then systems that support large volumes of both structured and unstructured data will continue to rise. Data retrieved from technological devices initially designed to perform simple tasks or provide tangential entertainment value, have now become fundamental to the way in which architects and architecture operates.

Whereas the previous chapter discusses how designers and automation can co-exist and asks where things are heading, this chapter highlights and examines the economic and automation trade-offs that will occur in the next phase of Web 3.0. Will organizations leverage data from the outset in order to drive value to their buildings and ensure transparency in sustainability and productivity, or will they use machine learning to build a backbone for their building systems in order to enhance security, maintenance, and optimization? Big data and machine-driven design in architecture raises many questions about the future of the AEC industry.

The case studies in this chapter demonstrate the importance of architectural CAD software to Web 2.0 and the Internet of Things (IoT), and allow us to examine its role in the ever more quickly paced digital turn of contemporary architectural design and the building industry in Web 3.0. This chapter also looks at how data has expanded at various scales and across platforms and specifically explores the lineage of architectural software consortiums that have contributed to digital fabrication, the expedition of manufacturing by the labor force, the mechanical realities of robotics, and the digital supply-chains that contribute to experimental architecture. Finally it examines the business of distribution and access of design in the digital world of open source and digital ledgers, and how open data affects the operation of supply-chains in our cities.

The evolving and experimental processes of blockchains have undergone various iterations. Today, blockchain is at a point at which we can apply its potential to access user-information and distribute design information through meta-data even in the fields of digital media and architecture. As Web 3.0 forges ahead over time, the market will demand platforms that help data custodians govern and secure big data gathered by both nation-state actors and privatized consortiums , while enabling end users to analyze this data with the Blockchain. Such systems will mature to operate well within enterprise IT systems and standards, while the architecture and real estate industry will need to adapt.

From Participatory Culture To Participatory Authorship

Architectural Distribution and the Maker Movement

Most of the infrastructure on the internet runs on open-source software. While *Free and Open-Source Software* (FOSS)-based systems run the internet on its digital infrastructure – data centers are the physical megastructures that process the work for architects around the clock and around the world.

According to Engelfriet **1**, Richard Stallman, Robert Young, Bruce Perens, Linus Torvalds, and many others, the likelihood that software licensing is going open-source is further affirmation that FOSS is here to stay. But why does FOSS **2** matter in architecture? It matters because it is the basic framework for all software on the internet, it is the same digital infrastructure that connects to the fiber-optic cable network, which connects the entire world.

Although open-source licensure and automation lead to advances in technology, such as drones, the cloud and sensors that enable artificial intelligence, the growing concern is the degree to which consumerism and capital-based decisions will determine the circulation of goods and phygital (physical and digital) property in the near future.

Digital infrastructures such as IBM Watson that enable automation and computational power to run Smart Homes, such as Alexa and various other modes of integration, have already been integrated into the building industry. Architecture has become more dynamic than ever, incorporating automation, robotics, coding, and various hybridized practices into the field. Phygital property transference

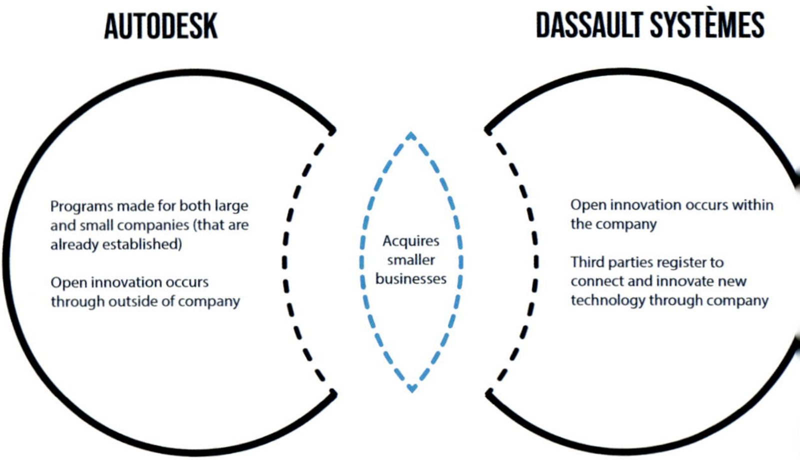

a

and integration are essential, not incidental. Architects and technologists are in many ways singular creators. Why limit our abilities as architects and designers when we can be creative technologists capable of far more than building buildings.

The future of the building industry and architectural practice will be dominated by the opportunities created by product efficiency, limited waste, and on-site pre-fabrication. While 3D printers and robotics will enable more intricate on-site construction, inefficiencies are inherent in their technology. Nonetheless, the automated delivery process, as seen in the advancement of *Kuka* robots at *Tesla* factories, facilitates streamlined product distribution processes. Drones and automation have the power to combine the opportunities of fabrication technology and participatory culture. Automation can provide the crowd with new motivation to build, make, perform, and organize.

The term "maker movement" was coined in 2005 or 2006 by Dale Dougherty, founder of the magazine MAKE and co-founder of *O'Reilly Media*, a technical publisher and conference organizer known for its advocacy of Open Source and Web 1.0 and 2.0. In 2006, O'Reilly Media, pushed the envelope of the appreciation for garage projects by "celebrating the right to tweak, hack and bend any technology to your own will" **3** (TED, 2015) and establishing the Maker Faire do-it-yourself (DIY) series, which has now evolved into an international empire and global network of makers. Chris Anderson, founding editor of Wired magazine, in turn, defines "makers" as the way in which the new industrial revolution will revolutionize the tangible world through bits and atoms and various forms of collaboration—a definition that differs from the MIT Media Lab's less precise understanding of the term.

As more designers and architects go beyond being the traditional single "maker models" of conventional craftspeople to becoming creators in the digital age, we shall see relevant technological changes implemented into the Architecture, Engineering, and Construction (AEC) industry by cloud systems, online structures, and collaborative platforms. These same technologies are already emerging in the present business models of Autodesk, Dassault Systèmes, Adobe, and various headlining building innovation CAD software companies.

For example, *3Dexperience*, which has been absorbed by Dassault Systèmes, is one of the few companies that explored the "platform" as a means of cloud collaboration in the AEC. Geared as a "business experience," *3DExperience* promised to provide software solutions for various scaled solutions in the building industry, from marketing to engineering services, based on 3D design, analysis, simulation, and intelligence through the platform's private cloud. Even Jonathan Mallie of *SHoP* architects has stated that, *"the benefit of cloud-based collaboration is speed and effiicency. You're increasing productivity. You're getting to the end of the project quicker."* **4**

Starting with the 1971 *Design Participation Conference* **5** organized by Nigel Cross, then moving on to *House_n* by Kent Larson of the MIT Media Lab and the *Open Source Building Alliance* (OSBA), the *WikiHouse prototype*, the *Open Architecture Network*, and the recent *Smart Parameter Platform* developed by UNStudio, this chapter presents a few projects that have set precedents for how architecture can promote thought-leadership, cultural distribution, online platforms, and open processes in both the physical and digital worlds of the built environment.

Architecture in the Age of Participatory Automation

While the future of participatory automation in the AEC industry may be prompting discussions of "cooler" toys, drones, and robots that can better assist in the construction of buildings, the buildings of the future may not be constructed, but rather manufactured. Phil Bernstein, former Vice-President of Strategic Relations at Autodesk offers insight on the future of automation and its role in the AEC industry, pointing out that, *"(r)evolutionary changes don't come along very often in the building industry, and when they do, usually a confluence of stuff pushes those changes forward. Prefabricated architecture sometimes also called "assembled architecture," looks to be one of those transformations. In the past decade, a few pivotal events shaped the transformation of "manufacturing buildings" from hyperbole (or desperate banality) to reality."* **6**

As Paul Mason of *The Guardian* notes in *"The End of Capitalism has Begun,"* due to the *"spontaneous rise of collaborative production: goods, services and organizations,"* **7** the market and managerial hierarchy of the economy is no longer dictated by goods or production. Instead, indication of economic power lies in the *information product*, in what I would describe as the *invisible intangible good*. *Open innovation* (OI) and the *internet of things* (IoT) in Web 2.0 has led to a language of daily operation and spending (economic / energy / time) habits shared by millennials, one that circles largely around social media networks, but also extends to the production trends that market the future of cities and the function of urban policy.

The communal attitude among millennials and their interest in the collective establishment of shared products and services encourages a participatory culture. The search for participation in our networked society also offers a means of authority in the architecture industry, since this trend (or movement) enables a new breed of contemporary designers and architects, who build their own design empire and buildings through resources such as the crowd-funding platforms of *Indigogo*, and *Kickstarter*, among others. *Wikipedia* alone has abolished the encyclopedia business and deprives the advertising industry of an estimated $3 billion a year in revenue as it is written by volunteers for free, enabling participants to author their own intangible information good. **8**

In architecture, the *Design Participation Conference* curated by Nigel Cross in 1971 gathered the likes of Negroponte, Bill Mitchell, and Yona Friedman because it encouraged a discussion on the participatory state of design in architecture and urban planning and paved the road for projects such as WikiHouse by the London Design Agency 00/, the MIT *Open Source Architecture* project by Carlo Ratti, and the MIT *House_n* led by Kent Larsen at the Media Lab. All these offer clear indication that the open movement in architecture is focused on greater collaboration, as indicated by cloud computing in BIM systems, but also by the ability of automation, crowd funding, and collective community effort to build more coherent cities.

In late 2003, an iteration of open-source construction was put through an academic test at the MIT Media Lab led by Professor Kent Larsen and his team in order to address the needs of the $800-billion-plus construction industry. The *Open-Source Building Alliance* (OSBA) began with the PlaceLab, an apartment-sized project. The next year it created *House_n*, a larger project that

b

addressed the construction industry's goal to utilize open source as a means of production and construction.

OSBA was founded with the objective of developing the key components of a more responsive residential model in which: (1) developers become integrators and alliance builders who offer solutions tailored to individuals; (2) architects work on design-engines in order to create thousands of unique environments in an efficient manner; (3) manufacturers agree on interface standards and become tier-one suppliers of components; (4) builders become installers and assemblers; and (5) customers (home buyers) become the "designers" at the center of the process and receive personalized information on design, products, and services at the point of decision. **9**

Albeit diverse, *House_n* began with the idea that the design of residential and work spaces must respond directly to the unique needs, values, and activities of the individual. With the goal of promoting social awareness and a means of leading technological impact, the project has focused on how the design of a home and the technologies, products, and services related to it should evolve to better meet the opportunities and challenges of the future. *House_n*'s larger goal is to merge a person-centric design methodology with the technological advances of everyday domestic life.

Launched in 2012 by London-based design agency 00/, *WikiHouse* became a poster child for an open-source construction project that integrated the needs of the individual with the exponential

components that it outsourced. Its "open-source construction set" allowed users to build their homes from slotted-together pieces milled from crowd-sourced, open-source designs that they could download for free from the web. The concept grew from the idea of making it easy for the general public to build homes from scratch, without power tools or specialized knowledge, and for the price solely of raw materials. **10**

The power in the developments of cities and the architectural process is so closely bound to the digital and open platform model. The public uses these digital forums to communicate and mirror the needs of collaborative manufacturing in prefabrication, and integrated project delivery, which are all means of production and automation in the construction and architecture industry. Robots are one form of such production. However, the digital open platform places a premium on information sharing. **11**

In the age of *shrink-wrap* **12**, license agreements are no longer valid due to cloud-based computing **13** and ISV model software license distribution **14**. Prosumers are no longer interested in clicking on *"I agree"* and blindly appeasing their EULA. Many times, they are savvier about their digital (intangible) and real (tangible) property rights than legal experts are. With the advent of internet proficiency and computer literacy amongst two-year-olds, the average child can now easily and dexterously delegate on most computer platforms **15** and user interfaces before starting their formal education. From participatory culture to participatory authorship, the new age of digital citizenship in the built environment lies in the promotion of active digital contribution through the interconnectivity of devices.

Digitizing the Supply Chain, While Tracing the Distribution and Demand

Often referenced as the *"Industrial Revolution 2.0,"* the current AEC industry has progressed beyond regional production. While global manufacturing has become the norm, the digitalization of processes along the entire manufacturing supply chain, starting with product design and development is driving the next industrial revolution 2.0. Robert Bodor, vice president and general manager of *Protolabs*, which makes low-volume 3-D printed, CNC-machined, and injection-molded custom parts for prototyping and short-run production, has been innovating with the notion of lean manufacturing. For several decades now, his company has served as the cornerstone of operational efficiency in manufacturing. **16**

Protolabs is creating a digital supply chain that enables producers, creators, and designers large and small to produce quality products with factory backing. It grants individual creators and medium-sized companies access to a digital supply chain and distribution channel, as well as quicker and more responsive turnarounds. By granting creators opportunities to react more immediately to market needs and remain competitive, the company improves operational efficiency through smaller batched production and prototyping output.

Mitigating Risk by Digitizing the Front-End

The manufacturing supply chain begins during a product's development phase. Designing a product with manufacturability, but also total production costs in mind, can have significant benefits further down the supply chain. For instance, the difficulty of manufacturing a product will definitely drive up its price and thus have a negative impact on its demand and consequently market acceptance. Knowing the manufacturability of its design during the prototyping phase, and understanding the eventual production costs from suppliers can save a company unproductive development time and help it hit its production cost targets sooner.

Companies thus resort to parallel prototyping, which permits them to test multiple designs simultaneously and determine the most viable option from both the functionality and production

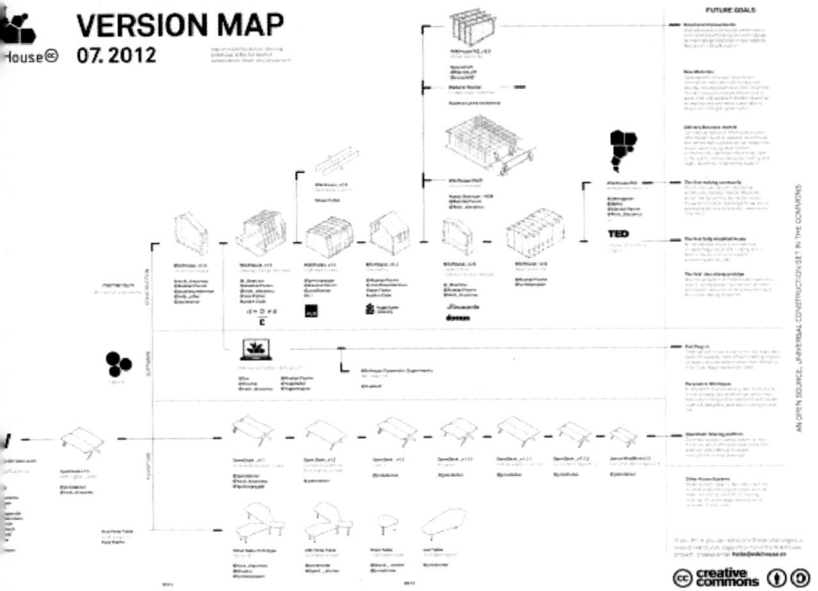

c

cost standpoint. Digital manufacturing can help the localized and regional supply-chain in various ways, as through simulation and rapid prototyping, for example. Many companies, including *Protolabs* and *Shapeways,* offer web-based software that can analyze a CAD model, write its build code, then virtually manufacture the part, giving design engineers nearly instant feedback on the manufacturability and production costs of their designs. This entire process is completely digital, on the cloud, and can take place in a few minutes.

Driving Revenue by Getting to Market Faster

Finding the most cost-effective and time-efficient way to go-to-market once the design is validated accelerates the path to revenue. Thanks to automation, digital manufacturing, in which the entire front-end process of design analysis, quoting, and tool pathing occurs with little to no human intervention, is not only an inexpensive way of building initial prototypes, but is also a bridge tool that can produce end-use parts in a matter of days. Instead of waiting for a costly production tool to be ready—a process that usually takes several months–the supplier can mold production-grade parts from a bridge tool, which reduces their lead times from several months to several days. The result is quicker appearance on the market and, ultimately, revenue. Identifying and eliminating non-value-added activities (e.g., waiting for tool production) from the procurement process is crucial to building a competitive supply chain. In addition to getting a product to market more quickly, a bridge tool can help manage sudden demand spikes or line-down situations, which further reduces the risks associated with high-volume production.

Reducing Production Costs Through On-Demand Manufacturing

By embedding agility into the manufacturing supply chain, companies can respond appropriately and swiftly to unforeseen market demands. According to Kathy Wengel, Vice President and Chief Global Supply Chain Officer at *Johnson & Johnson*, supply chain organizations need to improve their ability to pivot quickly so that they can meet changing market needs and expectations and get results that add value, rather than large, long-term projects.

Sourcing through traditional suppliers becomes challenging whenever product demand is difficult to predict. If a company cannot provide accurate forecasts in a timely manner, the supplier's ability to manufacture and deliver on time may be undermined. This, in turn, may lead to a lost opportunity due to a product shortage or delayed revenue caused by back orders. To mitigate against this or, better yet, completely eliminate the non-value-added time associated with traditional suppliers' long lead times, companies with greater demand volatility should consider manufacturing product components on demand and in lesser quantities. Such a strategy would enable them to meet demands effectively and reduce the operational expenses associated with logistics and inventory.

The incorporation of on-demand production into the manufacturing supply chain is also an effective strategy for regional and localized production when annual product volumes are relatively low. Manufacturing components in lesser volumes increases supply chain efficiency by reducing lead times and mitigating the risks associated with spoiled inventory or product obsolescence.

The digitalization of manufacturing processes has made the economics of on-demand production possible. Digital manufacturing provides flexibility by increasing automation and reducing the investments required, enabling lower volumes and customization. The benefits associated with lower tooling costs, no minimum order requirements, and faster lead times can outweigh the discounts that companies might receive when purchasing supplies at greater quantities. Additionally, there are significant supply chain benefits to procuring parts from a supplier that deploys a digital manufacturing model. One of these is instant digital traceability throughout the factory and supply chain as quotes and orders are processed, which reduces risk and ensures quality, in contrast to traditional manufacturing models. Digital manufacturing also requires a rigorous level of equipment standardization and automation in order for the economics of low-volume production to work. This, in turn, ensures production consistency and indefinite repeatability.

While many companies are still determining how to fully harness the impact of digital manufacturing on their entire supply chain ecosystem, those that have incorporated it into their lean initiatives have begun to realize the benefits of a more streamlined and cost-efficient manufacturing supply chain model.

Managing Digital Rights and Outcomes in Regulatory Markets

Laws should specify goals, rights, outcomes, authorities, and limits. Laws that do so broadly can withstand the test of time. Regulations specifying how these laws must be executed should be regarded in much the same way that code and algorithms are regarded by programmers, that is, as constantly updated tool-sets for achieving the outcomes described by the laws.

In today's world, this kind of algorithmic regulation is more than a metaphor. Consider financial markets: new financial instruments are invented every day and implemented by algorithms that trade at electronic speed.

Tim O'Reilly, the founder and CEO of *O'Reilly Media* founded a digital platform turned book and conference *Beyond Transparency* on the premise of a *"cross-disciplinary survey of the open data landscape, in which practitioners share their own stories of what they've accomplished with open civic data."* O'Reilly hoped to go beyond the *"rhetoric of transparency for transparency's sake"* *"towards a larger discussion and actionable account of problem solving."*

O'Reilly Media's research holds policymakers accountable and enhances legal regard for open data's movement in the civic domain, but also enables government agencies to gather enough opinions to develop a technological and innovative background on par with the research and development of private sector entities such as *Alphabet* (formerly, *Google*), the *Uber* Movement and *Tesla*, which at times harvest more data than governmental agencies do.

Private sector ownership of information, as in the widely successful example of *Facebook*, showcases the beneficial partnership between the private and public sector but also raises larger concerns about private access to information about the public. Were there no legal regimes protecting big data information and intimate details about citizens, would governments come under the thumb of corporate structures?

O'Reilly asserts that, *"(r)evelation after revelation of bad behavior by big banks demonstrates that periodic bouts of enforcement aren't sufficient. Systemic malfeasance needs systemic regulation. It's time for government to enter the age of big data. Algorithmic regulation is an idea whose time has come."* **17**

If data is provided in re-usable digital formats, the private sector can ferret out problems as well as build new services that provide consumer and citizen value. This is one goal of the US Treasury Department's "Smart Disclosure" initiative and is central to the efforts of the new Consumer Financial Protection Bureau. O'Reilly further notes that *"(w)hen government regulators focus on requiring disclosure, that lets private companies build services for consumers, and frees up more enforcement time to go after truly serious malefactors."* **18**

The rise of open data in the public sector has sparked innovation, driven efficiency, and fueled economic development. Thanks to high-profile US federal initiatives like Data.gov and the White House Open Government Initiative, more and more local governments are making forays in the field with Chief Data Officers, open data policies and catalogs. While the functions of open data are still emerging, we are seeing evidence of its transformative potential to shape the future of our civic life. As in the case of the US Census, it is at the local level that the government most directly impacts the lives of residents–providing clean parks, fighting crime, and issuing business permits. It is here that the greatest opportunity to use open data to reimagine the relationship between citizens and government lies.

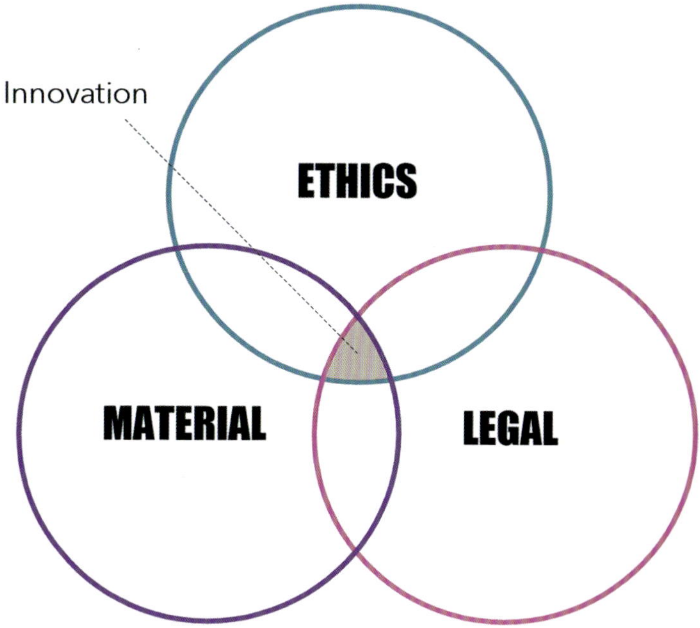

d

Opening the Future of Open Source for the Built Environment

Open Access Distribution

John Locke's classic *labor theory* of value **19** is rooted in the idea that people have the right to the fruits of their labor. Locke bases his argument on a hypothetical state of society prior to the accumulation of capital and in which nature is a common source for all. In his ideal commonwealth, the individual possession of property is a natural right. However, title to the property is secured through labor, which is the source of value. **20** In the *Second Treatise of Government,* Locke claims that nature has placed sovereignty in the hands of the people; people are equal and invested with natural rights, free from the state's infringement on those rights. Accordingly, it is natural law that governs behavior. Each person has the right to execute the law against anyone who infringes on these rights. Locke's basic tolerance for the exchange of property and rights is essential to our understanding of the contemporary landscape of digital property and ability to identify the inherent differences in the relationship between labor and value in the realm of authorship and ownership, a discussion that must now include digital and physical property.

Rapid advances in the technology industry have led to alternative business models that promote and incubate research and development beyond traditional brick and mortar spaces. Now that the digital sphere has become an active or extended space for play, the AEC industry too is seeing a shift towards the internet of things (IoT) as a mode of operation. The extension of physical into digital territory has thus altered the traditional norms of operating businesses.

Opportunistic variables that preclude open access as a form of property that allows ownership are often of concern to digital citizens interested in developing virtual and intangible goods, especially those designing such goods with the help of software and computational tools. Property within this realm of design can therefore be interpreted in various ways. Peter Suber outlines the basic concept of Open Access (OA) with the availability argument, claiming that because it makes *"research literature available without price barriers and without most permission barriers,"* its accessibility can be extended to a wider audience. OA allows

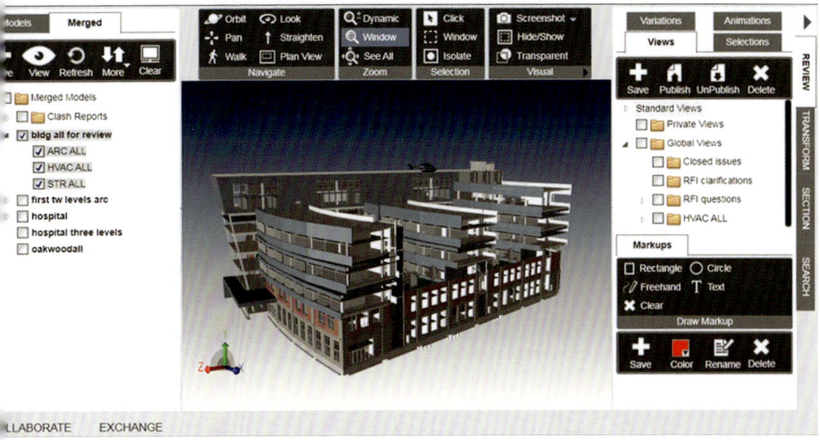

e

digital property to be *"available online, digital, free of charge, and free to most copyright and licensing restrictions."* **21** Why, then, would a copyright holder consent to OA? According to Suber, OA is possible only by consent of the internet and copyright-holder.

Building Information Modelling (BIM) software has created a large divide amongst those architects, engineers, and builders who use it. With new add-ins, such as Dynamo for Revit, BIM is taking on the next level of parametric design and constraints. Most of the building industry understands that because algorithmic and parametric design require highly customized construction methods, it is extremely difficult to reconcile these projects with traditional construction methods. Computational design and advanced BIM methods can generate alternative forms of construction, which challenges the building industry to become more progressive.

One actively researched example is *Building Ops*, developed by Autodesk's R&D team in Toronto, Canada. *Building Ops* is a mobile-first asset and maintenance management solution for building owners and operators, and Autodesk's first commercial "Internet of Things" (IoT) application. The program and digital platform is directed at developing more efficient technologies for the AEC industry and evaluating construction management. This means that the program actively relays feedback on HVAC and data systems to the project management team in case of problems or building deterioration before, during, and after the construction of a building. This allows future building owners to manage the life cycle of their buildings and anticipate potential issues and scenarios. Building Ops offers managers and technicians, including project management teams in the AEC industry, real-time delivery of information on the building they are working on. Building Ops also allows managers to access and update asset information instantly and directly from mobile devices. Teams can import their building's assets and associated data straight from BIM 360 Field or a .csv file and into the process.

Computational design can be understood as a form of applied research that exploits quantitative data. Programs and add-ins, including *Grasshopper* (a McNeel product), *Dynamo* (an Autodesk product), and *Vasari* (experimental beta software developed by Autodesk) can be used to gather information on things such as sun orientation and building codes, as well as to schedule and analyze a building's performance. Many BIM users and firms have yet to unlock all the capabilities of this emerging technology, which can save the industry time and money. By learning this parametric system, firms can devote more time to creativity and design.

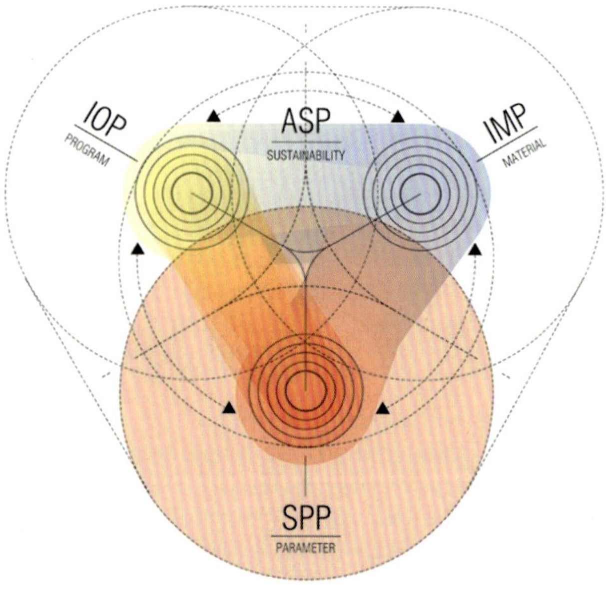

f

On the other hand, private practices and architectural design firms have started the digital journey to open innovation platforms. *UN Studio*, led by Ben Van Berkel and Caroline Bos initiated the Smart Parameter Platform to probe various areas of sustainability, innovative building technology, material exploration, and more. They created the platform to broaden the field of architecture. Not only does it allow contributors to increase interaction and collective participation within UN Studio's Research and Development (R&D) team, but it also provides publication of white papers and conference presentations that help outside participants better understand the firm's research.

In addition, *Foster and Partners* have established internal Applied Research units that are led by Francis Aish of the Applied R&D team. Working within the larger firm's factory, these exploratory and innovative teams of engineers, architects, and data-scientists look into future alternative building technology in the AEC industry. Much of the R&D process lies in technological analyses conducted through experimental projects, governed mostly by data.

In 2017, Autodesk similarly invested heavily in the development and applied research of bio-Nano technology. The AutoDesk Research teams have continued to focus on performance analysis, optimization, digital media, and fabrication technologies in

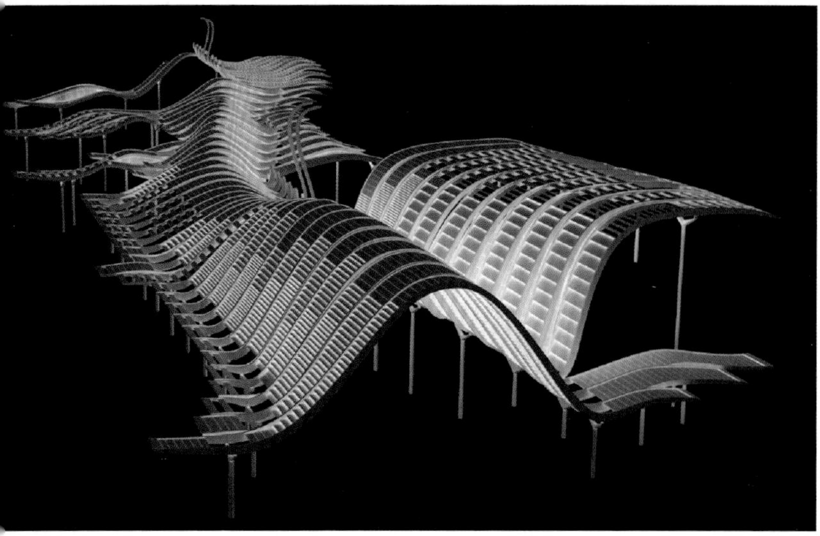

g

the AEC field. These variable teams function as collections or collective agencies within the larger Autodesk Corporation. They are comprised of acquired start-ups led by the SPARKS team or internal teams (a mash-up of existing Autodesk team members, researchers, and employees and/or created from institutional partnerships that are later brought to the larger Autodesk Research unit located in Toronto, ON or San Francisco, CA.) In 2018, Autodesk opened a larger, more concentrated AEC and robotics manufacturing research center in Boston, MA.

Whether developed internally in private firms *(UN Studio)* or by larger corporate entities (Autodesk), these applied research and development units are significant to the future of architectural tooling and design. They help architects become product developer rather than simply service providers, and thus garner considerable importance in today's era of digital deliverables. However, as architects and designers offer professional expertise in the realm of digital product development, questions emerge regarding the liability and legality of the transference of transitional digital (intangible) resources to physical products. The current role of architects in producing digital goods–on-demand product development, alternative modes of fabrication, and online platforms for the digital delivery of manufactured goods–places the responsibility of ownership and authorship on the architect themselves.

Blockchain and the Future of the AEC Industry

How the AEC industry can futureproof itself with blockchain

Currently, finance offers the strongest use cases for blockchain technology. Take international remittances, for instance. The World Bank estimates that over over $430 billion USD in money transfers were sent with blockchain in 2015, and $702 billion in 2020. It predicts that by 2026, the number will rise by another $200 billion to total over $930 billion. Indeed, Bitcoin is now accepted as official currency in El Salvador and other emerging markets.

Architecture, engineering, and construction can be future-proofed through the integration of financial technologies, alternative digital property ownership systems, and cryptocurrency models, such as the blockchain. This section discusses the technology, premise, and use case of intellectual property in AEC, as well as how equity and ownership could be implemented in the field. More importantly, it looks at how the blockchain technology and framework apply to the AEC environment.

What is blockchain? Why should the industry care?

The blockchain is an open, distributed digital ledger in which transactions made in Bitcoin or other virtual cryptocurrencies are recorded chronologically and publicly. The technological framework at the heart of Bitcoin enables individuals using the digital ledger to seamlessly transact between two parties or more without using intermediaries. It can be used to automate and potentially change the way we understand the ownership of equity and physical property transactions. More significantly, it may represent the future inter-dependence of digital and physical property exchange and how this may automate the architecture and construction industry silo. **22**

The digital currency known as Bitcoin emerged in 2008 from a white paper allegedly published by Satoshi Nakamoto. According to the Bitcoin exchange Coindesk, in August 2017, one Bitcoin was worth approximately $4,300 USD, up from $800 in August 2016, and $350 in January of that same year. While the volatile digital currency ranged between $30,000 to $65,000 during the span of 2022 The use of cryptocurrency is growing in parallel. In 2016, there were 10 million bitcoin wallets in existence and the number of daily transactions increased from 80,000 to over 200,000. While in 2022, the numbers expanded to 81 million bitcoin wallets. Bitcoin is expected to attract 100 million users in coming years. Built on a peer-to-peer network, the digital currency relies not on a single, centralized database or server, but rather on the blockchain, a ledger that exists across a decentralized network of machines, each acting as a node on that network.

As author William Mougayar explains in his book *Blockchain: The Business, Promise, Practice, and Application of the Next Internet Technology*, blockchain decentralizes the sharing of information:

> The traditional way of sharing documents with collaboration is to send a Microsoft Word document to another recipient, and ask them to make revisions to it. The problem with that scenario is that you need to wait until receiving a return copy before you can see or make other changes because you are locked out of editing it until the other person is done with it. That's how databases work today. Two owners can't be messing with the same record at once. That's how banks maintain money balances and transfers; they briefly lock access (or decrease the balance) while they make a transfer, then update the other side, then re-open access (or update again). With Google Docs (or Google Sheets), both parties have access to the same document at the same time, and the single version of that document is always visible to both of them. It is like a shared ledger, but it is a shared document. The distributed part comes into play when sharing involves a number of people. Imagine the number of legal documents that should be used that way. Instead of passing them to each other, losing track of versions, and not being in sync with the other version, why can't all business documents become shared instead of transferred back and forth? So many types of legal contracts would be ideal for that kind of workflow. You do not need a blockchain to share documents, but the shared documents analogy is a powerful one."

Simply put, the blockchain is a decentralized technology, meaning it operates on a user-to-user (or peer-to-peer) basis. The various forms of mass collaboration that it enables are just beginning to emerge.

More importantly, how does this affect the future of the architecture, engineering, and construction (AEC) industry? Most of the current AEC industry relies heavily on automation for production; 3D modelling software is produced by Autodesk, Adobe, Dassault Systemes, Gehry Technologies (Trimble), or McNeel, while formalized manufacturing is carried out mostly through digital transactions and foreign equity trades. If we can remove intermediaries, then the supply chain and architecture distribution system can push towards a class of active and creative designers and a revolution in decentralized ownership.

Now more than ever, the creative class is questioning its position in design, architecture, and the future of its entrepreneurial equity. By removing the middle party and connecting collaborators directly, blockchain technology supports the very foundation of this movement. Surveying over 1,000 individuals, I found that when offered a choice of equity or attribution, creatives were split on which options they would prefer for their digital designs. These same individuals were open to direct compensation (but, not solely through monetary compensation) of their design attributes.

Transparent and incorruptible, the blockchain network exists in a state of consensus, one that automatically checks in with itself every ten minutes. As a kind of self-auditing ecosystem of a digital value, the network reconciles all transactions at ten-minute intervals. Each group of transactions is referred to as a "block."

This results in two important properties:

Transparency
: Data is embedded within the network as a whole and is public by definition.

Incorruptibility
: Altering any unit of information on the blockchain requires a huge amount of computing power as it must override the entire network, making corruption relatively impossible.

The blockchain perspective has fascinating implications and potential for the emerging market. As indicated by Vitalik Buterin, inventor of Ethereum, another cryptocurrency built on the blockchain, *"Blockchain solves the problem of manipulation. When I speak about it in the West, people say they trust Google, Facebook, or their banks. However, the rest of the world does not trust organizations and corporations that much–I mean Africa, India, the Eastern Europe, or Russia. It is not about the places where people are really rich. Blockchain's opportunities are the highest in the countries that haven't reached that level yet."* 23

The software development sector of the AEC industry alone would reap benefits that blockchain technology brings to creatives and designers. This includes the possibility of increasing the developmental nature of shared CAD files, codes, and scripts that are co-authored and designed to innovate building typologies. Meanwhile, blockchains could lead to more direct relationships between creators and those who require access to sensitive and confidential design files. The technology allows for the design and history of a project's development to be iteratively documented to the final step of construction and manufacturing. The benefits of a digital ledger will help creatives develop their designs and track the contributions of their predecessors who have interacted with their files. More importantly, if any libelous contract decisions are made between parties, all details have been carefully maintained in the integrated file system of the incorruptible digital blockchain.

In the music and entertainment industry, several companies including *UJO music* and *ascribe* are trying to use a form of blockchain called *Ethereum*. (digital currency) to support creative work and ownership. *UJO*, a company devoted to revolutionizing blockchains for music transactions, has partnered up with musical talent Imogen Heap to usher in the next stage of the music supply chain on transparent digital currency. Simply put, *UJO* allows users to purchase music using a cryptocurrency called Ether, as well as to track the song's key, tempo, and stems. **24** More importantly, due to the transparency of the system and financial tracking, the money is directly distributed to the producers, writers, and engineers involved in the production of the music supply chain. Similarly, a Berlin-based company, ascribe, uses blockchain technologies to copyright the work of artist and creators.

For Imogen Heap, a music industry veteran, *UJO* and the benefit of blockchain technology lies not only in monetary reward, but also in data ownership and the distribution of information. *"There's a whole world behind each song…there's a lot of data there and a lot of wasted data that's not being harnessed to give back to the artist," Heap says, noting that this data offers valuable feedback for artists: "It's so, so important to be able to know where your fans are, what they are listening to, what is exciting to them about what you are doing."* **25**

The properties of blockchain that enable traceability and the distribution of wealth offer positive opportunities for creators. But first one must determine whether creatives want to transfer their intellectual property (IP) of their works in a decentralized space. And, more importantly, in a post-capitalistic scenario, whether the creative industry will be able to offer equitable and attributable causes for the creative beyond monetary compensation. If, in the future, tracking and technological advances improve on cryptocurrency as a means of decentralized payments for creators and producers, would intermediaries within industries still be required? Moreover, if users mitigate governance of digital currency and transfers would governance be purely a political policy change that leads to self-governance?

The transparency of blockchain will grant creators further access to the products and services aligned with designed and manufactured goods, but allow them to monitor their iterative process in real-time through smarter choices that can be edited and corrected. Creators will thus be able to produce and re-design more immediately, looking at the market value and real-time consumption of their goods, while seeing which trends are selling better.

For example, let us say that Jane creates an innovative brick. By monitoring real-time purchases and distribution of the product, she can simultaneously inspect various colors, materials, and techniques through which she can innovate the brick. By putting the brick on the market, Jane can see which colors, materials, and qualities are either selling better or working better with various applications. Thanks to the transparency of product distribution, supply chain, and monetary solutions and her direct, unmediated interaction with these, Jane has more options. She can choose either to offer better incentives to sell the brick in a material that is less popular, or change the stock of the material of the brick that she hopes to remove from the market. The transparency of a digitized supply chain and a system of limited mediation could thus benefit small- to medium-sized creators working with producers or a decentralized and on-demand manufacturing counterpart.

Futureproofing the AEC industry with Blockchain

The future of ownership in the built environment will require more self-initiative by creators on many fronts, as younger generations of both consumers and designers opt for experience-related markets rather than physical ownership. The former have now proven more relevant, as we can see in sharing economy models, such as *Airbnb*, *Uber*, and various new platform urbanisms and economies.

Blockchain overcomes many of banking's current limitations and has already disrupted the financial service sector through decentralization and digital distribution. Moreover, unlike banks, which require physical property and management, blockchain systems require no physical branches to function. Since blockchain operates on a distributed network, it has no need for complex and expensive private infrastructure. This saves on costs that banks and telecom companies pass on to users through fees and other charges for using bank accounts or performing mobile transactions.

The future of architecture will no longer be determined solely by the physical properties of brick and mortar. Architecture must be futureproofed so that designers, architects, engineers, and builders can adapt to the position of a digitalized, decentralized, and distributed system of organization, and push for more flexible and nimble operations, a more systems-oriented approach to design, manufacturing, onsite delivery, and construction.

The traditional architectural training requires us to be more than systemic thinkers; we need to be able to balance materiality and technicality. However, as the industry pushes computational design forward, it is not unusual for contemporary architects to be asked to develop a repertoire of skillsets that anchor the distributive models of computer science and software development, as in the case of Frank Gehry's *Gehry Technologies* twenty years ago or Jose Sanchez's more recent *Plethora Project*. Architects are constantly required to work with automation in order to manage, or at least, understand it. They must also operate closely with on-demand models of manufacturing and alternative forms of ownership, and develop an entrepreneurial savviness that goes beyond that of the traditional architecture studio or shop.

Automation and digitization on the blockchain minimize avenues of corruption as most robust systems maintain a record and footprint of all transactions. If private, many of these financial and design systems are still subject to manipulation, but blockchains can help combat poverty by limiting corruption and opening discussions to transparency.

By building a strong AEC base through the integration of *phygital* property in emerging or developed countries, blockchain as a distributed ledger can provide unprecedented transparency. The futureproofing of architecture, integrated with opportunities in financial technology (fintech), such as blockchain, can help us build both a tamper-proof economic and political system.

Industries like real estate and architecture could benefit a great deal from the technology offered by blockchain and its digital ledger. Real-estate-focused platforms as demonstrated by *DecentraLand*, *Metajuku* by *Republic*, and various new companies that are being pushed forward into Web 3.0 and phygital space, as early-stage examples of where meta space can be with smart contracts. The hybridized utilization of digital offerings and real property exchanges are challenging not only our built environment, but also the business model of who takes ownership of architecture. If not architects, then who?

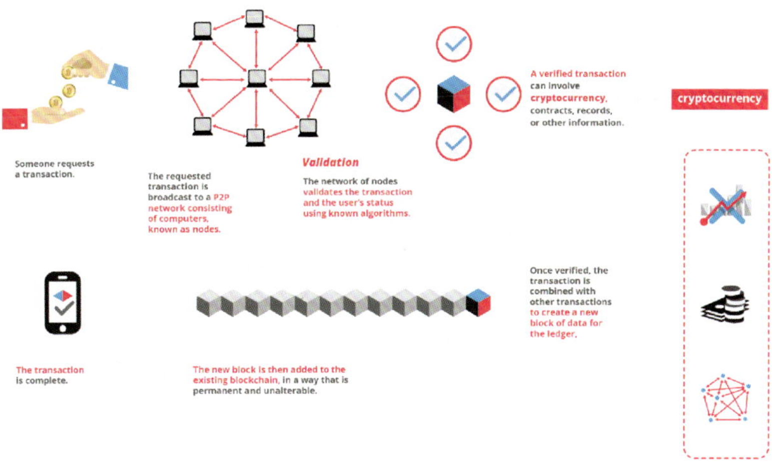

The introduction of smart contracts makes blockchain even more powerful. Payments are not the only types of transactions that can be stored in the transparent ledger. Proof of property ownership such as land titles and other asset certificates can now be stored in the blockchain as well. These types of integrated systems, designed as a holistic combination of fintech, digital property integration, and physical workforce, could strengthen the AEC field, while pushing forward the potential of new economies and entrepreneurial opportunities and thus ignite new practices.

Rather than allowing large architecture and construction software consortiums to take the building industry through open innovation and sharing economy models that value a collective intelligence mentality, architects must take a stand by offering more transparent business models and construction transactions. Aside from their utility, these software companies are solely transactional platforms for creation–tools that allow architecture to be built.

Although UN Studio, Fosters and Partners, and Gehry Technologies have tried to crack the software prospects in architecture, none have tried to build on the blockchain. If blockchains could be used to help phygital property ownership and distribution in architecture, then the technology itself could provide countries (and communities) suffering from inequality with access to transparent means of property ownership, such as real estate, in the future of Web 3.0.

References

1 According to Arnoud Engelfriet, an IT lawyer, European patent attorney, and author of the open sourced, *The International Free and Open-Source Software Law Book* available through the Creative Commons licensure, "FOSS shows no sign of slowing down."21 Linux is widely in use in embedded environments (mobile phones, televisions, cars, robots), and the open-source Firefox web browser is the most popular alternative to Microsoft's Internet Explorer, currently known as Edge.

2 Consensus has it that the principles of FOSS are legally sound. FOSS licensing is also being recognized as valuable by policymakers. Lawsuits in the coming years may address some open issues, such as the scope of derivative works and liability for FOSS developers. More is to be expected from voluntary compliance and a growing maturity in the ways that the legal community approaches FOSS licensing principles.

3 TED Dale Dougherty - Profile. Accessed, December 20, 2014 https://www.ted.com/speakers/dale_dougherty

4 3DExperience - Dassault Systemes - White Paper. 3DS SHoP Case study. October 2013. http://www.3ds.com/fileadmin/customer-stories/pdf/3DS_SHoP_CaseStudyEnglish_Oct2013.pdf

5 Cross, Nigel (Editor). *Design Participation*. Proceedings of the Design Research Society's Conference, Academy Editions, London, 1972. Retrieved from: http://www.participativedesign.com/design-participation/

6 Bernstein, Phil. "Future of Construction Is Manufacturing Buildings." *LINESHAPESPACE*. Autodesk, 25 Aug. 2015. Web. Retrieved from: http://lineshapespace.com/future-of-construction/

7 Mason, Paul. "*The End of Capitalism Has Begun*." The End of Capitalism Has Begun. Economics. *The Guardian*, 17 July 2015. Web. Retrieved from: http://www.theguardian.com/books/2015/jul/17/postcapitalism-end-of-capitalism-begun

8 Lakhani, Kevin J. Boudreau Karim R. "Using the Crowd as an Innovation Partner." Harvard Business Review. Harvard Business Review, 27 Aug. 2015. Web. 20 Feb. 2017. <https://hbr.org/2013/04/using-the-crowd-as-an-innovation- partner>.

9 Open Source Building Alliance (OSBA) - *House_n*. Kent Larsen. *MIT Media Lab*. 2004. Web. Retrieved from: http://web.mit.edu/cron/group/house_n/

10 Kingsley, Jeremy. "How the DIY WikiHouse May Revolutionize Architectural Innovation." *Future Tense*. Slate, 22 Feb. 2012. Web. Retrieved from: www.slate.com/articles/technology/future_tense/2012/02/wikihouse_the_diy_movement_and_architectural_innovation_.html

11 Robert Bodor, "How Digitalization Is Changing the Economics of the Manufacturing Supply Chain," *Supply & Demand Chain Executive*. N.p., 14 June 2017. Web.

12 *Shrink-Wrap Agreements* - Shrink wrap contracts are boilerplate contracts packaged with products; usage of the product is deemed acceptance of the contract. Web-wrap, click-wrap and browse-wrap are related terms which refer to license agreements in software which is downloaded or used over the internet. A software license agreement is commonly called an end user license agreement (or EULA). A shrink wrap license is an end user agreement, concerning the use of a copyright work that is enclosed with software in plastic-wrapped packaging. It includes pre-drafted terms and conditions of sale that consumers are required to agree before unpacking and using the work, usually a software product. The terms and conditions are usually non-negotiable. They are generally displayed on a piece of paper than can be read through shrink-wrap packaging. Once the end user opens the packaging, a consumer is deemed by the copyright owner to have agreed to the terms and conditions of use. 2015. Web. Retrieved from: http://definitions.uslegal.com/s/shrink-wrap-license/

13 "The cloud delivery models that present the most software-licensing challenges are infrastructure as a service (IaaS) and platform as a service (PaaS). Software as a service (SaaS) is less likely to cause problems because, as the name suggests, the software is part of the cloud provider's services. With IaaS and PaaS, though, the customer has shared control over what is run in the cloud environment, including third-party software. In the case of IaaS, the customer does not manage or control the underlying cloud infrastructure but may have control over operating systems and deployed applications. With PaaS, while the customer typically doesn't have control over the operating system, it may have control over the deployed applications."

Trappler, Thomas J. "Software Licensing in the Cloud." *Computerworld*. Cloud Computing, 2013. Web. Retrieved from: http://www.computerworld.com/article/2496855/cloud-computing/software-licensing-in-the-cloud.html

14 ISV License - from Chapter 3 , Section: Absence of History in Licenses–Modern day CAD software is increasingly dependent on subscription based software licensing and the metadata exchange, between the software provider and the user such as *Independent Software Vendors* (ISVs) - more detail regarding

Independent Software Vendors (ISVs) will be described in the following *Foundation of Royalties* section.

15 Robinson, Helen Mele. *Emergent Computer Literacy: A Development Perspective.* 2009. Routledge. New York

See Also: Gee P. *A sociocultural perspective on early literacy development.* In S. B. Neuman &Dickinson (Eds.), Handbook of early literacy research (pp. 30-42). Guilford Press,New York. 2002

Prensky M. 'Digital natives, digital immigrants', *On the Horizon*, vol. 9, no. 5, pp. 1-6. 2001.

Subrahmanyam K1, Kraut RE, Greenfield PM, Gross EF. *The impact of home computer use on children's activities and development.* Future Child. Fall-Winter;10 (2):123-44. 2000. Retrieved from: http://www.ncbi.nlm.nih.gov/pubmed/11255703

16 Robert Bodor, "How Digitalization Is Changing the Economics of the Manufacturing Supply Chain," *Supply & Demand Chain Executive.* N.p., 14 June 2017. Web.

17 O'Reilly, Tim. 2013. Chapter 22. "Open Data and Algorithmic Regulation". *Beyond Transparency.* Edited by Goldstein, Brett, Lauren Dyson, and Abhi Nemani. San Francisco, CA: Code for America, 2013. p. 289-300. Print.

18 O'Reilly, Tim. 2013. Chapter 22. "Open Data and Algorithmic Regulation". *Beyond Transparency.* Edited by Goldstein, Brett, Lauren Dyson, and Abhi Nemani. San Francisco, CA: Code for America, 2013. p. 291 - 296. Print.

19 Karen I. Vaughn, "John Locke and the Labor Theory of Value," *Journal of Libertarian Studies* 2. No 4 (1978): pp 311.

20 George Lichtheim. Marxism and beyond: On historical understanding and individual responsibility. Journal of the History of Philosophy 7, No. 4 (1969): pp. 474-477.

21 Suber, Peter. Open access / Peter Suber. Cambridge, Mass. : MIT Press, c2012. pp 4 - 11

22 By BlockGeeks. "What Is Blockchain Technology? A Step-by-Step Guide For Beginners," Blockgeeks, 29 Aug. 2017. https://blockgeeks.com/guides/what-is-blockchain-technology/

Audrey Watters, "The Blockchain for Education: An Introduction," Hack Education, 07 Apr. 2016. https://hackeducation.com/2016/04/07/blockchain-education-guide

Blockchain Details
- Fact: 1 Bitcoin = about $415 USD (2017) / Now about $22,000 USD (2022)

Brief History
- In October 2008, Bitcoin, a virtual currency, was invented by an unknown. However, Satoshi Nakamoto is linked to the invention as he published the paper, "Bitcoin: A Peer-to-Peer Electronic Cash System," released at the same time.
- By 2009, Nakamoto had mined the first Bitcoins, thereby activating the Bitcoin network; Nakamoto removed himself from public view in April 2011.
- In 2013, Bitcoin took off as more websites began accepting the currency. This led to a price surge–$1108 per Bitcoin–in November of that year, generating interest among investors eager to invest in Bitcoin-related start-ups.
- "The Department of Homeland Security shut down the Bitcoin exchange (formerly a Magic the Gathering exchange) Mt. Gox in 2013, which at the time was handling nearly 70% of Bitcoin transactions. Mt. Gox declared bankruptcy the following year amidst reports that some 744,000 bitcoins had been stolen from the site."
- Mike Hearn wrote, *"In the span of only about eight months, Bitcoin has gone from being a transparent and open community to one that is dominated by rampant censorship and attacks on bitcoiners by other bitcoiners."* In its coverage of the fallout, *The New York Times* cautioned that *"The current dispute, though, is a reminder that the Bitcoin software–like all computer code–is an evolving product of the human mind, and its deployment is vulnerable to human frailties and divergent ideals."*

People Involved / Blockchain Capital Leadership
- Anthony Jenkins - Board Director
- Peter Smith - CEO and Co-Founder
- Michael Jackson - Board Director
- Jeremy Liew - Board Director
- Nic Cary - President and Co- Founder
- Arthur Levitt - Board Advisor

- Bob Wigley - Board Advisor
- Salil Patroda - Board Advisor

Technology
- A distributed database that exists in multiple copies across multiple computers; a decentralized network where each is a node on that network.
- Public key cryptography permits transactions that can be signed digitally.
- *"Because of the distributed nature of the blockchain database, data about all new transactions must be propagated to all nodes on the network so that the blockchain stays in sync as one "world wide ledger," and not as many conflicting ledgers. That means that in order to update the blockchain, these multiple, distributed copies of it must be reconciled so that they all contain the same version. This happens in the blockchain via a consensus process: the majority of the nodes in the system must concur. (Note: there are other synchronization methods for distributed databases.) This consensus process is one of the key innovations of the blockchain: it is "emergent," rather than happening at a scheduled time or interval as each new transaction and block are verified computationally."* Watters, Audrey. *"The Blockchain for Education: An Introduction." Hack Education. 07 Apr. 2016. Web.*

Intellectual property premise of Blockchains
- Blockchain transactions are immutable; therefore, registered works cannot be lost or altered.
- Smart contracts are a useful feature in blockchain; they are code that automatically facilitates, executes, and enforces contracts.

23 Vitalik Buterin, inventor of Ethereum. BlockGeeks, "What Is Blockchain Technology? A Step-by-Step Guide For Beginners," Blockgeeks, 29 Aug. 2017. https://blockgeeks.com/guides/what-is-blockchain-technology/

24 Lily Kuo, "Imogen Heap Wants to Use Blockchain Technology to Revolutionize the Music Industry," *Quartz*, 19 Feb. 2016. https://qz.com/620454/imogen-heap-wants-to-use-blockchain-technology-to-revolutionize-the-music-industry/

25 Lily Kuo, "Imogen Heap Wants to Use Blockchain Technology to Revolutionize the Music Industry," *Quartz*, 19 Feb. 2016. https://qz.com/620454/imogen-heap-wants-to-use-blockchain-technology-to-revolutionize-the-music-industry/

Image Credits

a Open Innovation Competition between Autodesk & Dassault Systemes. 2016.

b MIT House N - Open-Source Building Alliance (OSBA). PlaceLab Elevation.

c WikiHouse Version Map. 2012. Image Credit: WikiHouse.cc

d Wendy W Fok. Ethics. Material. Legal. 2016, 2022.

e Wendy W Fok. Autodesk BIM 360 Field Platform. Web. 2016.

f UN Studio. Smart Parameter Platform. Web. 2016.

g Foster and Partners. Applied Research Unit. Web. 2016.

h Blockchain transactional diagram. Blockgeeks. Web. 2017.

i Seven Layers of the Metaverse - JJ Jin & Wendy W Fok (2022), Jon Radoff (2021)

j Locked Cryptocurrency - Rachel Pendelton

The Seven Layers of the Met

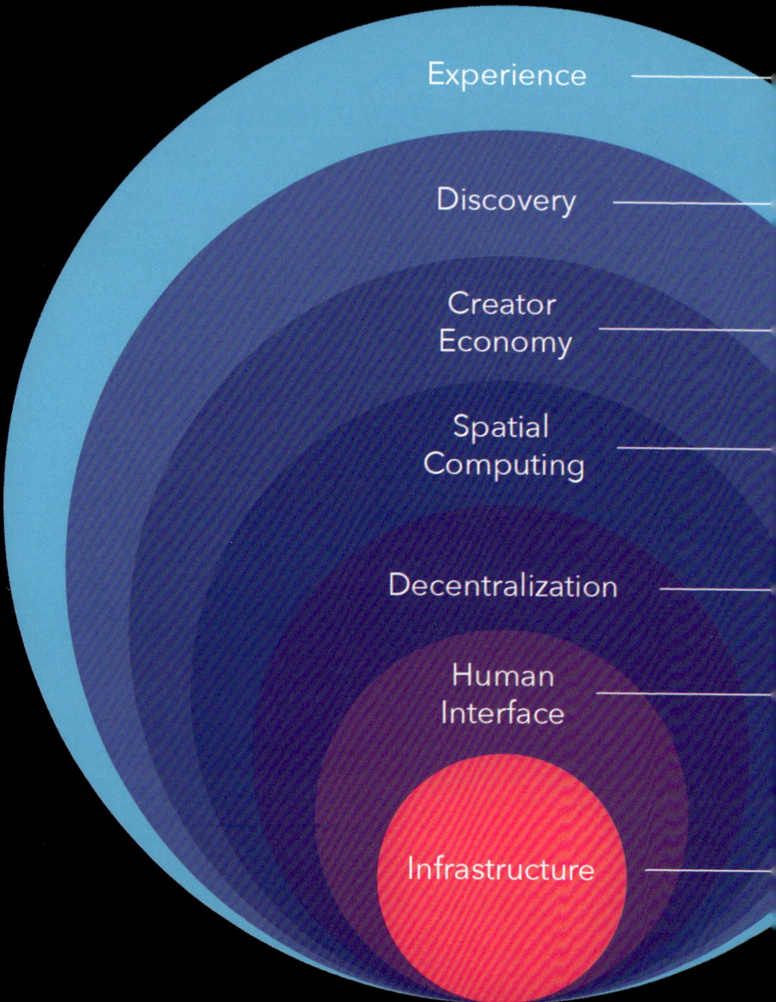

se

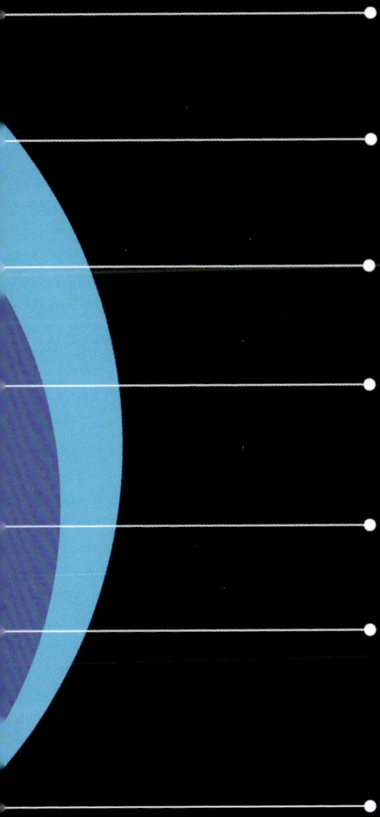
Games, Social, Esports,
Theater, Shopping
Ad Networks, Social, Curation,
Ratings, Stores, Agents
Design Tools, Asset Markets,
Workflow, Commerce
3D Engines, VR/AR/XR, Multitasking
UI, Geospatial Mapping
Edge Computing, AI Agents,
Microservices, Blockchain
Mobile, Smartglasses, Wearables,
Haptic, Gestures, Voice, Neural
5G, Wifi 6, 6G, Cloud, 7nm to 1.4nm,
MEMS, GPUs, Materials

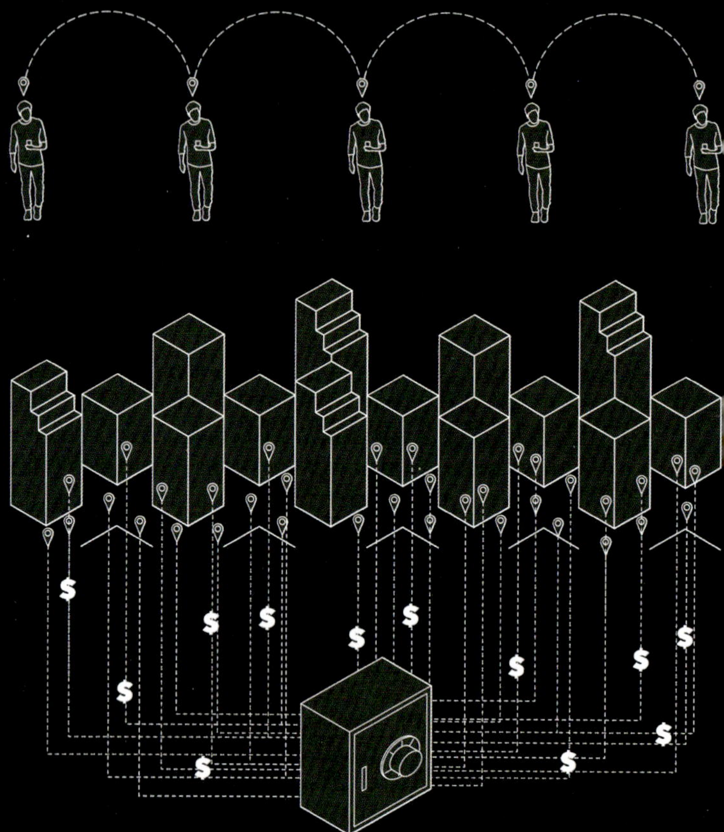

j

Dapper Labs - Digital Kitties, the NBA, and Beyond

Mik Naayem

By the end of 2021, conversations about digital kitties, punks and apes and an artist named Beeple were ubiquitous. NFTs had captured people's attention and brought the conversation about cryptocurrency and blockchain to the mainstream.

A year prior, when our company, *Dapper Labs*, launched NBA Top Shot, a digital collectible that irrevocably transformed the nature of fandom (500,000 fans spent nearly $1B in a year), most had never heard of NFTs. Until then, conversations about crypto were firmly anchored in the financial realm centered around *Bitcoin* and *decentralized finance* (DEFI). It wasn't until blockchain was applied to consumer products that the true possibilities of Web3 started to come into focus.

How Did We Get Here?

The journey to this new and exciting ecosystem began in 2017 when a group of us became convinced that a decentralized blockchain defined by distributed databases and fungible tokens (cryptocurrency) was the future of the web.

Although bullish about the possibilities, we also recognized that a core component of a decentralized web was missing, the ability to represent purely digital assets online. We set out to solve that challenge by building a proof-of-concept via a simple and accessible collectibles game that we called *Cryptokitties*.

Our goal was two-fold: encourage consumers to embrace the idea of buying, owning, trading and selling a scarce digital asset online and to do so using crypto currency instead of fiat. Not only did our test work, Cryptokitties rapidly grew into a $40M digital economy with some selling for upwards of $100,000 in Dec. '17, shortly after our launch.

The outsized and unexpected success of our *Ethereum* based blockchain game, built with ERC-721, today known more widely as a smart contract, represented a significant change in consumer behavior. It demonstrably proved that you could establish irrevocable provenance, rarity and digital ownership online. Put more simply, people embraced the idea of true digital ownership of rare digital assets, in this case, NFT ownership facilitated via a game of rare breedable digital cats.

What Does All This Mean?

It means that a better, more equitable and trusted online future awaits us all. While many believe that the current architecture of the Internet is "good enough", at *Dapper Labs*, we believe that it's irrevocably broken and that a crypto-enabled web, one defined by decentralized ledgers (distributed databases), fungile tokens (cryptocurrency) together with NFTs (a unique digital asset certified via smart contract) will bring outsized benefits to both consumers and businesses.

Today, most of our online activity is tightly controlled by five global behemoths (*Facebook, Apple, Amazon, Google* & *Microsoft*). Not only do they maintain a stranglehold on our data and our online activities, but they also restrict access to it, obfuscate their actions around it, build algorithms to amplify it unequally, levy fees and profit handsomely from data as well as IP and digital assets that they had absolutely no hand in creating.

One need only look at the headlines from the past several years (*Cambridge Analytica* data breach, Russian election interference, *Epic Games v. Apple*, the proliferation of fake news, the *Facebook* whistleblower, Frances Haugen etc.) and it's not hard to connect the dots back to a severely broken, monopolized web that resides in the hands of a few.

Now, imagine living and working in an online environment of radical transparency, collaborative decision making, real ownership and trust, at scale. One where creators, artists and business leaders are in complete control of their own data and digital assets, have crystal clear visibility with immutable assurances that it has not been tampered with and know that their original IP is tied to them in perpetuity along with future royalties. It's not only possible, but also happening.

What holds our future?

A $69.3M digital collage from a previously unknown artist, a digital collectible of a deep three drilled by *Dallas Mavericks* unicorn Kristaps Porzingis an animated cartoon cat might all seem like fun and games but make no mistake, the very nature of their existences is monumental and has already had a seismic impact across virtually all facets of business and society.

What began in obscurity (cryptocurrency) in the wake of the 2008 global financial crisis as a way for people to control their money without relying on banks and governments opened the door for *Dapper Labs* and a passionate community of Web3 evangelists to lay the groundwork for a decentralized Internet.

Today, not only has business been irrevocably transformed, culture and art have been impacted, industries have been upended (sports, music, entertainment etc.), the relationship between creators and fans has been transformed, the very nature of communities (DAOs) and ownership (ever bought a "fraction of an artwork"?) have been redefined and billions in new revenue has been generated, and it's just the beginning.

Mikhael (Mik) Naayem is co-founder and Chief Business Officer of *Dapper Labs* and served as a board member for its parent company *Axiom Zen*, even prior to joining company operations. He is responsible for business strategy, partnerships, and helping build out *Flow's* ecosystem in order to create powerful blockchain-based user experiences. His work has led to top-tier partnerships with organizations like the *NBA* and *Samsung*, as well as with well-known brands such as *UFC*, *Warner Music Group*, and the *NFL*. Prior to joining, Naayem founded and was CEO of *Fuel Powered*, a venture-backed liveops platform used by mobile gaming leaders including *SEGA* and *Bandai Namco*, with over 250 million monthly active users. *Fuel Powered* was acquired in 2017 by *Animoca* Brands, where he still serves in a non-operational role as President of Games. Naayem graduated from *Columbia University* with a BEng and MEng in Engineering.

Scan the icon to view dynamic content

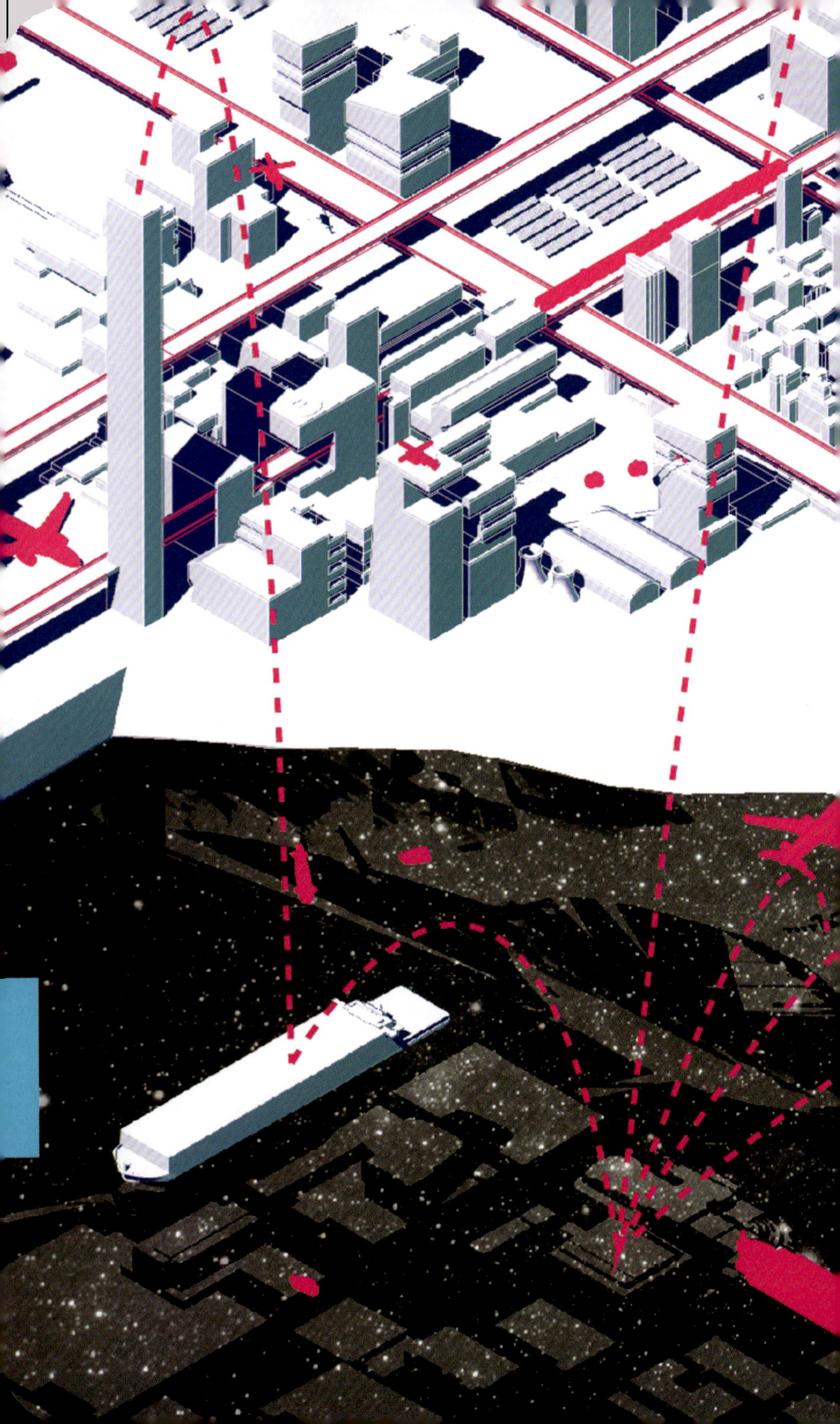

5. From Platform to Phygital

Realities of Web X.0 in Architecture

5.

> "Big data for cities is not new. Some might argue that data collection is as old as civilization itself. In its earliest forms, data gathered about property rights, land production, and assets was used primarily to control and extract value by those in power. James C. Scott's book, Seeing like a State, reminds us that units of measurement were developed to exploit resources."
>
> - Sarah Williams, *Data Action: Using Data for Social Good*

In 2006, *Time* magazine named the collective digital "YOU" as the "Person of the Year," thereby granting the honor to the millions of people who, in earlier iterations of the internet, had controlled and created the medium and financed the new digital democracy.

These same citizens of digital innovation have created new platforms– as can be seen in the early beta developments of *Kickstarter*, *Twitter*, *Wikipedia*, and *Facebook (Meta)*– and continue to contribute to the manipulation of international power and information exchange, while creating value propositions beyond the traditional complexity of products in the ideas and commodity market.

By the early 2000s, peer-exchange and crowd organizational strategy was being used to innovate the built environment. As the trend is growing, it would be good for the architecture and construction industry to recognize and benefit from it. This kind of open innovation and new media has proven valuable to the market of consumer goods and corporate vendors.

Whereas the previous chapter discusses the relationship of architecture-related software and applications, this one discusses theories based on the idea that digital collaboration can direct applied research to the realities of everyday urban life.

Case studies in this chapter demonstrate that the demands of how we use data in our lives are shifting in the Web 2.0 and Web 3.0 space. This includes how data is used in wide-scale adoption in emerging markets, and what consumers question the future direction of the built environment. Advances in data analytics have affected the growth of big data and phygital (physical and digital) space–in terms of what it means to engage with the metaverse.

Thus, this chapter elaborates on whether digital collaboration and the IoT will inform or disrupt the evolution of the building industry beyond 3D printing houses and the rise of architecture as a commodity. Finally, it will dive into the reality of what "digital" actually means and does in our digital culture, and ask how open data can generate public infrastructure and civic opportunities, and whether architects need to care about the environmental damage caused by data centers if they are not regulated soon.

Open Data / Civic Engagement - the Key to Open Innovation?

Technological Wave and the Growth of the Architectural Profession

As more and more mayors appoint *Chief Technology Officers* to innovate cities, the larger question is whether the technologist should encourage active and passive innovation and technologies so that these cities can be operated as "smart cities." Open Innovation (OI) and Internet of Things (IoT) in urban cities (versus suburban) have several benefits of offering the diversity of promoting theoretical, systematic, and prototypical approach of practical conditions to better understand digital design systems within cities. Much of my research is on the co-creation of experimental cross-pollination between open-data access and civic engagement, and on the role of citizenship in both digital and physical property in the built environment.

The term "Internet of Things" (IoT) was coined by Kevin Ashton in his presentation to *Proctor & Gamble* in 1999. Ashton, a brand manager, was trying to find a better way to track inventory. His idea was to put a microchip in packaging to let stores know what was on their shelves. Originating in the wireless networks of the

1990s, the networked sensors of the 80s, and the development of DARPA in the 70s, IoT is closely related to the phenomenon that the networked state of the current generation of "smart cities" is as relevant to the developed internet as are the Information and Communication Technologies (ICT) present in an Open Innovation (OI) framed system.

Cities are networked systems. They are formulated by various technological innovations that are often defined as "smart cities." There are four general categories that set cities in parallel with technological advances, although not every city may actively use technology to be "smart". City officials often predetermine a branded approach to the condition of which correlates as 'smart' factors are significant. Both Tim O'Reilly, in *Beyond Transparency: Open Data and Algorithmic Regulation*, and Boyd Cohen, in *The 3 Generations of Smart Cities*, have stated that cities must meet the following conditions to be "smart":

1 .*Open government in direct relation to open data*
2. *Connectivity in ICT infrastructure and mobile networks*
3. *Digital and e-skillsskills, meaning the city cultivates the citizens' digital competences and their resilience in a digital world*
4. *ICT community collective intelligence, and the sharing of knowledge and ideas*

In *IoT Mapped: The Emerging Landscape of Smart Things*, John Parkinson discusses several additional spheres that the IoT schema must take into consideration. Meanwhile, on November 19, 2015, the *US Department of Energy* announced that "renewable power economic potential has more than tripled." **1** Triggering this discussion is the lowering of costs of technology and technological advances.

Both Rio de Janeiro and New York City are operated and governed according to a technology-enabled, but city-led mentality. Both are actively engaged in ventures that are technologically savvy and promote awareness of the developmental offerings of energy and sustainable factors that drive their cities. By contrast, cities like Medellin, Colombia, the winner of the Urban Land Institute's Innovative City of the Year Award, promote citizenship as the factor driving innovation and civic engagement. The difference in

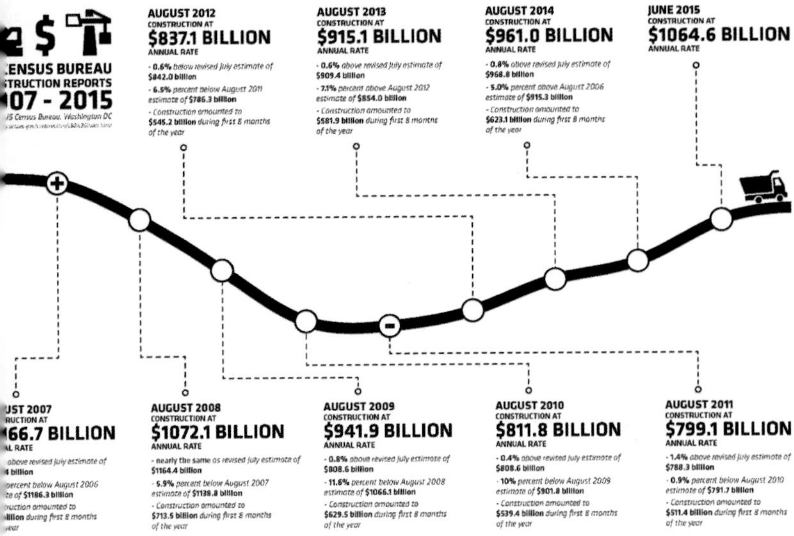

b

the approaches taken by various cities raises the question as to whether open data and civic engagement can one be attained through one means. Meanwhile, designers should embrace that there are multiple solutions on whether the digital or the physical concurrently could predetermine the sole outcomes of a 'smarter' citizenship.

The exploration of the crossover between architecture and urban public policy, open innovation and data access, the urban ecology and technological planning of cities should include critical analysis
2 based on the developmental nature of experimentation and applied research. The move towards smart cities must occur with thoughtful dialogue that considers how *Open Innovation* (OI) and the *Internet of Things* (IoT) affects the world of architecture/design, fabrication/construction, and urban development/real property.

Anticipating open data and civic engagement, open innovation in city planning emphasizes the analog as much as it does the digital and takes a methodological approach to design that lies between context and technique and is implicit in the process of design and integration into site. **3** Not only should city planners, majors, and policy makers be asked to develop investigative design methodologies with prototyping capabilities and to design digitally influenced projects that question citizenship in the urban playground, but they should also be required to gain from collaborative processes within a participatory framework and learn, document, and research theoretical approaches of earlier methodologies from data scientists, designers, urban ecologists, and architects.

Social Goals of Access to Open Data and Civic Engagement

The sharing economy: how will it affect architecture, urban politics, and the co-creative initiatives that drive economic production rates in the future built environment. What does Open Data mean for the building industry?

Most contemporary forms of public and civic engagement and policy planning for the built environment are based on data derived from citizens. This data is sourced from statistical accounts of financial orders, construction dollars spent, or production values based on the annual import and export of agricultural production of GDP (gross domestic product) or GSP (gross state product). In the world of the digital citizenship, however, data cultivation is a curious profession, often contextualized through industry, and biased based on source. Big Data on the other hand, is the science behind much of complex aggregation, that is, both structured and unstructured forms of traditional data processing that usually challenge the analytics, search, storage, transfer, sharing, capture, visualization, and information privacy, all grounded within the digital archives, sometimes for nothing, yet, often for the economic benefit of privatized corporations. Most Big Data discussions revolve around issues of online privacy and data accessibility, and are usually related to the question of how much data is accessible to the National Security Agency and various other governmental institutions. Many of the same unstructured data formats are useful to the *algorithmic regulation* of urban planning, which is based on the aggregated data.

The social good of the open-source movement is evident in the work of Pritzker Prize winner, Chilean architect, Alejandro Aravena, who has liberated the architectural designs of four of his housing projects. This decision flags a broader, more ambitious turn For Aravena's studio, *Elemental*, which has come up with *"the ABCs of incremental housing public knowledge."* Broadly speaking, the social good of open source lies in the power of public access and distribution, which private top-down residential developments do not offer. According to Aravena, the open sourcing of *Elemental* designs would also allow the designs to be modified to comply with local regulations and building codes as well as "local realities" and the availability of materials. This type of social shift in the mentality of architecture and design leads to an entirely new kind of transaction between the client and the traditionally service-based practice of architecture. These types of projects place ownership and empowerment in the hands of local communities, allowing them to take charge of their own developments and the future design of their communities.

Can we use Open Innovation and Data for Social Good?

> Census data is a political tool. It is used to plan infrastructure, understand citizens' needs, track economic and social health of communities... Every ten years, questions are added to track real and emergent trends, such as employment status, languages spoken at home, or access to the internet."
>
> - Sarah Williams, *Data Action: Using Data for Social Good*

Whereas in *Data for Social Good,* Sarah Williams claims that census data is a political tool, I would expand on this by saying that data and the census also serves as an infrastructural tool for gaining power – power to distribute, allocate, and provide access to digital infrastructure such as the internet. Those who have this power (to distribute, allocate, and provide access to Internet) can help deliver resources that are key to accessing knowledge and communicating with the rest of the world.

c

Intellectual property often stimulates creativity but at the same time holds back innovation. Much of my research therefore explores rigorous design methodologies and traces the development of the role that ownership and authorship play in the active participation of data and privacy in the digital age of architecture and open engagement of cities. Architects and designers, as much as policy makers and city planners, should be held responsible for creating opportunities in open innovation and alternative business solutions that include a range of models, such as open source, open innovation, and open data, and their critical dis/advantages to "all rights reserved" protection. These models provoke us to ask whether a) intellectual property, ownership, and authorship rights on various scales stimulate or hold back creativity and innovation, and b) open innovation initiatives are viable and competitive in today's proprietary world, and to consider their future. **4**

Open innovation in cities would enable groups to have an intelligence of their own distinct from that population as a whole. The goal of collective intelligence is to attract the mass participation of a diverse group of people who can solve challenging problems for the common good. Collective intelligence initiatives attempt to aggregate the contributions of individual to enhance their collective understanding of an issue, often through software on the Internet. **5**

According to a simplified visionary approach, the future direction of Internet of Things (IoT) lies in its ability to address its wide-scale adoption in many markets, its interception with advanced technology, the explosive growth of data, and the emergence of data analytics. IoT business applications span multiple vertical markets. Open systems aim to inspire creativity and collaboration among businesses in their naissance, such as architectural design firms that require external collaborative models, construction corporations that prefer to take more innovative approaches to building technologies, and/or entrepreneurs who breed innovation and deliver IoT solutions that can impact citizens positively by making business processes more efficient and improving quality of life. With the proliferation of smart-phones and social media, data generated by user wearable/mobile devices continues to be a key source of information about us and the markets around us. **6**

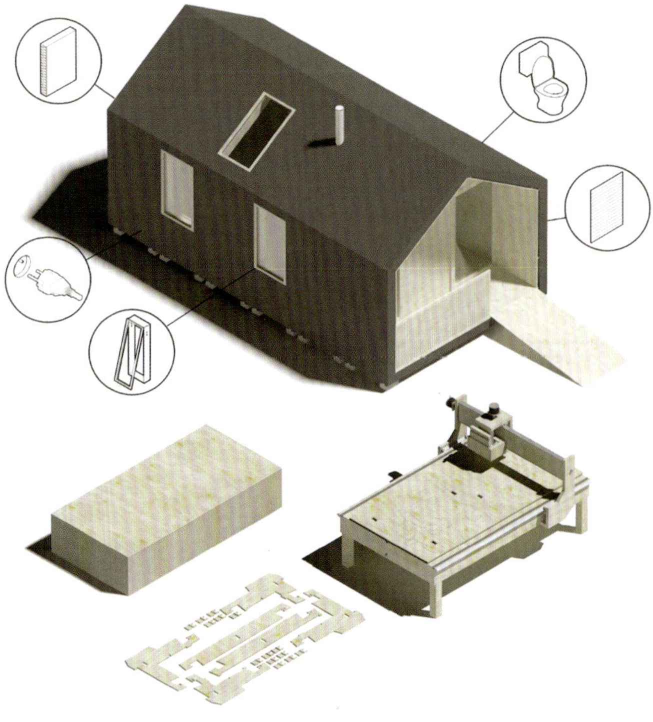

d

Operating between digital and physical, at the opposite end of the spectrum are innovative and semi-open-source digital platforms like *Wikihouse* and *Resilient Modular Systems* (RMS). These two types of digital platforms are social enterprise and impact platforms that straddle the digital community and physical production. More particularly, they challenge the role of production and labor in the realm of digital fabrication and construction.

As noted in Chapter 3, the *WikiHouse* is an *"open-source construction set"* that allows people to build their homes from slot-together pieces that they can mill from crowd-sourced, open-source designs that they download free from Web 1.0 and 2.0. Developed in 2012 as a spinoff project from a London-based design agency, 00/, the *WikiHouse* makes it easy for anyone to build a house from scratch. *Resilient Modular Systems* (RMS) on the other hand hope to become a leader in modular innovation and design that challenges the traditional model of the supply chain for a more regional and localized type of production. The company aims to empower local communities and minimize transportation and material wastes. The focus of the RMS's 2.0 digital platform lies in formulating a fascinating connection between the DIY community, vendors, and manufacturers, specifically in *emerging markets*.

Both projects are looking for a way of providing a digital and human model that could help resolve the global and fundamental flaw of our economic system that is arguably destroying sustainable and equitable urban development in the 21st century. **7** Both models transfer the ownership of home-building and modular innovation directly to communities in need through accessible digital platforms. Open source and DIY tools can help citizens in remote regions who are forced to bypass state policies that are incapable of fixing local urban building efforts. **8**

The operation and integration of open-source systems in both the IoT spectrum of Web 2.0, and the phygital of Web 3.0, are already actively functioning in our cities and infrastructures. In 2017, the New York Waterway (NYW), a private ferry company operating out of ports in New York and New Jersey, began using an Internet of Things-based platform built by *Hitachi Data Systems* to upgrade its security and efficiency. The sensor-driven system was intended to improve the capacity of its ferries to turn into emergency response

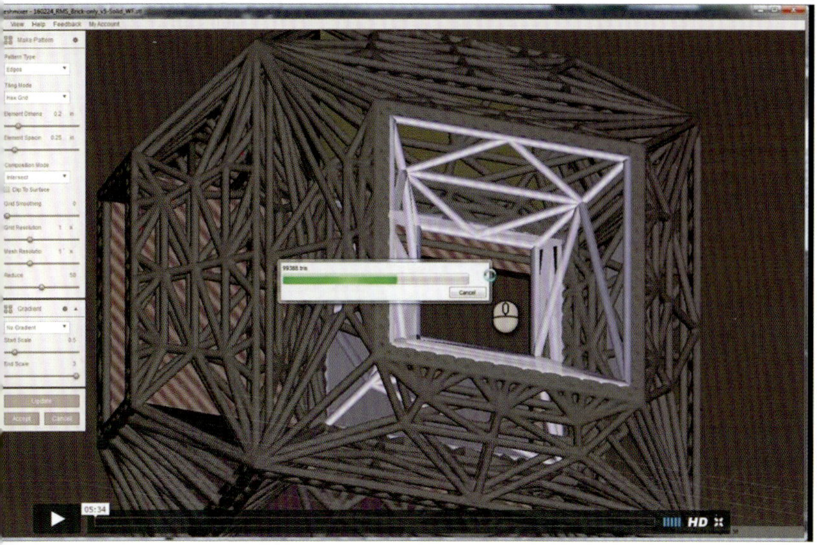
View Help Feedback My Account
05:34
HD

e

SAMSUNG
beta.resilientmodularsystems.com
MORE
Back
Home
Bookmarks
Tabs

f

vehicles. With the new program, explains Mark Jules, vice president of public safety and visualization at *Hitachi*, *"it's easy to share data with other agencies so that they can respond as quickly and as best as possible."* The company can offer shorter response times because managers know the exact locations of all of their vessels. Additionally, they can share live video feeds with other agencies. **9**

g

Moving closer to the citizen and body are digital platforms and systems such as *Body Labs*, a digital platform and software that looks to unlock the power of the body as a digital platform by using a data-driven process and advanced technology for analyzing human shape, posture, and movement. Born in a New York lab that does research on contemporary consumers who demand more personalized products tailored to their own unique body shapes, the company raised over $8 million in November 2015 but was eventually purchased by Autodesk. Before being sold, *Body Labs* was pushing the envelope to resolve the technological challenge of teaching a company's software or services to understand body shape and thus meet the emerging needs of customers.

If today's networked society is governed by no one and digital products are freely accessible online, how does one operate in a sharing economy? Since property titles can preclude equity and ethics online, the general concern of the creator are the laws that govern transferable rights pertaining to the ownership of and access to files and designs, and the distribution, equitable gain from and legal use of these products.

The provocation of legalism in architecture's digital state offers a critical lens through which to look at open innovation and digital property, automation in relation to labor, industrialization, intellectual property, and policy-driven design. Designers should be aware of the various copyright systems that are proliferating in the international arena. Two variable copyright and intellectual property systems divide the current American legislative and legal system from the ever-evolving Chinese copyright system, and these two systems are not quite analogous. Digital files transferred between the two are not governed by the same international trade standards; this inevitably casts a certain amount of uncertainty on designers and architects who are interested in manufacturing structures according to highly valued design specifications abroad. Manufacturing rights and distribution in the international arena and on digital platforms need to be a larger concern of their design work overall.

In the music industry, the distribution of digital music files is synonymous within the traditional model of music licensure and record production. **10** The streaming of software licenses is as commonplace in the AEC industry as the streaming of music licenses is in live radio broadcasting. Autodesk transitioned in 2017 from its traditional registration code licensing of software to streamed licensure–a customary practice in the Adobe software suite since 2014. Driven by market needs and the economic direction taken by prosumers, this types of floating software distribution will make software ownership more top down as it will increase both the regulation and surveillance of users in the digital realm. Users will be required to report to the networked community more regularly, while the internal meta-data recording of information will become more prevalent. Surveillance of user-information and data-distribution within the user interface is increasingly carried out and thus owned by developers. The large question in this scenario is whether the ownership of digital goods

h

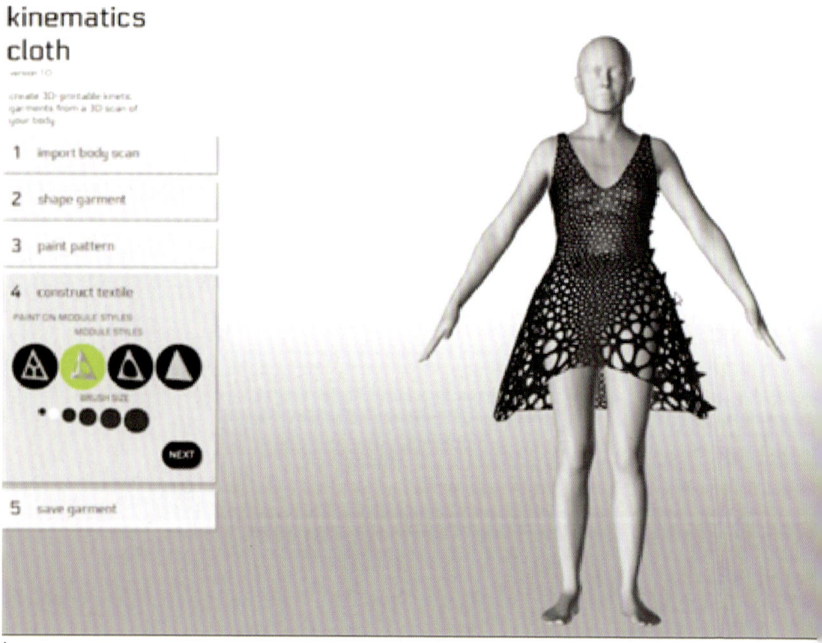
kinematics
cloth
1 import body scan
2 shape garment
3 paint pattern
4 construct textile
PAINT ON MODULE STYLES
MODULE STYLES
BRUSH SIZE
NEXT
5 save garment

i

prioritizes the creator (or designer) of the designed good, or the developer of the software.

Meanwhile, as the continuous development of technologies such as *OpenSim* **11**, *GitHub* **12**, BIM software **13**, and various other multi-user platforms **14** advance the state of participatory exchange and the collaborative nature of platforms, the question of property becomes more complicated for both the user and the creator of intangible goods, while the common ownership of file distribution grows more convoluted by these tangible and intangible forms of file exchanges.

Designers and architects need to take a stronger stand on the issues surrounding the participatory governance of designs on open platforms. Although patents and the ownership of goods (physical property and digital information) began with the intention to foster greater innovation–and thus increase the market for original goods–there is a growing anxiety about architecture as an intangible service-based industry. Both corporate and private digital practice focuses principally on the commoditization of labor and production in digital and computational design, and in doing so, neglects the issue of digital rights in the transference between the digital and real worlds.

Collaborative Digital Media in the Future of Cloud-Based Team Platforms

Should the AEC Industry work like Tech Companies do?

The future of digital media has sparked the creation of numerous companies that offer collaborative digital systems and platforms that enable the larger community to share and make digital contributions in a more transparent fashion.

Digital infrastructure in cities can potentially lead to a more connected and livable urban environment. **15** Smart and innovative cities have become ever better equipped to handle digital twins, **16** artificial intelligence (AI), Mobility as a Service (MaaS), and various intermeshed cloud and ground wired-platform-related services.

Cities connected through sustainable urban mobility planning can transform their data usage to their own benefit, but also encourage citizens to work towards a singular common good– that of engaging with and enabling public authorities to align investments in public infrastructure with policy goals on all levels of governance– local, regional, and national. Were multimodal engagement to offer collaborative digital media connections beyond the device and through architectural infrastructure, the grounded nature of buildings would allow architects to engage in a more hands-on approach to sustainable city planning.

As the AEC industry progresses towards cloud-based systems, which require various players in the industry to work across regions and continents, multi-sourcing control systems are offering its creators and designers more powerful systems through which to cross-collaborate. Autodesk and Google are two of several technology companies pursuing the potential of automated design.

During a keynote presentation at Autodesk University in 2014, Autodesk chief technology officer Jeff Kowalski said that his company was *"developing a CAD system that learns the same way we do, by referencing mechanical engineering textbooks, and building codes, and part catalogs, and even by observing real-world examples."* He also admitted that in his nine years as CTO, this had been *"the biggest, most fundamental change that I've ever seen coming our way."*

One result of Autodesk's research into automated design is *Project Dreamcatcher*. According to the company, *Dreamcatcher* is, *"the next generation of CAD. Dreamcatcher is a generative design system that enables designers to craft a definition of their design problem through goals and constraints. This information is used to synthesize alternative design solutions that meet the objectives. Designers are able to explore trade-offs between many alternative approaches and select design solutions for manufacture."* The powerful self-generating tools developed by Autodesk are competitively the key to the future of cloud-based tooling for the AEC industry with Dassault Systèmes, especially, with 3D Experiencity, *Virtual Singapore*.

According to, Dassault Systèmes, *Virtual Singapore* is a step in the "3DExperiencity" initiative, which too is trying to create 3D models of cities around the globe. Singapore's National Research Foundation is partnering with the company in hopes of improving the nation's security, disaster management capability, and infrastructure maintenance. The data aggregated in the virtual model will be used for many of the same objectives that cities integrating the Internet of Things (IoT) into their day-to-day operations hope to achieve. Meanwhile, in the United States we have *Flux*, a 3D visualization system for cities that is currently available only in Austin TX, where architects can view available spaces and development codes and place proposed projects interactively in the model.

Despite the quantity of digital tools aggregating in the cloud, how the management of these tools will be adapted in the future is still in question. Digital visualization and the aggregation of information through decentralized data distribution will inevitably question data-ownership and compensation models, as is already happening in the financial system with Blockchain. If the AEC industry hope to continue managing digital assets at the same speed as technology companies in Silicon Valley (California) or Silicon Hill (Austin, TX) do, then architects and designers will need to develop better management systems, or else partner with already established companies that are developing integrated digital management systems.

Firms and clients need to prioritize digital collaboration when developing decentralized compensation models for the future of AEC-technology. Management tools, like those used by many tech firms, should be adapted by architectural firms to help accelerate the design process and ease collaboration at the office.

A better developed decentralized control system for the AEC industry would incentivize architects, engineers, developers, and their clients to integrate themselves more deeply into system and build a more healthy, sustainable (both business and climate), and digitally collaborative future. Beyond digital tooling and platforms, architects need to make a more robust claim for digital territory and investment in the Blockchain.

Once architects can finally get themselves, their clients, and everyday citizens to use architecture to engage with multimodal data systems, then we will be at the table of those invited to collaborate and develop a sense of ownership over city planning. After all, other than capital, there is a reason why for over a decade, privatized tech consortiums have been building and planning cities of the future, such as Silicon Valley and Mountainview, CA, while their local governors allow policies to evolve with their needs.

Making, Capturing, Computing, and the Cloud

How Technology is moving faster than Legislation

Cloud computing requires physical data infrastructure.

Tech consortiums may want to advertise and market the elusive nature of cloud-computing as a seamless and invisible system, but data storage in the cloud is anything but clean, sustainable, and mechanical.

The world of 3D technology is rapidly changing. New cloud projects are springing up every day. With the advent of crowd funding, talented startups are moving quickly and disrupting traditional processes by the dozens on a daily basis. Unawares, we are entering the post-capitalist era. What is catalyzing this change is information technology, which has led to new ways of working and what is loosely defined as the sharing economy. Traditional forms of manufacturing and supply chains are being challenged as new methods of production are devised.

The sharing economy and DIY urbanisms are disrupting traditional business models and supply chains even within architecture and design. The maker community has grown significantly in the past decade due to visionary and community-based open platforms like Makezine and Maker Faires, but also because the public has transformed the global industry. Collaboration is not only key: it is essential.

3D printing, computing, and scanning have made companies, individuals, and other entities understand that there is no way

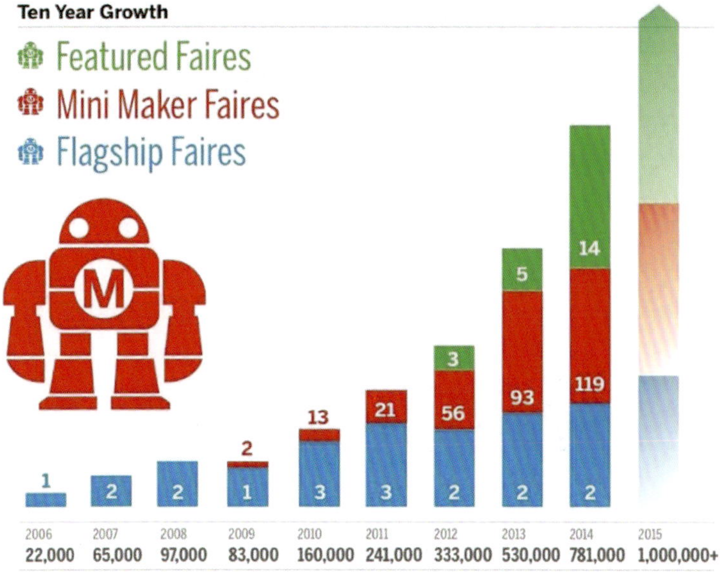

j

to navigate the convergence of 3D technologies for the general public. 3D tech is converging on many levels; companies like *3D Hubs*, *MeshWorks*, and a plethora of start-ups are offering a temporary autonomous zone, which, in the near future, will capture, compute, and create technologies that will move closer and closer to each other. They bounce off the internet and are amplified by absurd levels of computing power.

3D printing, capturing, computing, and processing can be said to be analogous to the rebellious Napster of the 1990s. They look to disrupt localized manufacturing processes and capitalistic prosumer consumption models. As 3D production develops, it is still unclear who it will truly benefit.

Two high-profile legal cases addressing 3D production openly undermine the rights of users in legal digital file transfer and capturing. Both *MeshWerks vs Toyota* and *Jerry Fisher vs Augustanta* College 3D Scanning Case unquestionably favor copyright holders or corporations that have the power to fight for distribution rights.

MeshWerks vs Toyota (2008) is a fascinating example of the current legal system's limited comprehension of 3D printing, scanning, and digital CAD files. Although adjudicated in 2008, the case displays a lack of comprehensive understanding of the extent to which the future of digital production and manufacturing could be affected since Toyota won the case, based on the court's decision that digital CAD files were analogous to photographs.

The Legal Framework

This case is significant for understanding the issues surrounding the current copyright regime and its lack of protection, and maybe even understanding, of the digital modelling world of creators.

The background: plaintiff, *Meshwerks*, a Utah-based digital CAD modelling agency, was hired to make digital CAD models of Toyota cars, the "base layers for computerized substitutes for advertisements." *Meshwerks* deliberately did not create any new designs, but only emulated the *Toyota* cars for use in *Toyota* advertisements. The court recognized the painstaking work that went into creating a model, as well as the fact that the artistic transfer from two-dimensional to three-dimensional modelling requires artistic effort and reworking, but hard work, it claimed, does not necessarily make copyrightable material. With the conclusion of the original contract for the digital models, *Toyota* and the advertisement agency proceeded to use the models for future advertisements without seeking permission from *Meshwerks*. Consequently, *Meshwerks* sued *Toyota* for misappropriation of intellectual property, namely, for using copies of its original wireframes from the digital files. *Toyota* countered and ultimately won the case by asserting that the wireframes lacked sufficient originality to be protected by copyright. No valid copyright meant no valid infringement claim.

1) Although this was work for hire between *Toyota* and *Meshwerks,* the tenth district did not have sufficient knowledge of whether the replication of design was equivalent–in terms of originality–to creating new design. If the designs had been made in another medium, would this case have been adjudicated differently? In my opinion, had the digital models of the cars been modelled out of

physical wax and cast, the replication may have been viewed as demanding "originality."

2) If the court had had a better understanding of the way in which digital tools are used for artistic expression and thus deserve intellectual property protection, then it would have agreed that *Meshwerks* was creating original content for *Toyota*. In such case, compensation or at least attribution would have been a possible resolution.

3) As a large corporate entity, *Toyota* has a stronger market hold than *Meshwerks*. This begs the question of whether large corporations should be setting the precedent for future cases involving digital CAD models in courts of law. If larger corporations continue to have a stronghold on smaller creators, how will the attribution of digital design and foundational compensation be distributed in the future?

The Environmental Framework

As discussed in previous chapters, cloud systems and data centers require monumental architecture. These systems are housed in colossal megastructures and machine-like landscapes that offer limited access to human beings. They are designed to store information, digital data, and provide seamless, high quality encrypted decentralized transfer via fiber-optics to their many ports of entry.

Yet, it is the *invisible* nature of the cloud that allows for the lack of awareness and responsibility that leads individuals to place items into the ether without questioning where it is stored. Although consumers and generators of data are not particularly concerned about where their data is stored, they are aware of *how* their data is damaging the climate.

As numbers show, the demand for data centers is increasing, and grew significantly during the pandemic **17**, especially in regions and rural areas far from mega cities and metropolitan areas. Savvy consumers know that the maintenance of data centers requires a vast amount of water and power (fossil fuel, electricity, natural gas, geothermal energy, etc.).

While consumers and new legislation pressure governments to build data centers, architects and urban planners need to pressure companies to choose more sustainable cloud providers and solutions. Although many companies are being pushed to reduce their carbon footprint, they are not being held accountable for the emissions generated by data stored on external cloud servers.

New legislation will oblige EU-based companies with over 250 employees to report on their environmental impact–just as they report their financial data–by 2023. Reporting, however, does not offer solutions. Once tech consortiums are concerned about data center construction and storage, which is now linked to cryptocurrency mining and blockchain advancement, architects will need to work on the development of such technology in this circular economy.

Climate awareness and advocacy must work together in which data is stored, and climate advocacy and awareness must change with the ever-increasing data consumption in our daily lives. We can no longer overlook the need to take action on the way in which data is stored on the cloud.

According to Andrea Hak, we can do this by:

– setting clear, universal environmental reporting standards for data centers
– including water consumption, IT or data center carbon emissions, and e-waste in calculations
– providing data centers with incentives to invest in green tech adoption and research (particularly in terms of new cooling techniques)
– making companies accountable for emissions tied to their external data and providing them with incentives to choose green data service options
– banning water towers throughout the world

Networks of Connection in Corporations & Outer Space

> "Space has become the ultimate imperial ambition, symbolizing an escape from the limits of the Earth, bodies, and regulation. It is perhaps no surprise that many of the Silicon Valley tech elite are invest in the vision of abandoning the planet."
>
> - Kate Crawford,
> *Atlas of AI*

By the time of this book's submission to print, in late-2022, 1,919 Starlink satellites had been installed in orbit around Earth **18**, according to *Spacexstats* a site that relies on *SpaceX* API data. Starlink was founded by Elon Musk, an entrepreneur, co-founder of *PayPal*, and the outspoken CEO hired by the founders of the electric vehicle company Tesla.

A spin-off of *SpaceX*, Starlink and its relevance to digital infrastructure was spawned from the intention to distribute accessible internet throughout the US to over 60 million individuals, and eventually to all remote and rural locations that have a difficult time accessing data. According to the University of Warsaw, by increasing its number of internet satellites by over 185 percent in the last 18-months, *SpaceX* has also obstructed the night sky for scientists studying space at the Zwicky Transient Facility (ZTF) at the *Palomar Observatory* in San Diego California. **19**

The latest application of the Starlink system was dispatched for the troubled citizens of war-torn Ukraine during Russia's invasion of Ukraine. On March 1, 2022, Elon Musk and his team confirmed that the system was successfully offering internet access in response to a plea via Twitter from Ukraine's Deputy Prime Minister Fedorov. This demonstrates yet again how privatized corporations in the US have overtaken public and government efforts to deliver basic internet access to citizens. It also proves that in the US the unparalleled efforts of privatized digital infrastructure and data distribution penetrate the market before governmental powers and abilities do.

The consumption and distribution of data through satellite technologies are limited and difficult to maintain. Alphabet's *Project Loom* and various social-good internet mesh networks in emerging markets have proved to be short-lived. Between 2020 and 2022 alone, various tech elites have demonstrated the commercial potential of accessing space through *Blue Origin, Starlink,* et al. The possibility of using outer space as the next location of data storage and colonization is no longer distant, yet the question that remains for architects is how to limit the environmental impact of data storage, whether in outer space or on Earth.

On the other side of the globe, China has spent the last decade quietly building over 100,000 miles of submarine internet cables under the oceans throughout the world. Stated funded, the project is being realized with partnerships with countries in North Africa, South America, and Western Europe. The *Peace Cable* is providing internet access to the North African countries along the coast as well as to neighboring countries on the Mediterranean Sea.

Open-sourcing Corporate Research Technologies

In June 2014, Tesla announced that *"all our patents belong to you, its customers."* **20** This was a bold move for the country and spearheaded by Musk and an attempt to bridge larger open innovation and grant the public access to Tesla's technology. By open sourcing its technology, the company is openly inviting the public to use its technology to innovate, so that down the road, when some engineer has an "aha!" moment, Tesla can devour the benefits and potentially buy out the company that comes up with the new invention.

Known historically for its innovation in electric-powered engines, Tesla Motors was named after electrical engineer and physicist Nikola Tesla. It was incorporated in 2003 as a Series A startup, long before the involvement of Elon Musk, and was founded and financed by Martin Eberhard and Marc Tarpenning. Today, Tesla Motors is a multi-billion-dollar empire known as the American automotive and energy storage company that designs, manufactures, and sells electric cars, electric vehicle powertrain components, and battery products.

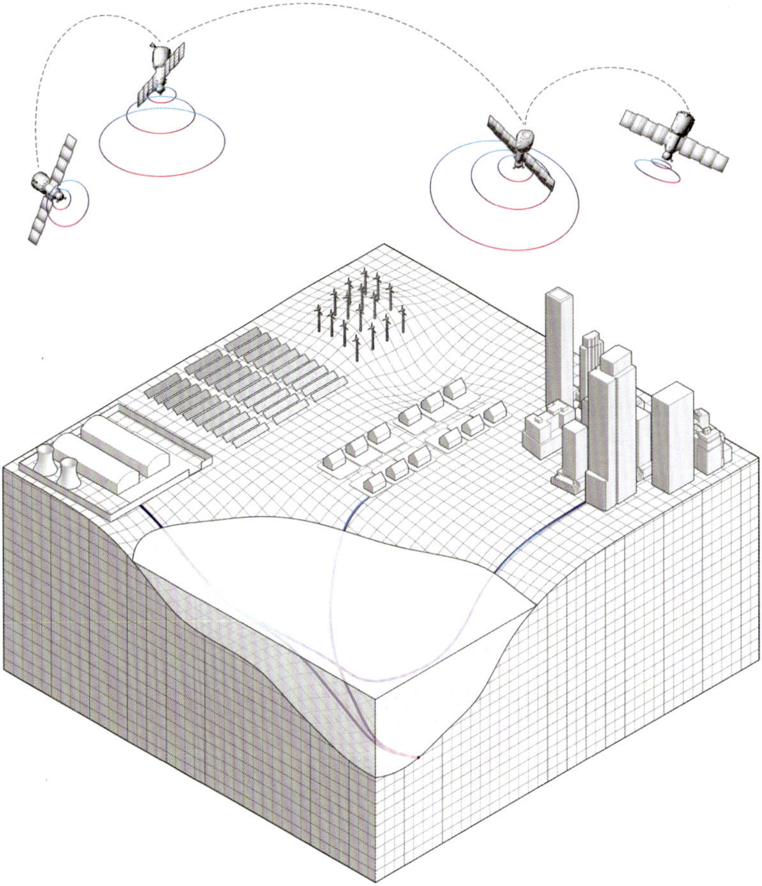

k

I

As operated by Elon Musk, Tesla has opened its doors to a variable model of open innovation. Musk's decision to open source the company's research on the battery system has allowed it to promote the future of automation and robotics. This could potentially affect use of energy in cities, while automated cars may impact the circulation of citizens in urban landscapes. The company places equal value on civic engagement and economic power.

Tesla and its current business model are committed to technological advancement. The company now funds many public projects that use innovative energy and electric power to fuel urban-scaled planning and residential homes with the help of the PowerWall. This invention was so popular that within its first week it sold over $800 million in units based on the high hope that it would enable cities and homes to be off-grid. PowerWall allows renewable energy to power the battery system and can be used as a "reserve" for most homes.

Digital Property in Web 3.0: Where Will it Land Us?

As Web 3.0 continues to blur the boundaries of Intellectual Property (IP) and digital communication in relation to labor (low-cost versus high-end) and production (rapid prototyping/aggregate manufacturing versus an unskilled workforce), we architects and designers need to explore and question the contradictions (and areas of conflict) at the intersection of digital technology, law, and policy.

Distributed and decentralized manufacturing breaks the mold of traditional supply chains. A decentralized system is already setting a precedent as more and more companies, including a flurry of startups, are breaking the digital barriers by selling information and data, rather than parts. Companies such *Hubs* (previously known as *3D Hubs*), *AtFab*, among others, are permeating the open innovation industry with digital platforms that enable manufacturing in a decentralized global supply chain system. The industry of localized manufacturing has come to fruition, introducing new jobs and challenging the traditional work mentality.

David Rotman recently wrote in the *MIT Technology Review* that *"(t)he economic anxiety over AI and automation is real and shouldn't be dismissed. But there is no reversing technological progress."* **21**

If we agree with this statement, then the solution lies not in dismissing the inevitable advances of technology or the innovative practices and inventions of automation that surpass the developmental potential of the human race, but in better integrating robotics and artificial intelligence in the practices of our everyday lives.

We do not need to live in a post-capitalist world without work, in which humans have no reason to exercise their muscles or brains. Instead, architects and designers should come up with new forms of exchange, and build communities or platforms of trust that integrate the way in which Web 3.0 and phygital space will work in the near future as digital property exchange becomes embedded in physical goods.

In 2022, *Republic's Decentraland* and *Metajuku* are just the latest to blend the technological real estate asset distribution of digital property with digital currency and cryptocurrency transactions that enable money and the digital land grab.

However, the opportunity to open up the larger discussion of transparency, accessibility, and accountability within this real estate has been overlooked by these platforms. If structured for social good, blockchain and its technology would be an excellent opportunity for new and emerging economies to engage with real estate–economies that have been disenfranchised and under-educated in the kind of learning needed to deal with the insular and "boys club" nature of the real estate industry.

The COVID-19 pandemic has demanded that the real estate industry be more inclusive in terms of both gender and race. Nevertheless, one of the oldest professions in history is still short on transparency and continues to bar admission. In New York City, for example, blockchain technology could offer a more transparent ledger of physical property titles, deeds, ownership transfers, condominium and/or co-operative board information, building maintenance histories–information that is traditionally difficult to access due to gatekeeping, prohibitive legal costs, and bureaucracy.

Digital ledgers and blockchains would promote easier access and accountability if city planning offices worked more closely with a decentralized system that would make both old and new ownership of property more seamless. More importantly, as mentioned in previous chapters, blockchain and digital ledgers are encrypted and thus difficult to corrupt. Hence, once they are part of the system, they stay with the system, eliminate human error, and prevent alteration.

Technology can lead to social adjustments that allow a decentralized logistical and supply chain manufacturing infrastructure to coexist with digital and physical architecture. And, technology should allow citizens to recalibrate with new modes of exchange between the phygital space in partnership with new platforms and needs.

Companies interested in how digital property can be integrated into new applications for blockchain technologies, which first blossomed in finance, will expand the cultural landscape, regardless of public acceptance. The *With Foundation*, founded by Kayvon

Tehranian and launched shortly before the COVID-19 pandemic, became one of the most successful NFT digital art communities in under twelve months due in part to its open welcome of cryptocurrency, cultural art exchange, and the bandwidth of access provided by Web 3.0. While initially it only allowed users to purchase and sell image-based content, the platform has now added performance art, music, 3D objects, augmented reality (AR), and beyond. The secondary DAOS market took an even deeper dive into what digital property exchange has made possible.

The technological shift from physical to digital is inevitable because more direct and dynamic business models will continue to grow in the next decade. The question, however, is where can architects challenge the unison of building out the physical and digital (phygital) space for the architectural speculation that Web 3.0 truly allows.

Travis Scott's digital concert on *Fortnite*, which allowed up to 50 people per instance, proved through numbers that it was one of the most attended online concerts in history. But what does that mean? Are people willing to plug themselves to virtual reality (VR) goggles and forget physical architecture? Not entirely. The adoption of the current Web 3.0's phygital reality requires physical architecture and space. Spatial planning will become more important, due not only to the growing demands of data storage, but also to new generation of users who are less trusting of consortiums of technological powers and nation-states that build submarine cable infrastructures and what we know as the megastructure of the internet.

Beyond using NFTs as a means for digital artists and designers to engage with the blockchain as an open ledger in the exchange of digital goods, we architects should look at how we can explore the functionality of blockchains in a relationship that could bond the digital (virtual) and physical (real) world in way that would be difficult to break. Data centers have come to serve as the glue for these two worlds, but beyond the utility and necessity of the data and information stored in these data centers, what role can architects and architecture play to challenge the digital version of the real?

During the COVID-19 pandemic, my students and I came up with several proposals and experiments with systems that investigate the potential of digital property and data infrastructural systems on an architectural scale. We focused on digital data storage of an individual's coveted digital files and proposed systems of exchange based on focused communities of localized trust. We asked whether individuals would rather opt for a decentralized local storage opportunity in a furniture system at a stranger's home that is within a 20-mile radius, or for digital data storage in the already existing infrastructure systems of the big 8 technology consortiums.

What if we could devise better interior architecture and architectural manufacturing systems that allow for localized and decentralized data storage? What if these same systems were engaged in furniture (such as chairs, tables, bedframes, etc.) and intermeshed with architectural systems (such as walls, columns, floorboards, etc.)?

Since consumers are willing to allow strangers into their homes, thanks to startups like Airbnb, which emerged in 2008, or were willing to share their couches in the 1990s with nomads, then why would they object to having data stored in furniture that is sold and exchanged in a decentralized manner and thus allow strangers rather than a large technology consortium store their digital files?

The premise is simple, but the question brings out larger questions of the anthropological and psychological system of which we are part in the world of Web 3.0. We trust larger tech companies more than we do our neighbors. Some individuals would prefer not to know where their data belongs than have daily access to their files. **22**

Although these systems of exchanges are speculative, the opportunity of novel data storage and exchange poses an alternative form of information storage, and utility. This proposal is to engage in another dialogue on digital infrastructures within cities, could promote both a local and interior architecture infrastructure integration.

Localized manufacturing will become a dominant competitor in the economic and policy-driven field. Due to ongoing issues with

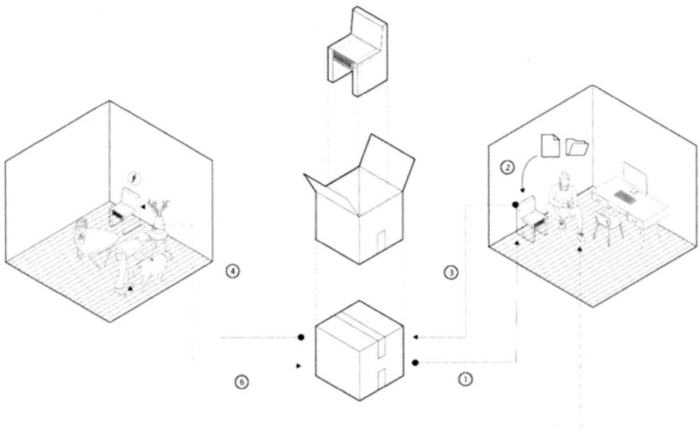

or ⑥

m

supply chain dysfunction (and malfunction) along with inflation during the COVID-19 pandemic between March 2020 and late 2022, companies, large and small, are going to need to find new modes of distribution and trade, by relying either on smaller factories in local neighborhood or cities, or other means of regional distribution. Prosumers will be able to pick up their goods locally, or even have them distributed by drones to their doorstep. The extreme model is one that is fully controlled by automated systems and robotics. In 2021, Amazon had a patent pending for a fully enclosed system with in-house operability inside a container, and a full-distribution drone dispatch system from the train container to the consumer. Thus the model of the traditional supply chain and distributed factories will have to be rethought, and potentially redistributed into compartmentalized regions or made local.

Whether it is a fashion company devising new forms and fabrics through manufacturing techniques based on the traditional crafts used by historic French houses, or innovative 3D printing that is part of the wearables trend that uses automation in clothing design, or larger corporations that are developing driverless technologies, it is the responsibility of the companies and of the individuals in those companies to develop a better language for training their workers to integrate, think with their tools, work with their technologies, and then apply their skill sets to their daily palette. This is the only option for a future in which automation has not left humans out of the equation.

The emphasis on conflict in digital/computational design and open-sourced information systems will continue to be exaggerated in the contemporary age of reproduction and commoditization. The most relevant discussion for architects and designers lies in

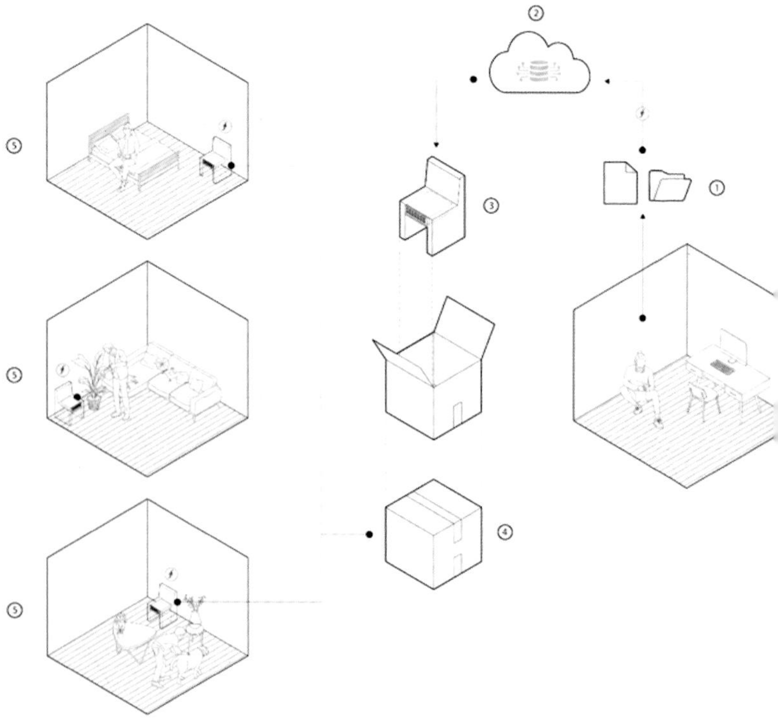

production, which now encompasses a larger (and more public) commercial audience. As automation becomes common in architecture, design, and construction, we must address how its needs in the digital era will continue to generate value for the architectural designer who engages in the open system of computational design in the phygital space of the world of Web X.0.

References

1 The United States Department of Energy. Web. Accessed: http://energy.gov/eere/articles/new-report-renewable-power-economic-potential-has-more-tripled

2 *IoT Mapped the Emerging Landscape of Smart Things* - by John Parkinson. Web. Accessed: http://venturebeat.com/2015/08/23/iot-mapped-the-emerging-landscape-of-smart-things/

3 Nigel Cross, ed., *Design Participation*, Proceedings of the Design Research Society's Conference, Academy Editions (London: 1972). Retrieved from: http://www.participativedesign.com/design-participation/

Paul Mason, "*The End of Capitalism Has Begun*," The Guardian (17 July 2015). Web. Retrieved from: http://www.theguardian.com/books/2015/jul/17/postcapitalism-end-of-capitalism-begun

4 *The 3 Generations of Smart Cities* - by Boyd Cohen. Web. Accessed: http://www.fastcoexist.com/3047795/the-3-generations-of-smart-cities

5 Jeremy Kingsley, "How the DIY WikiHouse May Revolutionize Architectural Innovation," *Future Tense*, Slate (22 Feb. 2012). Web. Retrieved from: www.slate.com/articles/technology/future_tense/2012/02/wikihouse_the_diy_movement_and_architectural_innovation_.html

6 Tim O'Reilly, "Open Data and Algorithmic Regulation," in *Beyond Transparency*, edited by Goldstein, Brett, Lauren Dyson, and Abhi Nemani (San Francisco, CA: Code for America, 2013), pp. 289-300. Print.

7 Fawzi Behmann, Kwok Wu, "*Collaborative Internet of Things (C-IoT): for Future Smart Connected Life and Business*". John Wiley and Sons. 2015

"as the source of use-value or utility (the reason people desire a good in the first place), it may attempt to explain the determination of relative prices (the exchange of value of goods) based on some measure of labor inputs, or it may claim that labor provides the only justifiable claim to receiving the exchange value of the goods it produces."

8 Lichtheim, George (1969). *Marxism and beyond: On historical understanding and individual responsibility*. Journal of the History of Philosophy 7 (4):474-477.

9 Mendelson, Zoe. *"Ferry Powered by the "Internet of Things" Pursues a More Efficient Ride."* Next City. Next City, 29 Mar. 2016. Web. <https://nextcity.org/daily/entry/new-york-waterway-ferry-smart-platform>.

10 Fisher, William. *Promises to Keep: Technology, Law, and the Future of Entertainment*. Stanford University Press 2004, http://cyber.law.harvard.edu/people/tfisher/PTKChapter6.pdf / The Copyright System for Music in the United States. Web. Retrieved from: http://cyber.law.harvard.edu/people/tfisher/IP/Music.pdf

11 OpenSim: OpenSimulator is an open source multi-platform, multi-user 3D application server. It can be used to create a virtual environment (or world) which can be accessed through a variety of clients, on multiple protocols. It also has an optional facility (the Hypergrid) to allow users to visit other OpenSimulator installations across the web from their 'home' OpenSimulator installation. In this way, it is the basis of a nascent distributed Metaverse. Retrieved from: http://opensimulator.org/wiki/Main_Page

12 Git Hub: GitHub is the best place to share code with friends, co-workers, classmates, and complete strangers. With the collaborative features of GitHub.com, our desktop apps, and GitHub Enterprise, it has never been easier for individuals and teams to write better code, faster. Originally founded by Tom Preston-Werner, Chris Wanstrath, and PJ Hyett to simplify sharing code, GitHub has grown into the world's largest code host. Retrieved from: https://github.com/

13 BIM: Building Information Modeling (BIM) is changing how buildings, infrastructure, and utilities are planned, designed, built, and managed. Autodesk BIM solutions help turn information into insight and deliver business value at every step in the process. Retrieved from: http://www.autodesk.com/solutions/building-information-modeling/overview

14 In computing, cross-platform, or multi-platform, is an attribute conferred to computer software or computing methods and concepts that are implemented and inter-operate on multiple computer platforms. Cl3ver is a form of a multi-user platform that allows designers and architects to collaborate on visualization of products. CL3VER is the leading provider of real-time 3D in the cloud. Through our breakthrough technology, sometimes complemented by our consulting services, we help our customers tap into the power of interactive 3D to communicate more efficiently on web and mobile. The "secret sauce" is our proprietary easy to use cloud platform based on leading HTML5 standards that brings 3D content to life on any device. Retrieved from: http://www.cl3ver.com/

15 Shepard, Scott, *How Digital Infrastructure Promotes Sustainable Urban Mobility Planning,"* published by Urban AI, Web. November 2021.

Bernstein, Phil. "Future of Construction Is Manufacturing Buildings." *LINESHAPESPACE*, Autodesk (25 Aug. 2015). Web. Retrieved from: http://lineshapespace.com/future-of-construction/

16 Sarah Williams, *"Data is a Public Infrastructure,"* Data for Social Good (Cambridge, MA: MIT Press, 2021), p.189.

17 Data Center Market - Global Outlook & Forecast 2022-2027, Arizton Market Report. February 2022, Web. and, Pro, TechRadar. *"The Importance of Data Centers during the Pandemic."* TechRadar, TechRadar Pro, 28 May 2020. Web. https://www.techradar.com/news/the-importance-of-data-centers-during-the-pandemic.

18 Armstrong, Martin, *'The Growth of the SpaceX Starlink'*, Statista, March 2022

19 Armstrong, Martin, *'The Growth of the SpaceX Starlink'*, Statista, March 2022

20 Musk, Elon. Tesla. *"All Our Patent Are Belong To You"*. Tesla Motors, 14 June 2014. Web. Retrieved from: http://www.teslamotors.com/blog/all-our-patent-are-belong-you

21 David Rotman, "The Relentless Pace of Automation," *Technology Review*. MIT (13 Feb. 2017). Web. Retrieved on 13 Feb. 2017. https://www.technologyreview.com/s/603465/the-relentless-pace-of-automation/

22 Matthew Hockenberry, Nicole Starosielski and Susan Zieger, eds., Assembly Codes: The Logistics of Media (Durham, NC: Duke University Press, 2021).

Image Credits

a From Platform to Phygital - JJ Jin & Wendy W Fok

b Wendy W Fok and Kevin Hai, 2016. Based on data from the US Census Bureau Data Infographic 2007 - 2015

c Aravena's studio, Elemental. Chile. 2016

d WikiHouse Foundation. WikiHouse. Web. 2016

e Resilient Modular Systems x Autodesk Meshmixer Digital Platform. Web. 2016

f Resilient Modular Systems Smartphone Digital Platform Application. Web. 2016

g Hitachi Data Systems. Web. 2016

h Nervous Systems x Body Labs. New York. 2016.

i Nervous Systems x Body Labs. New York. 2016.

j MakerFaire. Make Magazine. Web. 2015

k Relational Satellite and Submarine Cable network - Yarzar Hlaing, Isa Dabrowski, Wendy W Fok

l Tesla Robot Factory. AD Journal, Digital Property: Open-Source Architecture (2017) Slash Gear, (July 2013)

m Domestic Data Infrastructure Storage Clouds - Yvonne Fu & Wendy W Fok

n Domestic Data Infrastructure Storage Clouds - Yvonne Fu & Wendy W Fok

o Internet and 5G Infrastructure Rollout Diagram - Yarzar Hlaing

p Metaverse Rooms - Yarzar Hlaing, Rashi Gupta, & Wendy W Fok

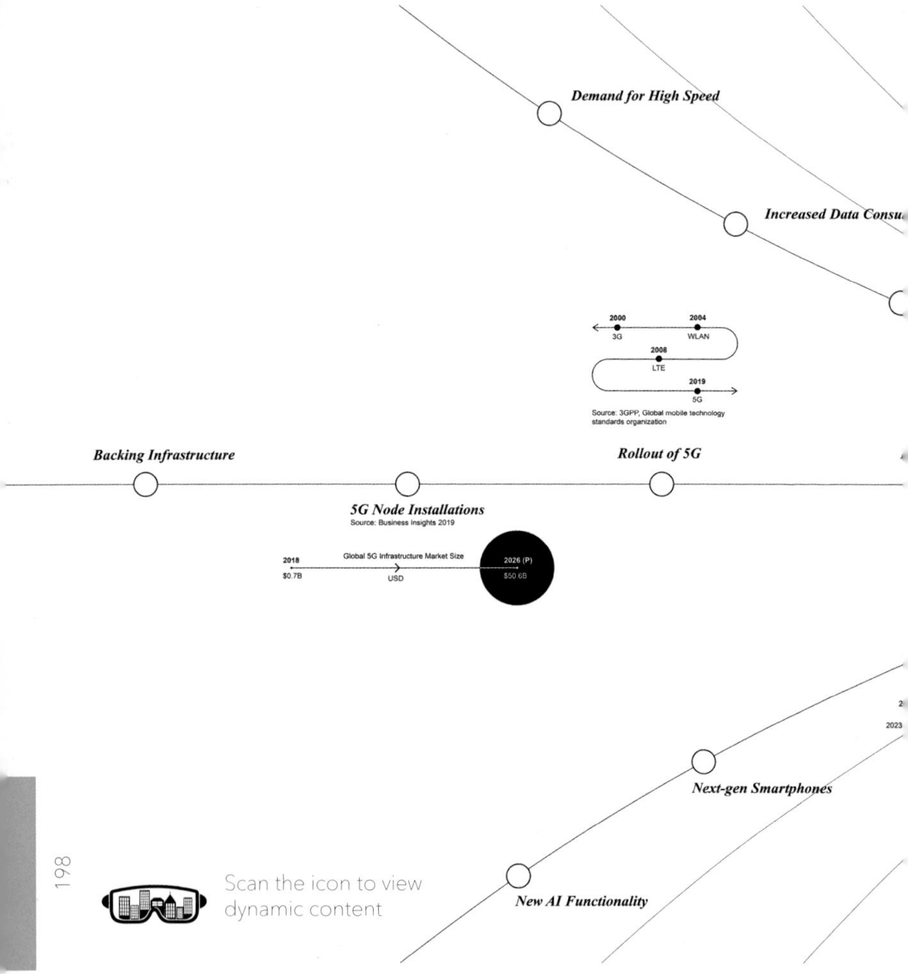

Scan the icon to view dynamic content

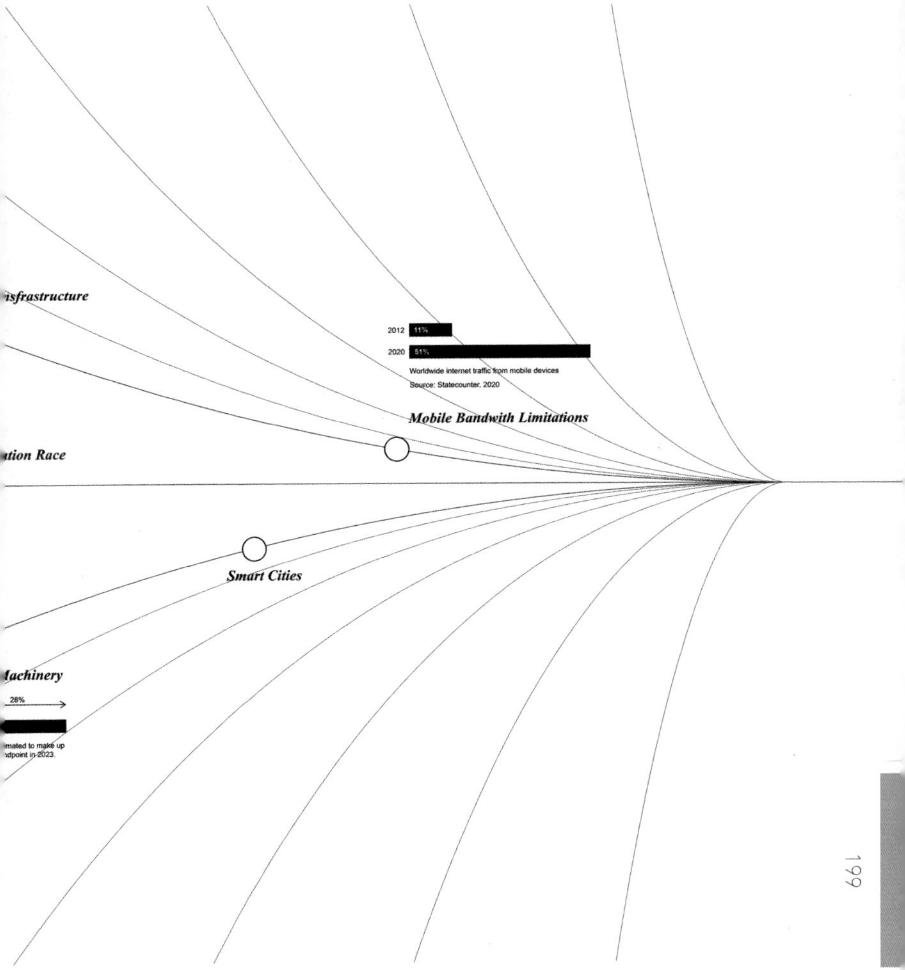
sfrastructure
2012 11%
2020 51%
Worldwide internet traffic from mobile devices
Source: Statecounter, 2020
Mobile Bandwith Limitations
tion Race
Smart Cities
achinery
28%
mated to make up
dpoint in 2023.

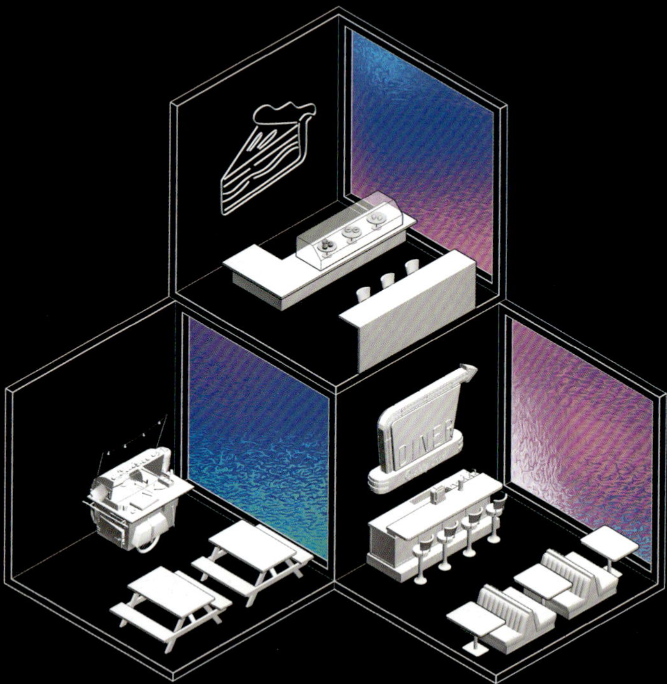
DINER

Zoom In, Zoom Out [Abridged]

Lydia Kallipoliti

Within the short course of a few days, we've all come to meet and live on Zoom.1 Its windows constitute portals to the outside—more operable than the windows of our homes—that peer deep into private spheres that were previously guarded and hidden.

In spatial terms, our daily mental journeys parallel the infinite invisible axis vertically to the earth of Charles and Ray Eames's Powers of Ten (1968). Crossing scales from the atomic to the galactic, their documentary envisaged a systemic analysis of the universe where all patterns could be imagined as interlinked. The Eames's vertical journey between scales and layers reflected the Earth view that had only just become visible to the public eye.2

Today, we reenact a similar type of movement every day: from the voluntary containment of our households, we navigate from the micro to the macro non-stop. Our feed tells us how Covid-19 spreads and how long it stays on different types of material surfaces while transporting us to the other ends of the world, giving visual forays into the devastating burials of Bergamo, the US Navy's hospital ships in New York, and other epicenters of the virus. We have never been more connected and never more apart.

This paradox of virtual connectedness while experiencing a severe corporeal detachment is a telling blow not only to those that originally denied the gravity of the virus, but also to those that deny climate change. Although there is no concrete evidence that directly links Covid-19 to the environmental degradation of natural habitats, the privileged logic of unaffectedness that has propped up such acts of ignorance is severely damaged. Anyone, anywhere, can be infected. There is no place to escape to.

This age of extinction is also a telling blow to the denial of "climate" in a broader sense, as a material condition that impacts all human and non-human beings. In 2017, Bruno Latour claimed climate change, inequality, and deregulation to be indivisible and intertwining problems, and envisioned the triad's materialization as a process of landing "down to earth."3

What is arresting at this very moment, unlike the recent past, is the impossibility to displace "evils," to move them far away from our current physical locations to a territory that we cannot, nor do we wish to see. Consider, for example, how New York City–which has aspired to achieve carbon neutrality and to operate as a leading city in its environmental objectives–exports the vast majority of its human excrements to Birmingham, Alabama, causing major methane clouds 900 miles away.6 The treated sewage–euphemistically known in the industry as "biosolids"–travels by a "poo train" to a landfill causing what the locals and the mayor's office call the "death smell."7 Yet this dislocation of waste from privileged to disenfranchised territories cannot be orchestrated with Covid-19. Any human is a potential vector of transmission. Zooming in and out parallels the logic of the virus' transmission: both inwards–in contracting the virus–and outwards–in relaying the virus to others.

In revising how we navigate territoriality, from inside to outside, renewed protocols to leave and enter the house–or any space, really–have arisen. The process of departure and reentry expands the threshold of the door to an elongated and operational space of decontamination steps. The door is now an airlock, necessitated to enter the unfriendly and unforgiving void of a foreign planet outside. Our households have become spaceships, while urbanity has transformed into a constellation of "essential" places. Supermarkets, gas stations, hospitals, and pharmacies all now make up a defamiliarized, non-cohesive space, while everything else has become obscured in a newly formed mental desert. The city today is a vast array of disconnected bedrooms, microcosms that come together in an abstract digital space, physically enabled by vital and essential data farms.

In experiencing containment, we have never been more viciously aware of our bodies in space: bodies relative to other bodies, to objects touched by foreign hands. As writer and clinical psychologist

Hala Alyan suggests, in pandemic times, all physical relationships can be seen as networks of intersection: bodies intersecting with other bodies, body parts intersecting objects touched by others, et al.[8] The fear of breach vividly renders the porosity of our bodies, not to mention national borders. Yet it was never as if the containment of the former by the latter meant that we would be safely shielded inside an unbroken preserve. Containment is observation, monitoring, and control. In this sense, bodies, as expressions of change, are carefully mapped and supervised. Within the premises of quarantine, bodies are unpacked: they are not simply discrete physical entities, but field distributions of droplets, germs, and pathogens within an expanded ambient environment. While moving from inside to outside, strict protocols of spatial jurisdiction and hygiene are instituted to administer porosity.

In this new world, we are in dire need of a new kind of criticism, of new ways to fathom interiorization and different methods of narrating stories through the design of our environments. We need to zoom in and out, now that returning to normality as was is no longer tenable. We need to open our eyes to the bubble inside which we voluntarily contain ourselves, and develop an erotic, yet resistant relationship with it. It might then be possible to penetrate our barriers and imagine other ways of being; even imagine some ground for hope beyond the market of euphoria for the few.

This text is an abbreviated version of "Zoom In, Zoom Out" published in e-flux architecture platform in April 2020.

Lydia Kallipolliti is an award-winning architect, engineer, scholar and curator and an Assistant Professor at the Cooper Union in New York. Prior to Cooper Union, Kallipoliti was an Assistant Professor at Rensselaer Polytechnic Institute where she directed the MSArch Program, an Assistant Professor at Syracuse University and an Assistant Professor Adjunct at Columbia University [GSAPP] and at the Cooper Union, where she served as a Senior Associate at the Institute for Sustainable Design, and as the Feltman Chair in Lighting. Her research focuses on the intersections of architecture, technology and environmental politics and more particularly on recycling material experiments, theories of waste and reuse, as well as closed and self-reliant systems and urban environments.

Scan the icon to view dynamic content

6. Conclusion

Whose Digital Property?

6.

> "Digital Infrastructure is just one of those things that, in its ubiquity, often becomes more obscure. Infrastructure space is, as the word suggests, customarily regarded as a hidden substrate - the binding medium or current between objects of positive consequence, shape and law, yet is also the point of contact and access, the spatial outcropping of underlying laws and logics."
>
> \- Keller Easterling **1**

Data is not fossil fuel, it is not a limited resource, but it does take a lot of energy to store and keep it alive.

In architecture and the world of Web 3.0, it is practically impossible to delineate the future of work without taking into account data infrastructure and questions regarding digital property. Power is forged from and against the contingencies of invisible labor, the inoperability of platforms and automation, disruptions in the supply chain, fractures in infrastructural systems, etc.

Innovations in and the rapid development of the Internet since 1989 have allowed architecture to overcome the traditional limitations of physical space and professional hierarchy. Today the discipline is practiced increasingly in digital space. By facilitating the distribution of electronic files and the exchange of information across borders, online collaboration across industries has led to innumerable advances in both global manufacturing and architecture. Yet, it has also increased the vulnerability of creators and innovators, who can do little to protect themselves from the dangers of duplication, illicit file-sharing, and high-speed transfers.

For me, the key takeaway from all the research I conducted over the past decade and a half lies in the details of how our information is linked to both the physical and digital properties of a data-infused world. Neither law, policy, and/or design can immediately solve these issues. Today, the practice of architecture and design has a more difficult time defining itself (or removing itself), from both the human generated data and the data generated by its automated and artificial intelligence systems (be it GAN style text-to-image software, processing, Grasshopper, G-codes, etc.). Architecture has evolved into larger data-hungry machine-learning capabilities.

Although we may not always have an opportunity to take ownership of this data, we should still be aware of how data is owned, where it is stored, and what it is doing to our world.

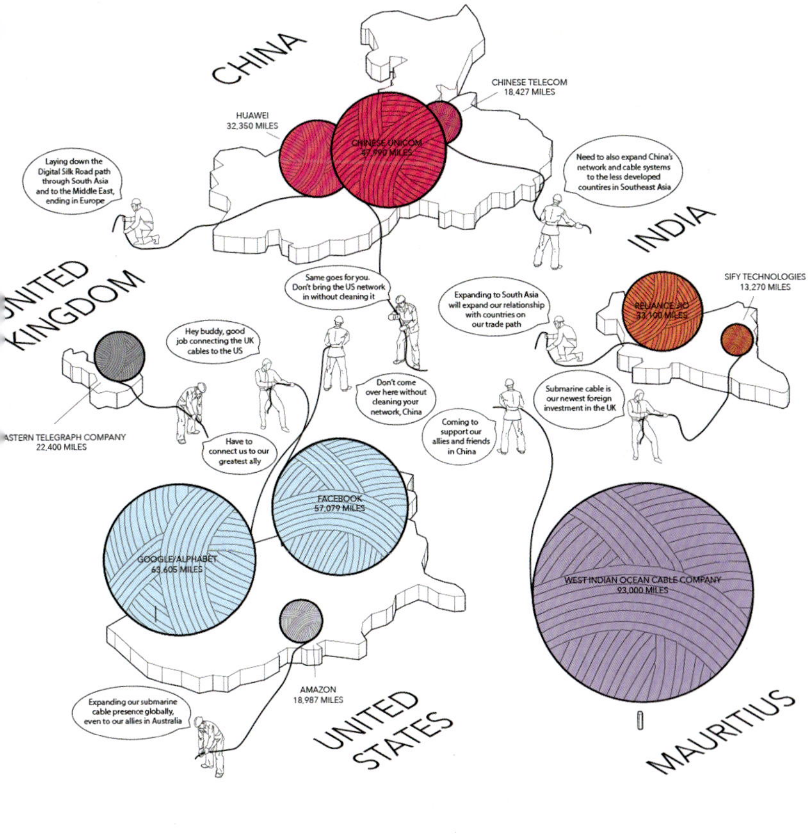

a

Property Exchange as Cultural Ledger

Data has become a form of digital property that works in tandem with cultural currency–whether conceived as a form of fragmented ownership, distributed network, or now, as NFTs.

In 2010, when I first started formulating research on issues surrounding blockchains, digital property, and data infrastructure and architecture, the culture and discussions surrounding Non-Fungible Tokens (NFT) barely existed.

Bitcoin really got people thinking about how a whitepaper (a theory) transitions into applied research, then explodes in digital finance as a practice such as cryptocurrency, which was launched in the world of operations alongside Ethereum and DAOs, and was later developed and embraced by digital arts through marketplace and third-party auctions.

AEC (architecture, engineering, and construction) can come to a better understanding of its own multifaceted practice by examining how other disciplines–e.g., computer science, music, art, fashion, economics, and law–have come to regulate the ways in which ownership and authorship are attributed to various forms of creative activity.

Architecture and fields tangential to it can also benefit from transparency, better use of open innovation systems such as blockchain-like file management systems, and collaboration across the digital realm, as, for example, through the sending of files to suppliers and manufacturers for machining fabrication parts, or through the global file sharing required by cross-team management of large international projects with multiple players.

Code-based designs, which include many CAD-designed objects, seem irrelevant in the current legal and design protection system. Creators, innovators, and publishers, who have little understanding of the cross-licensing procedures of the future, create incentive structures through extra-legal means or depend solely on copyright law. Meanwhile, policy makers and lawyers are establishing legal measures and standards, without any actual knowledge of the design process and methodology that makers and creators currently use to navigate their world of production. It is thus essential that architects and designers become part of the decision-making process of digital governance.

A gaping chasm currently exists between these two worlds. Closing it requires more effective and greater communication amongst trades. Questions remain as to how these newly created design works and technologies are fostering innovation, but remain reliant on antiquated laws in the books. The current state of law requires proof that the design is utilitarian or original, and is thus primarily about providing evidence that it has never been created before, and about hiring a lawyer to sort through thousands of previous inventions in the Patent Trademark Office (PTO) database.

At present, cultural currency business models only cover a small percentage of design rights for creators that are start-ups or early adopters of innovations. Design works created in an open-source system are often projects still in the ideation phase. Many new start-ups on NFT marketplace platforms ask creators to front and fund their own gas (the digital currency needed to place their creations on the digital ledger). This further reveals the flaws and issues of this allegedly ideal world, in which creators are still fronting the capital for emerging markets.

As we enter this new era of technological advancement in architecture and design, many new digital technologies are aiming to decrease turnaround time for design (quicker remodeling, greater collaboration within firms, use of crowdsourced designs and information databases, etc.). Consumers and the pro-automation audience push for quicker production rates and manufacturability even as questions regarding the need to improve turnaround time continue to linger. Consequently, we hurtle ever faster into the brave new world of design. Yet, given the pressure to become increasingly quicker and better, we designers and architects need to ask ourselves who should bear accountability for mistakes or flaws in project plans?

Architecture and Real Estate as Digital Exchange

> "Data Action makes a call for building data, which reminds us that even in the era of big data some data is missing or inaccessible – and sometimes purposely so. We must therefore fill the gaps in data so the voices of people, often on the margins of society, are not left unheard. Building data also creates a powerful voice for people whose perspective may be disregarded at the policy table."
>
> - Sarah Williams **2**

As a distributed ledger, blockchain provides unprecedented transparency. It is also built to be tamper proof. The introduction of smart contracts makes blockchain even more powerful. Today not only payments, but also proof of property such as land titles and other asset certificates can be stored in this kind of transparent ledger.

The traditional construction business model as well as the purchase of physical properties are nebulous concepts. In New York City, for example, they serve as huge barriers of entry for people of color not only for legal, economic, and political reasons, but also due to infrastructural limitations. Individuals who do not operate in the field of architecture and construction have a difficult time understanding conventional land titles and deeds. Do we need or might we benefit from a more transparent blockchain system for real estate and architecture, especially in communities populated by disenfranchised, *Black and Indigenous People of Color* (BIPOC)? Yes, we do.

Paper documentation of real and physical property enables unscrupulous groups to engage in corruption and manipulative business tactics and build on unethical practices. Due to fraudulent or falsified documentation, emerging and developing markets continue to be at risk of land grabs and eminent domain. Taking small farms away from agricultural workers and owners lets such land be converted to urban use **3**.

By contrast, thanks to the mitigation and structure of blockchain, ownership models can be tethered to transparent records of land titles and registry and now lie between digital and physical property. Since individuals and networks can be held accountable and are able to view every transaction, records will have to be documented in an exact and systematic fashion so as to impede tampering. As Nikolai Kuznetsov reports in *Forbes*, *"Sweden is currently testing the use of blockchain for land registry. Japan is also trying the technology out to facilitate government contracts. Governments of developing countries would do well exploring blockchain to provide transparent means of recordkeeping. Developing countries stand to benefit most from ways that could combat corruption as it remains to be a key problem for these markets, contributing to continued poverty and stymied progress."* **4**

New forms of ownership, new forms of lending, new legal contracts: a whole business subculture has emerged in the past ten, fifteen years, one that the media has dubbed the "sharing economy." Although buzzwords like the "*commons*" and "*peer-production*" are thrown around, few have bothered to ask what this development means for capitalism. I believe that new forms of legislature that benefit from a more thorough and subtle understanding of design and architecture may offer answers to this question, but only if these micro-level projects are nurtured, promoted, and protected by a fundamental change in governmental action. Such a disruption in mentality and policy must be driven by change in the public's manner of thinking about technology, ownership, and work. As we create the elements of this new system, we can say to ourselves and others: *"This is no longer simply my survival mechanism, my bolt hole from the neoliberal world; this is a new way of living in the process of formation."* **5**

Much effort has been placed in generating architectural (digital) collaboration and bringing Web 2.0 IoT to homes and cities that are concerned about environmental goals (rather than merely increasing the the number of ideas or design iterations that go into architecture projects). Examples of such efforts include databases that help buildings achieve energy efficiency, internal illumination that automatically responds to changes in the building's use and amount of natural light, etc. Is it possible that global environmental concerns coupled with digital technology are encouraging architects and urban planners to design more collaboratively as well as more mindfully of the sites of their buildings within the network of people and other structures that surround them?

This is the decade in which innovators must demand comprehensive design law catered to designers and architects. There is a real need for a niche methodology for digital and real property that protects both intangible and tangible designed goods. The current copyright regime is too limited to protect various architectural rights, the emerging rights of 3D printing and scanning, and the issues surrounding 3D CAD files. The present Patent Trademark Office (PTO) process is too unaffordable and time-consuming for the average designer who lacks legal support. This new form of design-focused protective legislature, or incentive-based reformist initiative should promote a form of governance for the built environment that lies between copyright legislation and the rights protected by the PTO. Existing congressional legislation on the protection of design rights does not motivate innovation and protects only corporations with deep pockets.

Now in its two-and-a-half-decade pilot, open source is not going to stop. It is time for governmental agencies and policy makers to recognize that private and public entities must be better educated on what open-source systems actually are. Open-access systems and blockchain ledgers enable transparent permission-based distribution systems for all. As a field, architecture has always relied on a system of exchange among many players, all the more so in contemporary construction, which requires so many internal and external consultants. Were the system of digital exchange more open and transparent, open innovation would increase the significance of management systems and cloud-based digital file transfers, push for better governance on the global distribution of digital file transfers, and possibly lead to a better system of governance among manufacturers, vendors, and creators **6**.

Society's current notion of fair compensation for intellectual property would benefit from better laws based on a deeper understanding of how designers and architects operate beyond drawing technical floor plans, and ones that take into account the holistic practice and industry of construction as it pushes the envelope of technological innovation with features such as robotics and 3D printing—practices that are currently governed by no legislature or regulation.

To ensure further legal protection, we need to consider the extra-legal norms of data and databases, the directive rights to manage and balance the interests of designers (design) and right holders with that of rightful competition (economics), and society (policy). We also need stronger digital management of property rights in the international arena–across the United States, Europe, and Asia–in order to governs the virtual distribution of data behind artefacts that could be used in international manufactural processes. Digital transfers of files with meta-data and information pertaining to 3D producible properties, like those containing g-codes generated by a CAD program that can be 3D printed or produce a physically 3D produced entity, in the case of these files, governance (i.e. laws and policy) should be restricted/reduced in order to ease international distribution from designers to manufacturers and vendors.

Existing contemporary notions of owner- and authorship cannot accommodate the environments and conditions of architecture and design in the digital age. The present lag in the legal and political treatment of digital ownership risks stifling new and innovative collaborations between various makers and players within the digital realm, especially in architecture and design, which rely ever more on digital platforms for production and construction. Further the legal and social ramifications of automation on ownership and authorship in these fields demand that we resolve the ethical divide between the production of digital file and the replacement of human with robotics and automated devices.

Additional measures could include apparatuses in the PTO and Copyright offices that protect designs and designers devoted to the research and development of content in confidential or restrictive settings with third party software, or that date and time the invention of designs **7**. "First to file" policies and laws in the current PTO and intellectual property systems no longer encompass the future of designer needs. Indeed, the "first to file" system only benefits those with the monetary means to file and often place limits on authors and owners' rights to distribute their creative content. Just as computer programmers obtain a natural copyright of their code by scripting, creators who use innovative technologies should be granted special rights that govern their inventions and creations as data and the transference of information and thus go beyond the current filing system for utility or design patents.

Due to the ongoing pandemic, inflation, and demand for a more streamlined supply-chain system, the global economy needs to come up with a new way of distributing goods and services and exchanging physical property. Although architects may not be the immediate answer to this larger problem, architecture could provide the infrastructure for the framework that hosts the digital ledger and the physical (urban) network system.

Does Architecture Need Data Center Urbanism?

> "The city is the nexus of material and informational flows, developed within multiple infrastructures of transportation, distribution, culture, and knowledge. The increasingly interconnected world has produced cities where global systems are intermeshed in local environments and scale shifts rapidly from local to the regional and international."
>
> - Jesse Reiser & Nanako Umemoto **8**

Today, solutions and products are derived from intangible goods in the form of digital tools with multi-user capabilities.

When it comes to the development of design, professional codes of conduct and legal regulations are a means to an end since digital barriers eliminate many of the necessary precautions required to authenticate the construction and fabrication of three- dimensional computer-aided-design (CAD) files. The *Digital Millennium Copyright Act* (DMCA) covers many of the intellectual property issues arising from the dissemination of technological devices or services, such as broadcasting, radio, and software, while the *Digital Rights Management* (DRM) ensures the protection and ethical use of digital technologies by hardware manufacturers, publishers, and copyright holders, as well as the after-sale use of the digital content commonly found in music and software. Architecture, on the other hand, has not adopted any such practice, and, as a discipline faces the difficulty of maintaining critical control over global practices in the built environment–from duplication, copycats, and faux reproductions to ongoing issues with the the supply chain and the onsite delivery of construction material.

The shift to digital and computational methods of design and production poses new legal, ethical, and economic challenges for architecture. It has now become normal for members of the profession to engage in collaboration that transcends physical borders as more and more work is conducted in cyberspace. Cross-border design development, which has been around for decades, is hardly a new concept. What causes friction, however, is the geopolitical command of territory, intellectual property, and data exchange across borders, especially when it comes to the competition over automation and the development of artificial intelligence between private companies in the US and state-owned conglomerates in China.

Machine learning and artificial intelligence has shifted the field of architecture in so much as it has provided a groundbreaking opportunity for new and emerging computational advances in AEC and new players entering the field. Nonetheless, the extraction, accumulation, and analysis of data by competing firms across borders faces criticism as it remains unclear how our digital infrastructure will continue to be built and who will own that data.

As discussed in this book, it is non-architectural, huge US tech consortiums such as *Alphabet*, *Microsoft*, *Facebook* (now, *Meta*), several gaming companies, etc. that dominate and build submarine cables in competition with or in partnership with China's *Huawei Marine*. On the one hand, capital driven by the earnings of the technology sector allows these infrastructures to be built without architects. On the other, it is the fact that most of these data centers and information warehouses are built by non-architects that the inhumane and sometimes uninhabitable machine landscape has come into existence.

If the internet and the submarine cables are the digital and physical infrastructural glue between the nations and continents that constitute the physical ports of connection, and hubs of megastructure, then when will architects start planning environments that allow us to live in tandem with these data megastructures. When, will architects start planning more livable conditions with or in tandem with these data megastructures?

Should architects be the ones designing cities for data storage and digital exchange? And what if they could come up with alternative means of data collection and embedded digital structures?

As Elon Musk's *SpaceX* and *Starlink* come ever closer to establishing internet connectivity in outer space and space colonies, we must ask ourselves whether our information and data continues to require a physical presence on earth. Simply put, could *Starlink* replace submarine cables?

Although most machine-landscapes of data center megastructures are built by and for the technology sector and its data hungry customers, it is the responsibility of architects and designers

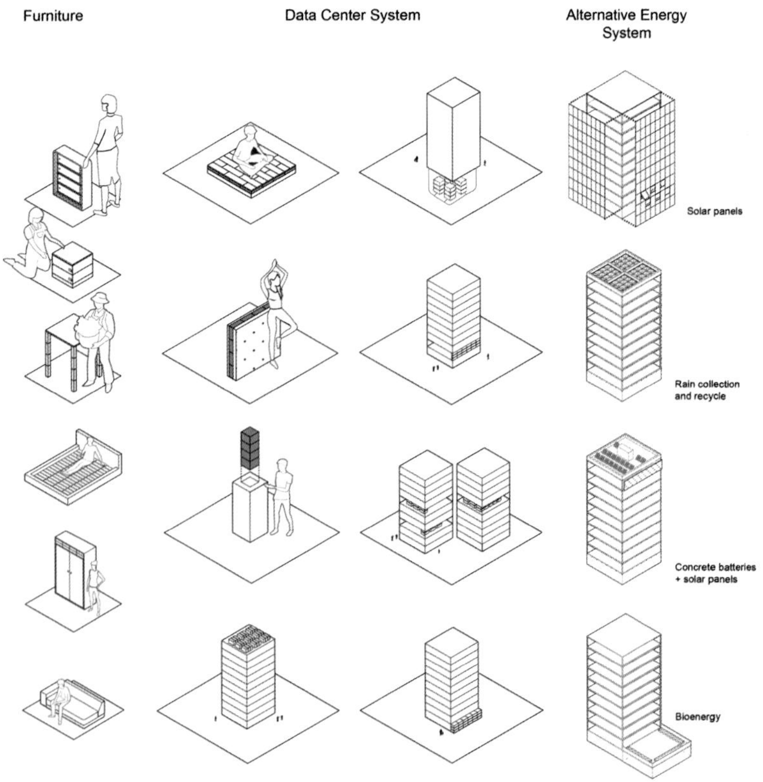

b

to engage with urban policymakers and real estate developers to construct more livable neighborhoods that integrate these landscapes.

Architects need to spend more time interrogating equitable (business) and ethical (legal) measures. We need to explore the tangibility and intangibility of digital (electronic) files, analyze creative systems of idea exchange, compare the concept of 'service and ideas' to that of 'commodity and product based' manufacturing, and decipher the various approaches to collective ownership and the authorship of design.

Where Is Architecture Going?

> "Space has become the ultimate imperial ambition, symbolizing an escape from the limits of the Earth, bodies, and regulation. It is perhaps no surprise that many of the Silicon Valley tech elite are invest in the vision of abandoning the planet."
>
> - Kate Crawford, *Atlas of AI*

The next phase of futureproofing the AEC industry lies in the question of the data ownership of "smart" homes, as in the initiatives driven by the research labs responsible for *IBM Watsons* and Amazon *Alexa* models, as well as the cities–perhaps even regions–designed by privatized tech consortiums rather than public (civic) urban planning officials.

Designers will need to think ever more in terms of systems, rather than assets. Those who develop novel systems will have to work with manufacturing partners in order to scale projects and systems. Certain structures may change partnership or ownership models. As the blockchain system enables transactions to be shared publicly, the extent to which design can be embedded in specific documents will impact those transactions. Moreover, the manner of deriving design value will also become more communal, accruing to a network as opposed to a specific designer.

In the future, creators of the AEC and larger design industry will be faced with a tougher question: how to develop IP so as to derive value from its adaptation. This is an issue that pertains not so much to user experience, as to the problems specific to industry. The AEC industry will need to play a more active role to evolve itself to become more like the start-up industry. Due to the nature of global practice and the ever-changing interface of digital and physical projects, the designer no longer has an idea of what kind of product the client wants. When developing products in the future the designer will need to abandon the top-down model of designing and marketing products, and instead, engage in on-going discussion with the client and build a commercial relationship based on market needs. As decentralization makes on-demand tools available online, architects will need to become thinkers and makers more than ever before. Designs will no longer be developed in a vacuum.

According to Andrew Witt, the future of the AEC industry will not be based on one model. As indicated by *Gehry Technologies* (GT), eventually sold to *Trimble*, past models will continue to exist and adapt to change. But the value of architects who design commoditized building types will continue to erode, since the processes required to create these commoditized building types will increasingly be embedded in software and the design process will increasingly be by search. Designers should thus take the opportunity to develop a strategic focus, technological or otherwise. Design itself is a big and ever more crowded field, and without some unique approach, the office will no longer be competitively viable. Such a unique approach may lie not in technical IP, but rather in relationships, process, marketing, or anything else with tactical impact. An asset such as this will enable new services as well as generate value of its own.

In the next phase of Web 3.0, products, technologies, and structures that are part of the Internet of Things (IoT) Web 2.0 as well as software that makes digital representations of architectural designs easier to create and manipulate will have high network externality (i.e., the standardization of such products will be valued by consumers).

Designers must therefore grow accustomed to thinking and and work in ways that are increasingly systemic and ecological (in the sense of interconnected). This, however, may not enhance the designer's ability to monetize IP as, at the end of the day, most design is still fee for service, and will remain so in the short term. Yet, there are several ways in which designers can derive direct value from IP.

Witt proposes two. Neither of these totally replaces the service model, but rather enables it in different ways. The *first* is through

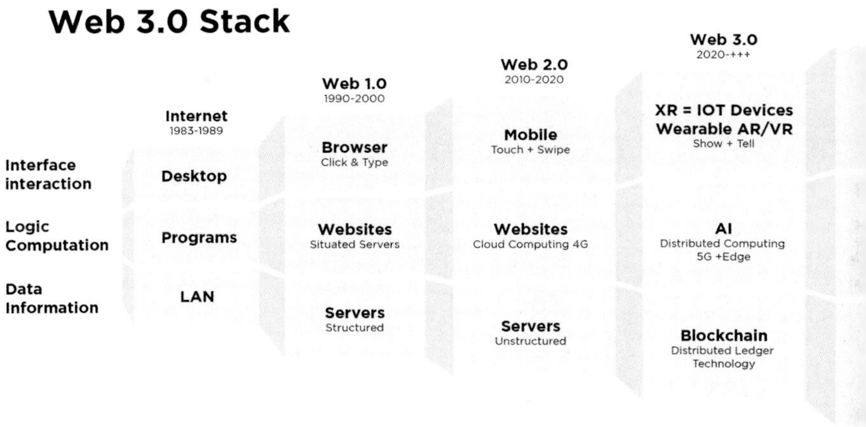

C

cultural value, which focuses more on thought leadership, bringing together disparate trends within society, and communicating strategic solutions for engaging them, as in the case of the business model proposed by *Cradle to Cradle* author, William McDonough. The *second* lies in facilitating the sharing and communicating of IP value in a piece of a design, as in the case of the Tesla open-sourced *PowerWall* battery model.

Do these examples and trends suggest that architecture and architecture-related software programming will become more collaborative in the future and require cooperation between companies? Yes, they do.

There is a sense of geopolitical urgency within architecture that is at the brink of rupture thanks to the field's intricate connections with the larger systematic source of data and information. Platforms and clouds of infinite kinds connect in minute daily operations that dictate the function of software and data storage. Today, architects and designers are often asked to serve as consultants and offer insight on both the physical and virtual real worlds–worlds that are being built by our invisible labor.

Our daily consumption of digital data has a significant impact on the surrounding physical world. Our current rate of data production and consumption is unsustainable in terms of both business storage and the ecological footprint of physical data centers erected to store information. This research also points to the greater appreciation of the field of architecture – in terms of both study and practice – with the emergence of Web 3.0, in which digital and physical property is intrinsically linked.

Nonetheless, my research on submarine internet cables reminds me that an invisible world of data and infrastructural technology constitutes our connective tissue of cause and effect and substantially intertwines all our realities (meta/virtual, and otherwise) and daily physical practices.

Is declaring the submerged internet cables beneath our oceans a megastructure built by private technology companies and nation-states enough to highlight the travesty of soft-power and digital colonialism in our daily lives? I would argue that the Internet is simply a product of data and infrastructure. Without built architecture and physical communities designed concurrently by architects, urban policy makers, and designers, we can look forward to a world dominated purely by digital governance, without corporeal sensibilities and meaning.

References

1 Keller Easterling, 'the Action is the Form', The Sentient City, Edited by Mark Shepard, The Architectural League and MIT Press, 2011

2 Williams, Sarah, Data Action: Using Data for Social Good, Pg 213 - 221, MIT Press, 2020

3 Kuznetsov, Nikolai. "How Emerging Markets And Blockchain Can Bring An End To Poverty." Investing. Forbes Magazine, 24 July 2017. Web.

4 Kuznetsov, Nikolai. "How Emerging Markets And Blockchain Can Bring An End To Poverty." Investing. Forbes Magazine, 24 July 2017. Web.

5 Kuznetsov, Nikolai. "How Emerging Markets And Blockchain Can Bring An End To Poverty." Investing. Forbes Magazine, 24 July 2017. Web.

6 Balter, Ben. "White House misses big opportunity with open-source push". 11 April 2016. FCW the Business of Federal Technology. Web. Retrieved from: https://fcw.com/articles/2016/04/11/balter-open-source-opinion.aspx?m=1

7 In September 2014, President Barack Obama committed to creating a federal open source policy to improve citizen access to software developed by the federal government. On April 11, public comments are set to close on a federal source code policy proposal that initiates a three-year pilot program to make as little as 20 percent of new government software available to the taxpayers who fund it and for whom the software's intended to benefit.

8 Jesse Reiser & Nanako Umemoto, 'On Infrastructural Urbanism (1998)', Projects and their Consequences, Pg 216 - 217, Princeton Architectural Press, 2019

9 Kate Crawford, 'Coda', Atlas of AI, Pg 234, Yale University Press, 2021

Image Credits

a Wendy W Fok & Thomas Wang, Connective Balls of (Internet) Yarn

b Wendy W Fok & Lin Zhu, *Live with Data* - Architectural Data Infrastructures

c Web 3.0 Stack - Wendy W Fok (2022), Yara feghali (2021), Deloitte (2019)

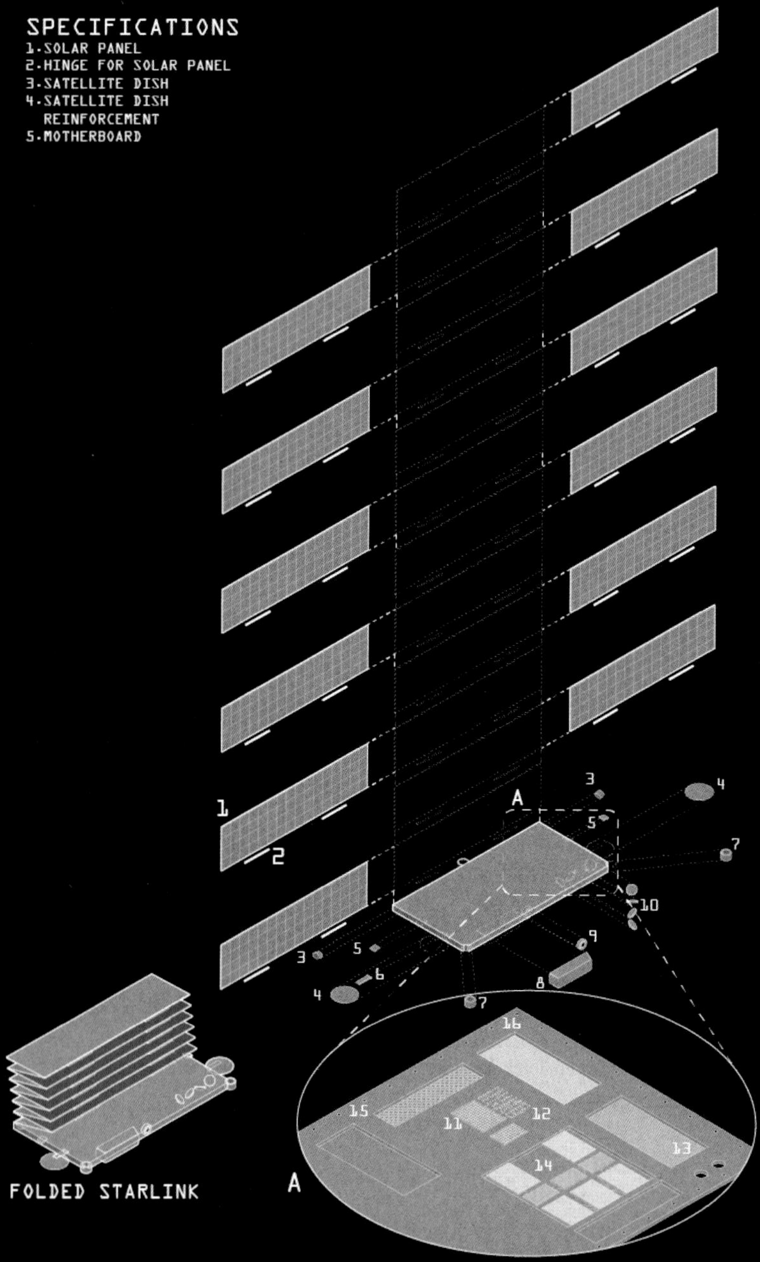
SPECIFICATIONS
1.SOLAR PANEL
2.HINGE FOR SOLAR PANEL
3.SATELLITE DISH
4.SATELLITE DISH
REINFORCEMENT
5.MOTHERBOARD
1
2
A
3
4
5
7
10
9
8
6
3
5
4
7
16
15
11
12
13
14
A
FOLDED STARLINK

Interview with Amber Bartosh

WF *What is the definition of a city for you?*

AB Ironically, I consider "city" as an awkward word in architecture. Because it broadly relates to a concentration of people and resources at the intersection of infrastructural components it has become generic – like "thing".

WF Do you feel like the definitions of cities have evolved since the beginning of your career, and how has that changed the post pandemic city to you, perhaps?

AB I think cities as they were historically understood have been replaced with urban networks. And those urban networks have evolved to be increasingly expansive and decreasingly nodal. The city used to be equivalent to access- i.e. physical proximity was key. What we see now is that access has less to do with a physical condition and more to do with agency and connection.

WF *Can you speak about the role of data and infrastructure in this conversation, and how you could suggest that designers, architects, policy makers, innovators, begin to better strategize for the future of our cities?*

AB It's irrefutable that data and infrastructure are key to the transformation of cities in multiple ways. 1) Cities are the primary sites for data collection. More data is collected about city behavior - both occupational and performative- than we can really even process or visualize, but the possible translations, mistranslations and responding directions that this data might lead to are profound. 2) Infrastructure has expanded into a virtual/digital realm that both links and frees users from physical locations - i.e. the mechanisms that allow us all to access the metaverse and remote work are on some level very much tied to very "grounded" power companies and data centers. So even as we expand our notions of cities to include digital twins and information layers, the constructs which enable that access and the realms from which we access it will continue to be of critical importance.

WF *It is difficult to talk about data without talking about privacy concerns and issues. How do you see the relationship of hackability and ownership of ones' data when it comes to urban policy and innovation?*

AB A rapid evolution of how we define property, ownership, and privacy is imminently necessary. There's a bit of a "Wild West" condition currently regarding the ownership of one's data which will only get wilder as metahumans and virtual real estate become more established.

Amber Bartosh is a LEED accredited architect and interior designer who constructs and examines the immersive infrastructures of the built environment using hybrid-reality and interactive design experiences. This research is supported by her professional practice and demonstrated through design-centric physical construction, exhibition, and installation. She has designed and managed award-winning projects for competition, bid & design build processes in the United States, China, Kuwait, and the United Arab Emirates and her work has been exhibited internationally in Australia and Italy.

Following her cum laude double major in Art and Architecture at Rice University she went on to graduate work in the M.Arch2 program at the Southern California Institute of Architecture (SCI-Arc) and as a teaching assistant for SCI-Arc's Applied Studies program. She completed her work at SCI-Arc with a Master's in Architecture and the Alpha Rho Chi medal. Amber is currently an Associate Professor at Syracuse University and Director of the Syracuse University London Architecture Program.

A Syracuse Center of Excellence Faculty Fellow since 2015, Bartosh is co-director of the Interactive Design and Visualization Lab (IDVL). The IDVL is a collaborative design cluster for interdisciplinary research, community outreach and professional partnership to create better living environments. Her visualizations communicate data related to phenomenology, building system performance, energy/fluid flows, and resource allocation. Custom-programmed environments couple digital simulation with video-game engines to provide interactive user interfaces via virtual reality, augmented reality and digital projection. Implementation ranges in scale from material investigations to urban geographies.

Scan the icon to view dynamic content

SPECIFICATIONS

1. IRON PIPES
2. DRONE DELIVERY SERVICE
3. LAND DELIVERY SERVICE
4. CLT PANELS
5. CONCRETE BAGS
6. BRICKS
7. METAL BARS
8. MAINTENANCE SERVICE ROBOTS
9. AIR CONDITIONER UNIT
10. TRAIN CART
11. INTERIOR PANELS WITH ELECTRIC LIGHTING
12. EXTERIOR PANELS
13. HINGE DOOR
14. HANDLE BARS

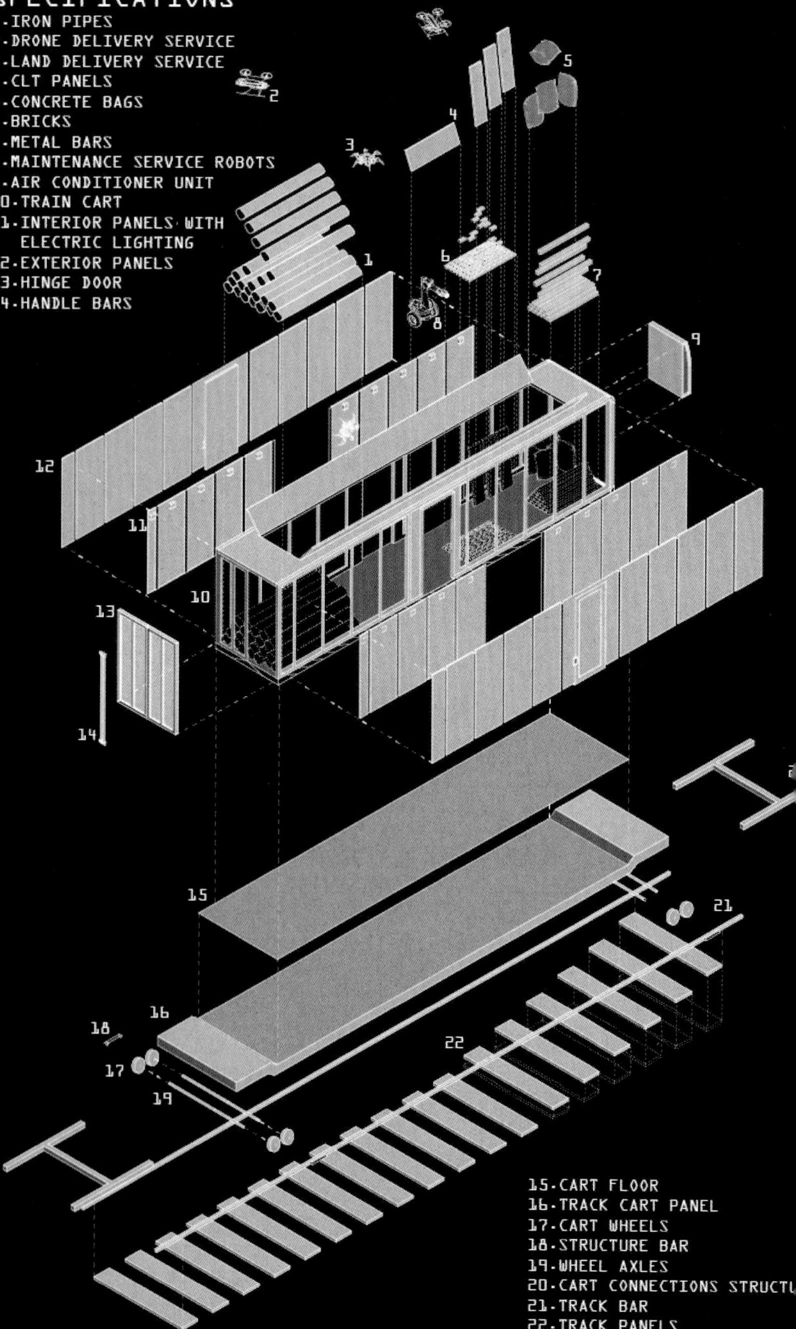

15. CART FLOOR
16. TRACK CART PANEL
17. CART WHEELS
18. STRUCTURE BAR
19. WHEEL AXLES
20. CART CONNECTIONS STRUCTU
21. TRACK BAR
22. TRACK PANELS

nterview with Michael Young and utan Ayata

F *What is the definition of a city for you?*

A For us as architects, the city is primarily two things:

One: The aesthetic appearance of the background of reality.

Two: The infrastructural connectivity linking flows of matter, energy, and information.

Architects believe they have influence over infrastructural systems, but primarily only have political agency through the aesthetics of the background. There is an interesting friction here especially given that infrastructures are increasingly invisible in the contemporary city. Raising awareness of these systems is not enough to constitute a shift in how architecture can respond to them. Wireless communication cares very little for the buildings it passes through.

Yet, this does not mean that there are not crucial changes in the technologically monitored urban environment that ask for design speculations on the part of the archite

WF *Do you feel like the definitions of cities have evolved since the beginning of your career, and how has that changed the post pandemic city to you, perhaps?*

YA One of the key tasks for architecture is to attempt a definition of its relations to the city. Our collective social interactions over the last twenty years have radically evolved through the advancements of digital technologies. While these resulted in new habits of digital mediation in our everyday urban experiences, a radical transformation of the physical environment would be harder to pinpoint. In many respects, Architecture is often slow to evolve, clumsy in adapting to the realities of emerging technologies and world events. Even though there are currently discussions about the city post-pandemic, we have yet to see this clearly formulated, nor have we done so ourselves. One area requiring a rethinking is in sensing technology. The dominant model is established from the point of view of capitalism and surveillance; that we are all marketed and managed as data opportunities or risks. But what is also at stake is that the city is now doubled depending on who, or what, the sensing entity is, and the tension or gap between these two cities is what needs to be described in terms that architecture can engage.

WF *Can you speak about the role of data and infrastructure in this conversation, and how you could suggest that designers, architects, policy makers, innovators, begin to better strategize for the future of our cities?*

YA For us, we always start with the aesthetic questions that a change in technology may raise. It's important to note that our position is not positivistic, nor techno-determinate, many technological changes have no aesthetic implications, while others suggest startling transformations. For instance, we have recently become involved in photogrammetry and AI image analysis. These are typically understood as surveillance technologies with the critical questions being how they operate and for whom is the resultant information valuable. From an aesthetic point of view though there are several interesting qualities that fallout. These stem from how environments are sensed and then how these sensations make sense, aesthetic questions. For most scanning technologies, edges and corners are not sharp breaks but jumps in data points, which means that corner or edge of a form becomes a fuzzy scumbled zone where the confidence in spatial accuracy is diminished. These points are also primarily color information created by how the scanner/camera detects electromagnetic information. In this, color is now a primary not a secondary quality, prior to space or form. There are shadows, gaps, and hidden zones that exist behind, or outside of the energetic thresholds, these are pockets undetected, a possibly new aesthetic of poche. Depth is calculated based on pixel differences between two images over time, not by projecting perspectival diminution, but by statistical analysis of thousands of previous images. Since so much effort has gone into facial recognition software, much of these analytical technologies are biased towards isolatable motifs of local symmetries such as exist in a human face. These are all aesthetic questions and are fundamental to architectural design in the most traditional manners yet appear now as altered concerns given that the primary sensing and evaluating entities are no longer human.

WF *What do you think the difference is between the digital (virtual) and physical (real) property of cities? Are there discussions of ownership and authorship, or issues of public literacy on how that could be part of designing architecture within cities?*

YA In keeping with some of the themes from the previous responses, we'd say that most of the traditional physical infrastructure of the city, even when billed a service to a client, was considered as held in some form of quasi-commons. This is not the case with digital infrastructures. These are private, for-profit enterprises, where our labor, education, and leisure time are commodified through surveillance. Older surveillance models argued that we would "behave" because we do not know if we are being watched. With digital interactions, we know we are constantly monitored, but we behave as if we are not. There is something important in this inversion that has to do with the difference between virtual and real in relation to how our environments are "shared."

WF *It is difficult to talk about data without talking about privacy concerns and issues. How do you see the relationship of hackability and ownership of ones' data when it comes to urban policy and innovation?*

YA Of course we should own our own data, the question is where the boundaries exist between personal data versus "public" data, that is data owned by the company that is collecting it. Much of this is well outside the purview of architecture, but if we were to speculate on a few interesting conflicts, one that seems to have blossomed during the pandemic is the city as a public space to inhabit versus the city as a provider of services. Both aspects are much older than our current technologies and have existed throughout the history of urbanity in variable relations. What has changed during the pandemic is that the shared space of public interaction has moved even further online radically accelerating the value of the data collected by these "service providers." To value the city as a publicly shared space is dialectically linked with desires to collectively become anonymous. This anonymity requires both privacy and a commons. In our current situation, data services offer neither privacy nor publicity in manners valued previously. What kind of city emerges from this is a crucial question for the architecture of the near future.

Young and Ayata formed a partnership in New York in 2008 to explore the conceptual and aesthetic possibilities of architecture and urbanism. The practice is dedicated to both built commissions and experimental research. The practice views the reality of contemporary building as a provocation for architectural form, material and technology. In following these trajectories it is necessary to understand architecture in its historical processes. Both principals teach and view the educational experience as crucial to the continual development of architectural ideas.

Young & Ayata are the recipients of the 2016 Design Vanguard Award from Architectural Record. The Apartment building DL1310 designed in collaboration with Michan Architecture received the 2019 Progressive Architecture Award from Architect Magazine. In 2015 they were one of two first prize winners in the International Competition for the New Bauhaus Museum in Dessau, Germany. They were finalists in the 2015 MoMA YAP Program in Istanbul, Turkey. In 2014, the partners were the recipients of the Young Architects Prize from Architectural League of New York, and their entry in the open international competition for the Dalseong Citizen's Gymnasium in South Korea received an honorable mention. A manifesto titled The Estranged Object: Realism in Art and Architecture, written by Michael Young with the projects of Young & Ayata was published in the Spring of 2015 by the Graham Foundation. Recently, the firm's work was exhibited at the Museum of Modern Art, the Istanbul Modern, the Graham Foundation, Yale University, SCI-Arc, and Princeton University.

Scan the icon to view dynamic content

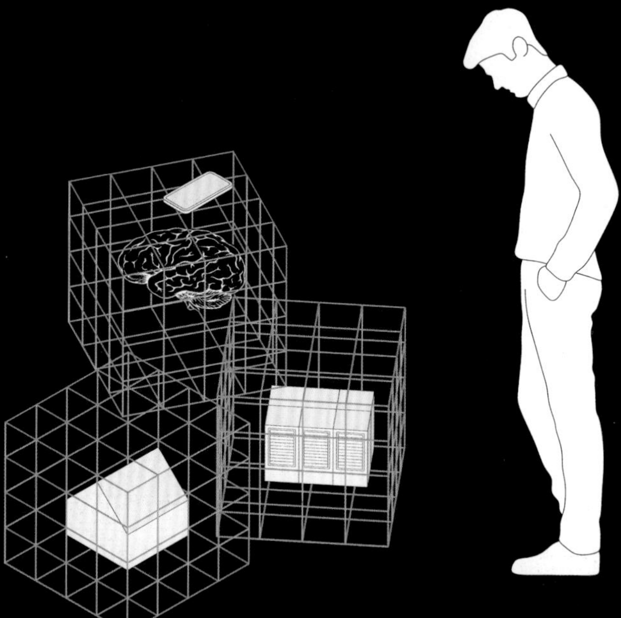

Interview with Jimenez Lai

WF *What is the definition of a city for you?*

JL The city is both a hardware and a software, moving at different speeds. The hardware is the physical material of the city: streets, buildings, and other constructed infrastructures. The software is the immaterial ideas of the people: politics, belief systems, aesthetics, and other desires. Some cities, like Dubai or Shenzhen, may have their physical hardware built over an incredible high speed, but with very little time for their citizens to formulate ideas about their cities. Meanwhile, cities like Rome or Istanbul may go through several cycles of idealistic, artistic, or political revolutions over many generations where people change their minds about things time and over again, yet the hardware would remain largely unchanged. This conflict of speeds between the hardware and the software is a constant friction in almost every city, and it is an experience that has defined the contemporary citizen of the society.

WF *Do you feel like the definitions of cities have evolved since the beginning of your career, and how has that changed the post pandemic city to you, perhaps?*

JL Remote work has transformed how people interact with the hardware and the software of the city. In Los Angeles, exclusively residential zones prevented commercial activities from taking place prior to the pandemic. However, since the pandemic, all domestic interiors effectively became mixed zoned spaces. This sudden state of emergency has become a flattening event: no one is near each other, and our new connections are both near and far. There is, at once, an expansive and contractive quality to this collapse of zones. On the one hand, the software of the city is more global than ever - the references and influences are not necessarily coming from the city where a person lives in anymore. On the other hand, the short walks people took around their neighborhoods for exercises shortened the physical experience of the immediately adjacent built environment to be as local as one would walk. This flattening event begs the oxymoronic questions: "does it matter where you live relative to where you work? doesn't it matter more than ever?"

WF *Can you speak about the role of data and infrastructure in this conversation, and how you could suggest that designers, architects, policy makers, innovators, begin to better strategize for the future of our cities?*

JL The strategy of our future cities is to represent our immaterial worlds more convincingly. Although we can visualize non-physical ideas much better than the centuries prior, high verisimilitude will not necessarily translate directly to conviction. The craft of clarity is a design approach that helps organize our minds, as well as how we develop where we can place our faith. In order for something to have any value or worth, first we must all collevely believe in it. Therefore, the infrastructure of how we design such belief systems, particularly when there is no physical material, is not so dissimilar to how religion is developed, how politics is structured, how bureaucratic language is written, or how currency is represented.

WF *What do you think the difference is between the digital (virtual) and physical (real) property of cities? Are there discussions of ownership and authorship, or issues of public literacy on how that could be part of designing architecture within cities?*

JL The belief system is a currency. How we believe we own what we own, whether it is physical or immaterial, is a method of communication humans have always found ways to represent. The idea of a deed to a physical property is not so different from a certificate to a degree, or title to a position, or a minted non-fungible token. The matter of worth is through the articulation of the belief, which is where texts, graphic design, paintings, graphic design, or buildings come into play. Imagine the early days of the stock market - what methods of displays must be necessary to communicate a sense of trust in investing someone's savings? In a world where the metaverse is being developed and NFT is starting to be traded, of course it is the designers and architects who would participate in the early developments of our immaterial cities.

WF *It is difficult to talk about data without talking about privacy concerns and issues. How do you see the relationship of hackability and ownership of ones' data when it comes to urban policy and innovation?*

JL I am not sure if there is any privacy in our current digital world. If there is a private thought, best to speak it into thin air.

Jimenez Lai works in the world of art, architecture, and education. Lai has lived multiple lives, working in a desert shelter at Taliesin, residing in a shipping container in Rotterdam, and working with MOS and OMA. Lai is a founding partner of Bureau Spectacular; his work continues to set stages for human stories.

Scan the icon to view dynamic content

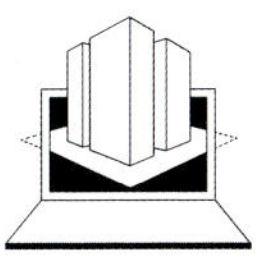

Patent Application Publication Jan. 27, 2022 Sheet 2 of 9 US 2022/0026931 A1

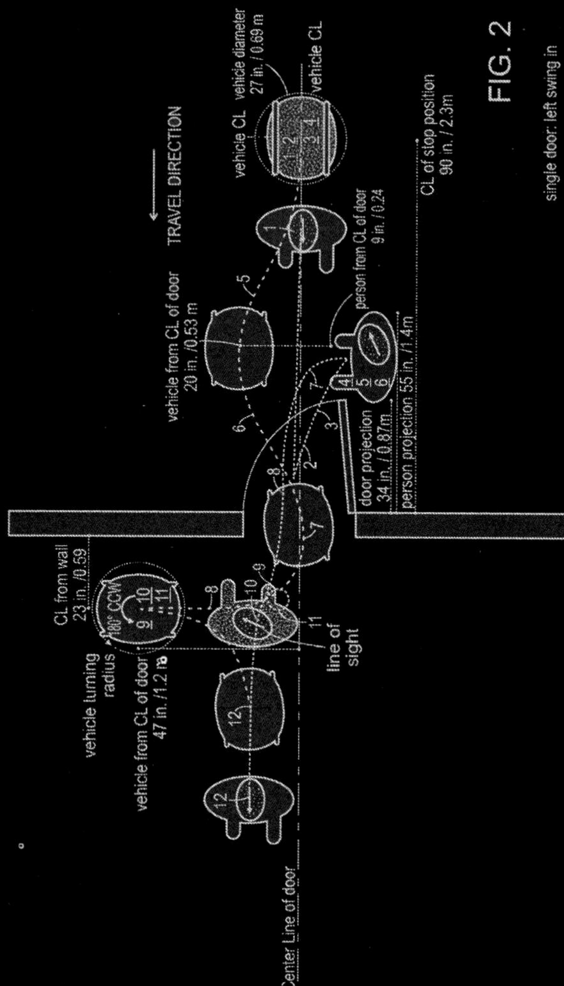

FIG. 2

single door: left swing in

What's Next?

Interview with Greg Lynn

WF *Straight to the point: what is the definition of a city for you? Do you feel like the definitions of cities have evolved since the beginning of your career, and how has that changed the post pandemic city to you, perhaps?*

GL In the United States there has been a shift in the last decade that has been accelerated by COVID and remote working and that is towards smaller cities, towns and what would have been considered suburbs that have the urban qualities of metropolitan cities. Similarly, in cities like Los Angeles and New York there is a rediscovery of neighborhood living and working instead of working in Central Business Districts and commuting from bedroom neighborhoods. In Los Angeles, many people don't need cars and commute by bicycle because they choose to live and work in the same or nearby neighborhoods. This is proving that a great transportation plan is a good land-use plan, and land use is trending towards neighborhoods, even in big cities.

WF *Can you speak about the role of data and infrastructure in this conversation, and how you could suggest that designers, architects, policy makers, innovators, begin to better strategize for the future of our cities?*

GL Walkability scoring, ESRI Tapestry Segmentation, U.S. Census Bureau "Journey to Work" and CTTP Data, U.S. Energy Information Administration reports are all incredibly useful resources for architects and designers to learn from when designing buildings that have a civic presence and impact. Hopefully all buildings address citizens and prioritize their effect on the quality of life of those in the local environment as much as the stakeholders of a specific building. In addition to masterplan and zoning guidance there are also more granular sources of data that can help give a picture of a community and context for designers.

WF *What do you think the difference is between the digital (virtual) and physical (real) property of cities? Are there discussions of ownership and authorship, or issues of public literacy on how that could be part of designing architecture within cities?*

GL Not really sure I understand the difference between the digital and physical property of cities. People navigate and experience buildings while looking at screens more than with their heads up and eyes open so it is difficult to make a distinction. With the devices we carry our location is often known and recorded down to the number of steps we take while the built environment has intelligent controls and monitors the interior and exterior environment. Making distinctions between virtual and real is not something I am able to do in all honesty.

WF *It is difficult to talk about data without talking about privacy concerns and issues. How do you see the relationship of hackability and ownership of ones' data when it comes to urban policy and innovation?*

GL PII or Personal Identifying Information should not be stored and recorded by the built environment and I would not want the built environment selling my data for marketing or targeting. Anonymized information is incredibly valuable for the improvement of the built environment.

WF *With the advent of digital technologies that are so seamlessly embedded to our digital domesticity, whether it be a smartphone, instant order buttons integrated with their home cloud systems, or automated robots that carry your groceries, what's next in architecture and urban development?*

GL Regarding domestic life, self-driving cars, on-demand services, and food and goods delivery are all conspiring to have us spend more and more time on screens where we are stimulated by content while our behaviors and reactions are recorded for more stimulation. Even travel, leisure and entertainment activities are designed to promote sharable experiences that will confer status and pride to us among our followers and friends. This is already what is next for domestic spaces, and we can expect more. The marketing of more time spent socializing in the "metaverse" by social media and advertising companies points to what we might expect people to do with more and more of their free time.

Greg Lynn was an innovator in redefining the medium of design with digital technology as well as pioneering the fabrication and manufacture of complex functional and ergonomic forms using CNC (Computer Numerically Controlled) machinery. The buildings, projects, publications, teachings and writings associated with his office have been influential in the acceptance and use of advanced materials and technologies for design and fabrication. As design opportunities today extend across multiple scales and media, his studio Greg Lynn FORM continues to define the cutting edge of design in a variety of fields. Because of his early studies in philosophy and architecture he has been involved in combining the realities of design and construction with the speculative, theoretical and experimental potentials of writing and teaching. In addition to designing consumer products utilizing new materials and manufacturing technologies with companies like Vitra, Alessi, Nike and Swarovski he is also a co-Founder and Chief Creative Officer of the Boston based intelligent lightweight mobility company Piaggio Fast Forward. In 2002, he became an Ordentlicher University Professor at the University of Applied Arts in Vienna. He is a Studio Professor at UCLA's school of Architecture and Urban Design where he is currently spearheading the development of an experimental research robotics lab. He was the Davenport Visiting Professor at Yale University from 1999-2016.

Scan the icon to view dynamic content

Postscript

This book is incomplete. It is incomplete in the diagrams that are drawn, maps that are produced, dialogues that are included. It is incomplete in the ongoing research and obsession I have on the topic of how architecture relates to digital property, infrastructure, megastructures, and beyond.

It is incomplete in terms of how inclusive the conversations and interviews are, and therefore, to continue the evolution of this dialogue, it was necessary for me (and, to Gordon) to, rather than believe that this is solely a printed book, but also to make it a mixed-media project that prolongs its shelf-life long after its first edition print.

The complementary digital platform and (audio/visual) interviews that survives on the digital platform allows those who have been approached, suggested, and invited, but did not have the bandwidth at the time of publication, to also contribute to future iterations of the open-access dialogue compendium of the book, that will hopefully survive long to come in the database of the internet.

One question that I constantly referenced back to is:
If Banham, Rudolph, Otaka, et al, were alive today, would they consider the Internet a megastructure?

digitalstructures.cc

Scan the icon to view
dynamic content

Acknowledgements

The research for this book would not have been made possible without the generous support of the Kluge Center at the Library of Congress, Ford Foundation, City Artist Corps Grant by NYC Cultural Affairs & New York Foundation for the Arts (NYFA), MacDowell residency fellowship, and various academic institutions of which I have been affiliated with, including but not limited to, Harvard University's Graduate School of Design and the Harvard Law School; University of Southern California's School of Architecture; Pratt Institute's School of Architecture, and many others over the past decade.

Jesse Reiser first opened my eyes, nearly a decade and a half ago, to the ubiquitous nature of urban infrastructures; yet, it was Michael Webb, during my undergraduate studies who fostered and seeded the thought of architectural infrastructure (or, perhaps even megastructures) into my architectural studies. It took a very long time for me to realize how much phygital infrastructure is part of our daily lives, independent of the study and practice of architecture.

Outside of the practice of architecture, this book would not have been possible without the efforts of my doctoral advisors, especially Prof William Terry Fisher and Prof Martin Bechthold, and informal reviewers such as Prof Yochai Benkler and Prof Peter Suber at the Harvard Law School.

Finally, I would like to thank Gordon and Jake for their patience in publishing this book, my language editor Irina at a time of war, and my partner for patiently reviewing architectural jargon. More importantly, my longtime friend and cover designer, Jung, and my team of emerging designers Jessica, Yarzar, Rachel, JJ, Lucy, Juan, Tara, and Isabel, of whom I had the pleasure of collaborating with.

More importantly, much of this research would not have been made without the current paradigm shift and mass cultural support into the metaverse and web3.

Index